Springer Proceedings in Business and Economics

More information about this series at http://www.springer.com/series/11960

Jorge Marx Gómez • Marie K. Aboujaoude •
Khalil Feghali • Tariq Mahmoud
Editors

Modernizing Academic Teaching and Research in Business and Economics

International Conference MATRE 2016, Beirut, Lebanon

Springer

Editors
Jorge Marx Gómez
Department of Computing Science
University of Oldenburg
Oldenburg, Germany

Marie K. Aboujaoude
Faculty of Economics and Business Administration
Lebanese University
Beirut, Lebanon

Khalil Feghali
Faculty of Economics and Business Administration
Lebanese University
Beirut, Lebanon

Tariq Mahmoud
Department of Computing Science
University of Oldenburg
Oldenburg, Germany

ISSN 2198-7246 ISSN 2198-7254 (electronic)
Springer Proceedings in Business and Economics
ISBN 978-3-319-54418-2 ISBN 978-3-319-54419-9 (eBook)
DOI 10.1007/978-3-319-54419-9

Library of Congress Control Number: 2017934915

Printed on acid-free paper

This Springer imprint is published by Springer Nature
The registered company is Springer International Publishing AG
The registered company address is: Gewerbestrasse 11, 6330 Cham, Switzerland

Preface to the Conference Proceedings

It is our pleasure to present to you the Proceedings of the International Conference "MATRE 2016," held in Beirut, Lebanon, on September 8–9, 2016.

This conference entitled "Modernizing Academic Teaching and Research in Business and Economics" was organized by the Lebanese University in collaboration with Oldenburg University in Germany and has been foreseen as a final network event within the MATRE (Modernizing Academic Teaching & Research Environment in Business & Economics at Lebanon and Syria) project. This project is funded by the European Commission under the TEMPUS IV–Sixth call for Proposals (Project Number: 544001-TEMPUS-1-2013-1-DE-TEMPUS-JPHES).

The main objective of the Conference was to bring together researchers for a corporate discussion about the contemporary issues in research, academic teaching, and education in the context of globalization. Another purpose of this event was to provide an international forum for the exchange of knowledge over the broad spectrum of fields covering the following topics:

1. Leadership and Sustainability in Higher Education
2. Quality and Governance of Higher Education
3. Internationalization of Higher Education
4. Labor Market and the Modernization of Business Education
5. Contemporary Trends and Challenges in Business Schools
6. Forging Research Links Between Business and Academia

The abovementioned topics have resulted in twelve accepted and presented papers including one industrial paper. These papers are arranged in the order of presentation in the conference.

We would like to take this opportunity to express our gratitude to all those who have made this conference possible and successful. We would like to express our sincere thanks to all authors who submitted their papers to the conference, to the board of reviewers, to our partners in international program committee, and to all speakers, session chairs, and attendees, national, regional, and international, for their active participation and support of this conference.

We hope that the papers contained in these proceedings will inspire more research in this field and will prove helpful toward modernizing academic teaching and research in business and economics.

Finally, it is our pleasant duty to acknowledge the support from the European Commission which is the project's funder and one of the drivers behind this conference. Our hope is to make this conference a recurring event in years to come.

Oldenburg, Germany — Jorge Marx Gómez
Beirut, Lebanon — Marie K. Aboujaoude
Beirut, Lebanon — Khalil Feghali
Oldenburg, Germany — Tariq Mahmoud

The Program Committee

Prof. Dr.-Ing. Jorge Marx Gómez, Oldenburg University, Germany (Chairman)
Assoc. Prof. Dr Jurgita Raudeliūnienė, Vilnius Gediminas Technical University, Lithuania (Chairman)
Prof. Dr. Vida Davidavičienė, Vilnius Gediminas Technical University, Lithuania (Chairman)
Dr.-Ing. Tariq Mahmoud, Oldenburg University, Germany
Dr. Oana Madelina Driha, University of Alicante, Spain
Prof. Dr. Khalil Feghali, Lebanese University, Lebanon
Dr. Marie K. Aboujaoude, Lebanese University, Lebanon
Dr. Sulaiman Mouselli, Arab International University, Syrian Arab Republic
Dr. Serene Dalati, Arab International University, Syrian Arab Republic
Dr. Chadi Azmeh, International University for Science and Technology, Syrian Arab Republic
Dr. Mohammed Koder, International University for Science and Technology, Syrian Arab Republic
Prof. Dr. Adnan Ghanem, Damascus University, Syrian Arab Republic
Dr. Majed Sakour, Damascus University, Syrian Arab Republic
Dr. Latifa Attieh, Modern University for Business and Science, Lebanon
Dr. Guitta Abou Khalil, Modern University for Business and Science, Lebanon
Dr. Nabil Sukkar, Syrian Consulting Bureau for Development & Investment, Syrian Arab Republic

Organization Committee

Prof. Dr. Charbel Kfoury, Lebanese University Lebanon
Prof. Dr. Khalil Feghali, Lebanese University, Lebanon (Chairman)
Prof. Dr. Jorge Marx Gómez, Oldenburg University, Germany
Dr. Marie K. Aboujaoude, Lebanese University, Lebanon
Dr. Tariq Mahmoud, Oldenburg University, Germany
Mr. George Kfoury, Lebanese University, Lebanon

Contents

Seeds of Sustainability in Lebanese Universities: An Empirical Study

Mireille Chidiac El Hajj, Ghassan Chlouk, and Richard Abou Moussa

Abstract Meeting the needs of the contemporary world, without jeopardizing the ability of future generations to meet their own needs, will not be actualized unless an educated population and an oriented workforce task are prepared to face the rapidly growing new challenges of the twenty-first century. Thus all Lebanese universities, public and private, are invited to integrate sustainability in their campuses. Our qualitative research demonstrates that seeds of sustainability are present in varying degrees in universities that have been continuously functional in the service of higher education in Lebanon for a period of 50 years or more. However, more is needed to prepare present students and the future community to rely on available sources. Change occurs when a sense of urgency for a relevant vision is created. Providing the right policies and resources can enhance sustainability practices. Nonetheless, many obstacles are found, like shortage in funds and human competence. Moreover, Lebanese universities are still not aware that sustainability may improve their profits. This point is crucial because it creates the motive for the private sector in Lebanon to cooperate with universities to support sustainability and form a partnership to convince the relevant public policy makers to adopt sustainability in their strategic plans. More universities are to be studied to extend the data and complement this research, and to allow further comparison of initial findings.

Keywords Sustainability • Lebanese universities • Change • Policies • Obstacles

1 The Framework

Nowadays, deteriorating environmental conditions, and natural resources depletion are prevalent. Meeting the needs of the present without compromising the ability of future generations to meet their own needs [1], will not be actualized unless an

M.C. El Hajj (✉) • G. Chlouk • R.A. Moussa
Faculty of Economics and Business Administration, Department of Management, Lebanese University, Beirut, Lebanon
e-mail: mireillehajj@hotmail.com; ramoussa@gmail.com

J. Marx Gómez et al. (eds.), *Modernizing Academic Teaching and Research in Business and Economics*, Springer Proceedings in Business and Economics,
DOI 10.1007/978-3-319-54419-9_1

educated population and an oriented workforce task are prepared to face the rapidly growing challenges of the twenty-first century.

Many conferences around the world have recommended improvements of public and personal knowledge related to sustainability issues. The UNESCO reports are calling for elevating education and are covering topics concerning sustainability in different domains: in Business, Science, Health, Agriculture, Engineering, and others. Yet, few of these recommendations have been fully implemented in some countries, especially in Lebanon, where the lack of awareness, and lack of initiatives are currently leading to widespread environmental problems; "jeopardizing the ability of futures generations to meet their own needs" [2].

Important guidelines that identify implementable educational strategies related to sustainability have been issued since the last quadrant of the past century. However, so far in Lebanon, little has been done in terms of recognizing the implications of environmental problems. Therefore, a close re-examination of conferences, such as the UNESCO Tbilisi conference held in 1977 [3], can help "bringing education nearer to the environment" and start the necessary momentum for addressing sustainability.

According to the 1977 Tbilisi conference, environmental education can be achieved through:

1. Developing an increased awareness and understanding of environmental problems among the general public (children, youth, and adults);
2. Preparing certain occupational groups whose responsibilities bear directly on environmental problems and opportunities (for example, engineers, planners, architects, medical personnel, teachers, administrators, industrial managers);
3. Training specialists for research or work related to environmental sciences.

Most specialists are formed at universities. Therefore, and in general, it is up to universities to shape the concept and define the guidelines of sustainability. Remodeling universities' curricula through the introduction of special courses and seminars on environmental issues, and preparing specialized educators and researchers who can cover sustainable development issues.

The main objective of this paper is twofold: (1) to investigate whether historically eminent Lebanese universities, that have been continuously serving higher education for at least 50 years, are integrating sustainability courses in their curriculum; and (2) to discern whether the universities' administrators are currently, or in the foreseeable future, addressing sustainability concepts and tools in their respective universities.

2 Universities Play a Major Role in Inspiring and Teaching Sustainability Concepts

2.1 Can Higher Education Independently Implement Sustainable Development

Many institutions of higher education worldwide are attempting to become more sustainable by signing different declarations and by providing courses, conferences and tools to prepare students to deal with sustainability issues. Over the last decade, a growing number of committed universities have ensured the integration of sustainability in their curricula, and across disciplines that were not traditionally associated with sustainability [4–7].Thus they materialized the multidisciplinary approach to sustainability where all can benefit from such a framework. Integrating sustainability in universities arose mainly as a result of signing and implementing policy statements and agreements, such as The Talloires Declaration stated by UNESCO to "provide leadership and to mobilize internal and external resources so that their institutions respond to this urgent challenge" [8]; or The Halifax Declaration [9] which indicated that universities play a "leadership role" in improving the capacity of countries to face environment and development issues, and to contribute to sustainable development on local, national and international levels. Charters were also influential, like the Kyoto Declaration [10] and the Copernicus Charter [11], which contain important guidelines for sustainable development in Higher Education. But the dilemma still exists. For example, while some international universities are currently implementing The Talloires Declaration within their institutions, and some others are incorporating the umbrella principles of the declaration; yet the majority of signatory universities did not implement The Halifax Declaration, and only a few incorporated its general concepts and value statements [12].

Even if some universities provide varying forms of such environmental education, others are not responding to change. To support sustainability development over time, tight collaboration is needed with the governments, enterprises, NGOs, syndicates [13, 14], mass media [3], and even students and other relevant entities to fully raise awareness, urge cooperation, and implement a general strategy for sustainable development. Evidently, universities alone cannot achieve the desired objectives. Rather, multi-sector partnerships including the private and public sectors can more effectively tackle sustainability problems. Accordingly, "because of their potential to combine resources, skills, and knowledge from a wide range of stakeholders to address the challenges of creating a sustainable planet [13], universities are called to play a major role especially in inspiring and teaching sustainability concepts. Yet, to teach, one should first know. Questions can be asked whether universities in Lebanon "know"; whether they have the required system thinking; whether they have an internal shared vision to deal with the sustainability concept; whether they are convinced of the need for a move towards sustainable development.

2.2 Developing Organizational Learning at Universities

Authors such as Argyris and Schon [15] focused, through their loops models, on organizational learning as a tool to qualify learning and learning outcomes; and implied that "learning systems" institutions must be invented [16], but they did not create a model for group or system learning. Peter Senge discussed system thinking and shared vision in his Learning Organizations and offered a model in his Fifth Discipline [16], which best depicts how the whole university's climate can nurture learning. Five cornerstones enhance the university's capacities: personal mastery, mental model, shared vision, team learning, and system thinking that integrates all other components, fusing them into a coherent body.

A shared vision develops awareness and commitment to scan and solve issues. It empowers organizations to develop an image of the required future. It helps the stakeholders to believe in the organization's projects, not because they "have to" but because they "want to." With team learning, the whole system develops a greater ability to address and solve problems, and, through dialogue, the team members enhance their capacities as they "suspend assumptions and enter into a genuine Thinking together" [16, p. 10]. The practice of team learning highlights solutions for problems, and pushes towards action. This leads us to another pillar of Peter Senge's Organizational learning: the mental models. They "are deeply ingrained assumptions, generalizations, or even pictures or images that influence how we understand the world and how we take action" [16, p. 8]. The presence of a vision-appropriate mental model is at the heart of transformation in any organization [17]. The last cornerstone, the "personal mastery", is essential to Learning Organizations and is associated with an energetic commitment to and capacity for learning. Thus, a "special level of proficiency" is produced [16, p. 7]. Hence, Senge's approach offers universities, the framework for their learning process.

However, creating Learning Organizations requires a change in prevalent perspectives, and results in a transformation in the universities' approaches to education and administration. The success of such renovations is dependent on the accomplishment of several phases. John Kotter [18] draws a roadmap for successful change that starts with three necessary and sequential steps: establishing a sense of urgency [for the issue]; forming a powerful coalition; and creating a relevant vision (and communicating it at a following phase). Kotter's phases resonate with Senge's model for a Learning Organization, but more importantly they guide the discerning eye to possible gaps in the successful launching of innovative and transforming concepts like sustainability.

2.3 Reviewing Some Existing Tools of Assessment

The literature reveals that universities can attain sustainability practice through the five criteria of David Orr's measurement system [19]:

1. What quantity of material goods does the university consume on a per capita basis? (e.g., how much paper, water or CO_2 is used/released per student)
2. What are the university management policies for materials, waste, recycling, purchasing, landscaping, energy use, and building?
3. Does the curriculum engender ecological literacy? (e.g., do graduates know the "stories" behind their food, water, and discarded materials? Are there opportunities to restore local rivers and degraded lands?)
4. Do university finances help build sustainable regional economies? (e.g., do food purchases come from regional farms? Are endowment funds invested in enterprises that employ sustainable practices and produce goods that truly benefit society?
5. What do the graduates do in the world? (e.g., does the work they do contribute to a sustainable culture?)

Orr's report provides tools of assessment and indicators that can serve as a learning curve in raising awareness of sustainability issues at both micro and macro levels. Based on these tools, The Penn State indicators report [20] divided sustainability practices in universities as follow:

1. The university has a comprehensive strategy to adopt sustainable practices; high profile issue with strong leadership.
2. The university has taken many significant measures to adopt sustainable practices but still lacks a comprehensive strategy.
3. The university has taken only limited measures to adopt sustainable practices.
4. The university has taken no significant measures to adopt sustainable practices.

Orr's indicators ignore both the link among the university, the students and the regional economy, and viewing sustainability as a whole perspective that links educational activities to operational ones: for it is said that universities can optimize their role as agents of change for a sustainable future by adopting a whole-of-university approach to sustainability [21]. Although they are not exhaustive, those indicators are still adequate to help researchers understand what universities are doing, and how they are doing it, in terms of sustainability [22].

Therefore, when assessing tools to measure sustainability, universities should define how to provide learning experience to students, how to sparkle creative projects, how to build leadership and how to develop the students' skills to permit soft transitions to sustainability [21, 23, 24]. There is a great need to develop a broadened vision of educational goals to meet the challenge of a rapidly changing world in an information-intensive age, and to achieve the goals of quality education [25].

The above administrative actions ripple to the pedagogical practices at universities. The Halifax Declaration [9] provided an action plan based on eight practical tasks for clear sense of direction in a number of core activities. One of these tasks is to review curricula and research agendas to see how sustainable development might be integrated in and between disciplines. The courses' content, perspectives, process, context, and design should prepare students with the "knowledge, skills, and values they need for creating more sustainable places and communities" [26]. Burns model of sustainability pedagogy offers a practical model, comprised of five key dimensions. The course seeks by its content "to increase learners' systemic understanding of complex sustainability issues. It provides learners, through perspectives, with opportunities to think critically about ecological and social issues. It enhances learners' civic responsibility and intentions to work toward sustainability through active participation and experience. It increases learners' understanding of and connection with the geographical place and the community in which they live. And finally, it utilizes an ecological course design process that weaves the other four dimensions together to create transformative learning experiences" [26].

3 Research Methodology

3.1 *A Qualitative Study*

This qualitative study followed a multimodal design for explorative and recommendation purposes:

1. Online research method is adopted to identify courses in the universities' curriculum. This secondary research approach permitted the selection of existing data.
2. Then, based on literature and online research methods European and USA universities that have sustainability practices were screened in order to compare them with Lebanese universities to indicate the gap and to deduce possibilities.
3. Finally, face-to-face semi structured interviews were conducted with several administrators to obtain primary data from historically prominent Lebanese universities. This in-depth qualitative interviewing helped us compare relevant data among universities in order to detect and recommend eventual strategies that can be adopted for sustainability.

3.2 *The Sample: Higher Education in Lebanon*

Lebanon's higher education was shaped in the nineteenth century. Its aim has been to provide education to youth and freedom for thought, influenced by foreign models and sectarianism. The changing national, regional and international context at social, economic and political levels has always had a profound effect on its development. Liberalism resulted from the limited contribution of the Lebanese government in establishing higher education organizations, and the close cooperation of private and public sectors, represented solely by the Lebanese University [27].

Third-level education in Lebanon is referred to as the "Higher Education" (HE), governed by the Ministry of Education and Higher Education (MEHE) and "protected under the Constitution" [28], through a main law passed in 1961, and composed of two groups: vocational and non-vocational. In addition, "Higher Education is divided into three categories: universities; faculties, necessarily attached to a university; and institutes which may be independent or attached to a university or a faculty" [27].

The four most prominent universities in Lebanon are the American University of Beirut (AUB), founded in 1866 by a Presbyterian mission, the American School for Girls (ASG), established in Beirut in 1835 by the American Presbyterian missionaries, and later in 1994 become the Lebanese American University (LAU), Saint Joseph University (USJ) founded in 1875 by "La compagnie de Jesus", and the Lebanese University (LU), founded in 1951 as the only public-sector university in Lebanon. In addition, and according to the official page of the Ministry of Education and Higher Education [29], there is a growing number of new universities, of up to more than 36 universities, 8 higher education institutions including L'École Supérieure des Affaires (ESA), and 3 institutes of formation and religious studies, lately licensed by the Council for Higher Education. The expansion of higher education is posing a problem because it is neither related to the needs of development of higher education, nor to the needs of a population of 4.5 million [30].

Overall, the academia baggage in Lebanon is homogeneous. The HE in Lebanon is contributing to building Knowledge-based society, social integration, and equal opportunities, and to providing students taxonomy of critical thinking and moral reasoning skills [28]. It shows "through the application of the US higher education system, the LMD system and the adoption of curricula and fields of specialization" [31].

However, within this research context, higher education suffers a threefold problem [30]:

1. The national policy of public and private higher education is not consistent with international guidelines. This is why many universities are in the process of adding a new system of external quality management to the national level, through accreditation systems;
2. Teaching in Lebanese universities focuses almost exclusively on academic issues and concerns. It hardly covers social changes or environmental challenges and hardly prepares students to cope with current issues;
3. The partnership frameworks and communication between educational institutions and enterprises is almost nonexistent.

Therefore, in the absence of a unified strategy, the objective of this paper is to explore how the aforementioned subject is deployed by each of the Lebanese universities under study, in order to answer the two following questions:

1. Are historically prominent universities in Lebanon teaching and drawing strategies and pedagogies to cover sustainability in their curriculum?
2. And more specifically, are historically prominent universities in Lebanon already providing students a learning experience that can permit a safe and smooth transition towards sustainability?

Results regarding these issues can be broken down into three key findings detailed below.

4 The Findings

4.1 Sustainability and the Current Curricula in Lebanese Universities

Online research concerning the integrated courses in the universities' curricula revealed that the topic can be split in two: (1) The American University of Beirut; (2) all other universities. AUB seems to be a pioneer in the field of sustainability in Lebanon: it has departments, units and courses that cover sustainability issues. This is made possible with the support of the International Development and Research Center (IDRC). AUB is the only university that has already established, since 2001, the Environment and Sustainable Development Unit (ESDU) with the main objective of promoting collaboration for sustainable development and acting as an interdisciplinary R&D center specialized in community development and sustainable agriculture.

Furthermore, at AUB the sustainability approach is integrated in other disciplines. Courses on responsible leadership, relying on Business Ethics and Corporate Social Responsibility and Social Entrepreneurship in the BBA, MBA, and EMBA programs, are ensuring the building of the next generation of "Responsible Leaders". Their objective is to build corporate social responsibility (CSR) awareness and to train students and professionals to develop sustainability practices within their organizations and engage them with their local community. The Faculty of Agricultural and Food Sciences is currently offering an interdepartmental Graduate Program, hosted by the Environment and Sustainable Development Unit, leading to the degree of Master of Science (MS) in Rural Community Development (RCODE, thesis or non-thesis). The Faculty of Engineering and Architecture offers courses such as Climate Responsive to address sustainability and climate responsive architecture, site planning, and sustainable design strategies. As for the Environment Responsive Architecture, it integrates green strategies in natural, rural and design settings. In addition, a set of online courses within a Pro-Green diploma, targeting candidates who work, are based on green economy, green technology and sustainable environments, water treatment, and energy efficiency. As for the faculty of Health Science, a special program weaves public health together with sustainable development in graduate programs.

As for all others universities, a quick look at the current curricula shows that all these universities adopt certain courses on sustainability in their curriculum, but have neither special units, nor specialized departments to teach it. Which reminds us of McMillin and Dyball's [21] statement critiquing most of the universities as "tackling sustainability issues in a compartmentalized manner, where sustainability education is only confined to specific courses, and where education is often isolated from research, and is likely to be linked to sustainable campus operations". In some of the universities such as the University of St. Joseph (USJ) and the University of The Holy Spirit (USEK), we found that the subject is addressed through conferences, and projects.

However, there is still a significant gap between AUB course offering on sustainability and the ones in other universities, particularly in two faculties: the Faculty of Engineering and the Faculty of Sciences. For instance, under environmental quality and control, a solely professional master of "Sciences and Environmental Management" (EMS) is offered in USJ; and an isolated course is given on the "Protection, Restoration and Sustainable Management of marine environment description" in the Science Department at LU.

Evidently, since its implementation in Lebanon in 2002, Tempus has contributed in the modernization agenda of the Lebanese higher education sector. Yet a lot is to be done.

4.2 *Benchmarking with European Universities*

The Higher Education Sustainability Initiative (HESI) was created as a partnership of UN entities (UNESCO, UN-DESA, UNEP, Global Compact, and UNU), and with a membership of almost 300 universities from around the world, including one of the Lebanese universities, which is Notre Dame University—Louaize (NDU).

The HESI network is committed to "(1) Teach sustainable development across all disciplines of study, (2) Encourage research and dissemination of sustainable development knowledge, (3) Green campuses and Support local sustainability efforts, and (4) Engage and share information with international networks" [32].

According to the European Commission [2], some universities such as Leiden, Delft and Rotterdam (LDR), are contributing in teaching Responsible sustainability. In their Strategic Alliance, established in 2012, they built "The Centre for Sustainability" that connects universities, companies and governments to provide research based knowledge and solutions for resource efficiency. Their objectives are to help students think proactively and flexibly, to teach them how to become socially conscious and understand dilemmas in responsible innovation, to forge their entrepreneurial spirit, and to make them drive value to contribute to financial, ecological, and social sustainability. In this context, universities, such as Edinburgh University in UK [33] are working on:

1. Procuring funds by purchasing new equipment to support sustainable labs that aim to improving science and maximize efficiency and effectiveness while minimizing social, environmental impacts.
2. Rewarding, supporting, and guiding students who are showing how, through collaboration, innovative solutions to everyday problems can be fostered.

"Key to this is giving students more opportunities to leave their institutions with the knowledge, skills and attributes required to critically challenge the world around them, and a desire and willingness to tackle social, economic and environmental issues and inequalities" [33].

In the department of Business Administration, Economics and Law at Oldenburg University [34], the Institute of Innovation Management and Sustainability was created. Its objective is to research the theoretical questions of evolutionary and interaction economics, as well as empirical and applied innovation management, the generation of sustainability innovations, and the creation of "green" markets and eco-entrepreneurship. Current research focuses on the joint projects: Nordwest 2050; green economy startup monitor; StartUp4Climate; SHIFT and NIK. In addition, there are courses on sustainability such as a bachelor course offering on "Sustainability Economics" and a Master thesis on topics like Corporate climate adaptation strategies, Eco-Entrepreneurship, and Environmental innovations.

To summarize, we can say that the gap between Lebanese universities and the above named European Universities is remarkable. On the one hand, whilst the integration of sustainability in Lebanese universities (with the exception of AUB) is still at its "seed level", European Universities are already offering units, projects, teamwork, publications, research departments, and courses to provide a coherent overview of European products and services in the field of sustainability. In addition, western universities are making more profits while working for the interest of their societies. In contrast, Lebanese universities are still not aware that sustainability may improve their profits. It is worth mentioning that empirical studies such as Orlitzky, Schmidt, and Rynes's [35], suggest a positive link between adopting social and environmental responsibilities and increased profits. It follows to wonder: what are the constraints and limits facing sustainability practice at Lebanese Universities?

4.3 To Modernize or Not Modernize Higher Education

Among all Lebanese universities, we have chosen for study (by alphabetical order): AUB, Balamand University, BAU, Haigazian University, LAU, LU, Sagesse University, USEK, and USJ for four main purposes. Firstly, all are classified as the leading universities in Lebanon [29]. All nine universities are over 50 years old and hence can play a role of influence on higher education practice. Secondly, to closely understand the current implementation of sustainability—if present—within the universities' disciplines and programs; knowing in advance, that the on-line research placed AUB as "leader" in the field. Thirdly, to explore whether the university administrators and directors—who are not fully covering sustainability issues in the curriculum—are aware of the need for sustainability practices and have the desire to integrate them in the foreseeable future. Fourthly, to discover the main obstacles—if any—that are constraining the development of a whole-of-university approach to sustainability in capable higher education institutions.

Table 1 Table of interviewed directors in different universities (by alphabetical order)

University	Name of person interviewed	Occupation	Date and length of interview
American University of Beirut (AUB)	Dr. Shady Hamadeh	Chairman, Agriculture Department. Director, Environment and Sustainable Development Unit—FAFS	Wednesday, January 27, 2016. 60 min
Balamand University	Dr. Habbouba Aoun	Co-Academic Programs, Faculty of Health Sciences, University of Balamand	Wednesday, February 3, 2016. 60 min
Beirut Arab University (BAU)	Dr. Hania Nakkash	Dean of Postgraduate Studies and Research. Professor of Physiology and Pharmacology	Tuesday, February 2, 2016. 45 min
Lebanese American University (LAU)	Dr. Raed El Khalil	Assistant professor. Consultant for several companies in the US like Chrysler, General Motors and Boeing, in the areas of operations management. Leading and influencing change and issues like sustainability at LAU	Monday, January, 18th 2016. 90 min
Lebanese University (LU)	H.E. Professor Adnan Al Sayyed Hussein	President of the Lebanese University	Wednesday, January 10, 2016. 40 min
Sagesse University	Rev. Khalil Chalfoun	President of Sagesse University	Monday, February 1, 2016. 45 min
University of the Holy Spirit (USEK)	Dr. Samar Azzi Achkouty	Chair of the Green Committee	Friday, January 29, 2016. 45 min

The Results of the Interviews

For 2 months: January and February, 2016, a group of researchers from the Lebanese University interviewed people in charge of sustainability in the selected universities. Two universities of the selected sample were not represented: USJ and Haigazian University. The others welcomed the interview, indicating that sustainability is of interest for their respective universities. The interviews were conducted with universities' directors as shown in the Table 1, which reveals that our platform for interviews ended up with seven university leaders arguing sustainability issues and vision at public and private Lebanese universities.

They provided their views on sustainability issues connected to Orr's different models, curriculum, policies and initiatives of cooperation (Appendix 1). Each of the contributors was asked separately to define whether the issue of sustainability is

Table 2 Enrolling universities in Penn state university indicators model

Model	Which statement suits the university best?
A. The University has a comprehensive strategy to adopt sustainable practices; high profile issue with strong leadership	Balamand University
B. The University has taken many significant measures to adopt sustainable practices but still lacks a comprehensive strategy	AUB, LAU, USEK (All B going to A)
C. The University has taken only limited measures to adopt sustainable practices	Lebanese University (LU) (the strong measures present are not applied in all faculties) Sagesse University (C going to B as the new leadership of the university becomes more established)
D. The University has taken no significant measures to adopt sustainable practices	BAU (D going to B in the next few months)

very urgent, moderately urgent, or not urgent. All of the contributors presumed that sustainability is not only a very urgent issue, but that there is no other choice left, considering the different environmental and social changes. They also highlighted the challenges and opportunities of this "obligatory" new trend.

Table 2 enrolls each university in The Penn State indicators model following each respondent's knowledge of his/her university:

Concerning the universities' management policies, Table 3 shows that answers varied as follows.

4.4 Converging Directions

According to the participants there is an urgent need to reform universities' systems. New strategies should be adopted to redefine their position on sustainability. They acknowledged the role of an urgent need of a Top-Down inspiring vision, and of a new dynamic of change not only of current policies, methodologies, curricula and practices, but also in mentality. Amidst a chaotic situation where lack of incentives prevails, the mission is hard with obstacles such as scarcity of funds and human resources. The will is there, yet the fear of change prevails because it demands a lot of work and perseverance to create a group of critical mass. The inability to do much, or enough, facing the problems in Lebanon, is creating a sense of frustration among all participants.

All expressed concern because of the inactive role of the government, and the erosion of any cooperation with NGOs, syndicates, enterprises, and universities, for it is only through unifying forces among different entities that sustainability is guaranteed.

Table 3 Universities' management policies

Management policy	AUB	Balamand	BAU	LAU	LU	Sagesse	USEK
Materials	Not clear	✓ Through accreditation	✓ for economic reasons	✓ Recycling cartridges	No	✓ Reducing paper work. Virtual magazines and electronic billboards	✓
Waste	✓	✓	✓	Recycling plastic	✓	✓	✓
Purchasing	✓	✓	No	No	No	✓	✓
Energy use	Yes and No	✓	No	✓ Classes equipped with motion sensors	No	No	✓ Green transportation and sensors
Green building	The green Hosler building	New buildings are built accordingly: Eco-friendly environment	No	With the cooperation of Italian companies	No	Not yet but measures for insolation and vision for new buildings	Not yet

4.4.1 The President of the Lebanese University: Professor Adnan Al Sayyed Hussein

One way of estimating the size of a university is to look at the number of students enrolled. Prof. Al Sayyed Hussein used this indicator to show the powerful position of the LU and the impact of its programs. He stressed on the emergency of implementing the sustainability topic. The issue of sustainability in LU needs more promotion, including social media exposure, to show the breadth of its current practices. Sustainability is already there: mostly in the curriculum of the Faculty of Agriculture; and in the human rights courses across the board.

The president of LU, expressed that following the Rio treaty in 1992, LU was inclined to teach sustainability in all faculties. To further elaborate, Prof. Al Sayyed Hussein asked Dr. Samir Medawar, Dean of the faculty of Agriculture, to contribute to the interview, in order to highlight the different current projects taking place in his faculty. According to Dr. Medawar, the faculty of Agriculture in the LU is accredited from Montpellier University, and is currently working on new projects, in the domain of Territorial Management and sustainability on the one hand and the domain of Marketing and the contribution in the civic society, on the other. These projects are funded by the French Ministry of Education. The objective is to prepare undergraduate and graduate students for proper civic engagement. Within this context, Prof. Al Sayyed Hussein highlighted the role of women in societal sustainability, confirming that a strong society cannot be built without the powerful contribution of women.

In addition, still according to the President of LU, the obstacles, hindering the adoption of sustainability practices, are the result of the current political environment and confessionalism. From his comments, it was evident that there is a struggle within the dominance of confessionalism preventing Lebanese people from moving forward.

The Dean of the faculty of Economic studies and Business Administration, Prof. Ghassan Shlouk, offered a variation in perspective asserting that the issue of sustainability becomes a matter of fact when there is an increase in the level of education particularly in related sciences. Therefore, the focus should be on education and sciences rather than on the sustainability concept per se.

In this context, Prof. Bashir El Murr, member of the scientific counsel in the Doctoral Institute of Higher Education at LU, proposes that the accent in universities should be on energy and environmental economics studies. This will educate people to optimize the use of resources in order to preserve them for future generations.

4.4.2 AUB Contributor, Dr. Shady Hamadeh

For Dr. Hamadeh, awareness was the key drive of the American University since the late 90s. He said: “It’s the problem of confessionalism that is ruining the country" (thus agreeing with Prof. Al Sayyed Hussein's view). Politicians resist change; they believe that change can ruin their security in power. Working on sustainability has become an individual endeavor. There is no need to refer to the government whose role is currently neutral (if not negative). "If we are to leave anything to future generations" said Dr. Hamadeh, "we ought to concentrate on universities, NGOs and civic contributions".

Accredited from American universities, and cooperating with different American and European universities—such as the university of Davis-California in USA, the RUAF in Holland, or the ZALF in Germany—AUB is seeking to implement sustainability in all faculties.

Civil Summer Camps, with the support of the Faculty of Engineering and Architecture, prepare students for community development and public work in remote areas. The camps are jointly conducted and co-funded by the Economic and Social Fund for Development (ESFD). The students are volunteers from the Department of Civil and Environmental Engineering (CEE). According to Dr. Hamadeh, there is a clear need for sustainable rural development in Lebanon, to prevent emigration from villages, where neglect or over-exploitation are the main mismanagement approaches to natural resources. Agriculture, the main resource management strategy in the rural areas, is currently at a near standstill, due its poor economic viability.

4.4.3 LAU: Professor Raed EL Khalil

Through his studies in USA, Dr. Raed EL Khalil naturally compared between American and Lebanese universities. He noticed the gap that exists in sustainability practices between the two countries. Sustainability in USA is based on indicators that measure progress. In Lebanon, there is a rampant lack of awareness. Dr. El Khalil stated: "We struggle because of the scarcity of skilled professors who can offer not only sustainability courses but also Knowledge. Only 1.2% of professors have an experience in the field. Most of sustainability courses are electives and most universities in Lebanon imitate each other."

Unlike Lebanon, the US government offers incentives and a long term vision. This is the reason why, US universities are taking more initiatives toward more sustainable campuses and green buildings; decreasing carbon emissions, conserving water and energy, implementing solar energy throughout buildings. Thus they offer both moral fulfillment and financial benefits.

According to Dr. El Khalil, LAU is highly ranked in terms of sustainability even though it does not have a specialized unit similar to AUB. This is due to LAU's expansion to the city of New York: the university has to abide by the directives of the USA, and follow special standards for campus life at all levels, i.e. social, environmental and economic. At the social level: committees, not individuals, work on sustainability, joining efforts, in system thinking that is based on trust and transparency.

Finally, Dr. El Khalil attributed the main limitation for successful sustainability to come from top administrators. If the Administration of any university is willing to provide the right policy, tools, materials, equipment, labs and other resources, then sustainability will flourish.

4.4.4 The Dean of Postgraduate Studies and Research at BAU, Professor Hania Nakkash

Professor Hania Nakkash sees sustainability as a new competitive instrument that can help the world and new generations to survive. It is a vision and a strategy for development. Even though no specific courses are observed in the university curriculum, Prof. Nakkash pointed to the different workshops and conferences taking place at BAU, such as the civic engagement conference due April 2016. Besides recycling, campaigns for students are conducted to raise awareness, ranging from volunteering to learn how to help disabled people, to participating in the Red Cross on-campus activities. However, according to her, sustainability needs more promoting.

Moreover, modes of behavior in Lebanon are disappointing while the absence of the government is widely recognized. Dr. Nakkash stated: "It is up to individual initiatives to raise awareness and to create new forms of solidarity. In this context, universities have to play a key role in contrast with the relative weakened part played by the government". However, the intensification of isolation felt by the community augments, according to speaker, the feeling of insecurity and of vulnerability, pushing people towards immigration.

Therefore Dr. Nakkash is determined to work on addressing the topic of sustainability in the curriculum and on promoting ecological literacy. "The approval of the Administration is firstly needed, but no worries," she added "since students come first."

4.4.5 Balamand University Under the Loop of Dr. Habbouba Aoun

According to Dr. Aoun, there is a lack of both motivation and commitment. Firstly she argued that sustainability is a challenge in all fields. Through her work with the UNDP programs, she experienced the Lebanese prevalent mentality and described it as the main obstacle towards implementing social improvements. She hopes that the youth within local communities will work on perceived needs and on empowering people, in a country where the governing system has failed in providing help and security to citizens. A top-down strategy along with enforced new laws and policies are needed to offer a more sustainable environment.

Dr. Aoun revealed that a new strategy was implemented at Balamand University 5 years ago, working on a green curriculum, integrating courses, workshops and field work in all faculties and departments. Following the Administration's vision and mission, new committees were created and regional development was conducted especially in the North area, where the faculty has implemented an Office of Development and Public Relations that serves the whole region for free. Securing and maintaining regions and villages is one of the main objectives of Balamand University, which is intensively working to offer a secure and safe environment to locals, helping them find stability, and preventing immigration.

4.4.6 President of Sagesse University, Rev. Khalil Chalfoun

Rev. Chalfoun emphasized the importance of sustainability, and indicated that the concept of sustainability is directly addressed in the Political Sciences department. Although an elective course in sustainable development is offered in the faculty of Business, the university is still making its first steps regarding sustainability in the undergraduate level. However, more is observed at the Master level due to the influence of a current agreement between Sagesse University and Bordeaux University in France, enrolling 50 students in a whole master program. This will ensure exposure of Master level students to sustainability practices abroad. Moreover, with an environmental focus, several forums for NGOs took place in the last couple of years.

Chalfoun maintains what hinders sustainability practice is the lack of awareness at all levels. He stated that he tried, without success; several outreach initiatives with local governments to cooperate in addressing environment issues. The municipalities apply poor pragmatic solutions with not long term vision for addressing pressing environmental and social issues. He also attributed the freeze in sustainability at a national level to the lack of proper functioning of governmental entities that may exert a top-down influence on institutions.

Nonetheless, the president of Sagesse University highlighted the urgency of addressing sustainability, and aspires to take several steps to ensure its implementation at a university level. For example, electronic media usage and recycling programs are already in place. He stated that the concept of sustainability should be addressed in the architecture and infrastructure of new buildings. Chalfoun also pointed to the importance of encouraging local businesses.

It is obvious that Chalfoun has sustainability as a priority as he launches his leadership of the University, which has started in September, 2015.

4.4.7 USEK Contributor, Dr. Samar Azzi Achkouty

Dr. Azzi said, "Sustainability is the only choice," and "Awareness got a proper body with the benediction of the higher authorities of USEK." The importance of the subject pushed the University Administration to establish new rules and policies to spread the concept of sustainability all over the campus. Different measures have been taken: from implementing sustainability in courses and curriculum, to creating a special committee, a special office, a green campus, with green transportation across the university in an eco-friendly environment.

Courses such as Civic and Citizenship Education, and Introduction to Ecology and Environment aim to teach USEK students notions, concepts and practical applications indicative of a civic commitment. These courses are built on acquiring the concept of commitment, on adopting the fundamental values of citizenship, on developing an understanding of the principles of ecology, and the life supporting and resource generating structures and functions of the ecosystems.

Awareness should be complemented with practical work. Posters, meetings and conferences are stimulating students to ensure sustainability on campus. The dilemma resides between going for a rewarding approach, to stimulate students to cooperate in building a green environment inside USEK; or going for coercive actions, forbidding students from neglecting their society and environment via punishment; or adopting both approaches.

5 Discussion

Triangulating observations, interviews and documents led us to the following:

1. Awareness is gaining more surfaces in the studied Lebanese universities, with efforts to follow, revise and optimize sustainability. However, redefining their own positioning, (passing from a lower to a higher level on Orr's Model), and presenting a vision to deal with this urgent topic, represent challenges in times of change. All contributors acknowledge the urgent need of change, while insisting on the importance of creating new policies, curricula, units, labs and research centers. They endeavored to recommend new frameworks to govern university operations. According to most participants, universities to develop their own strategies instead of copying others.
2. Remarkably, change was observed across some universities just as we took an appointment to discuss sustainability practices with the person in charge. This research raised awareness. The idea was there; in the minds of the upper level administrators, but the researchers created incentive that made it flourish. Sustainability issues are forcing universities to respond by taking fast action. But universities have limited funds and human resources. While calling for vital support from the government, universities need to increase their sources of funding and to hire qualified educators, who know how to transfer the principles of sustainability properly.
3. Collaboration with NGOs, syndicates, enterprises, and government helps building a whole system thinking based on collective intelligence to deal with current problems. However, according to the contributors, the lack of government incentives is essential to launch and support sustainability: an element that is missing with the current political situation in Lebanon. However, according to Senge's vision, we can only address a particular situation through our understanding of the underlying structure. It gives us the ability to identify the leverage points to change the system. As observed, things have to change, by

pushing people to step outside their comfort zone, without waiting for the participation of all actors.

4. Sustainability combines at least three elements: social, economic and environmental. Most National and International organization try to focus on one pillar at a time in order to solve problems. All participants pointed to the role of all three pillars, but insisted on the primacy of the social, followed by the economic and then by the environmental. Comparing the sustainability pyramid to that of Maslow, most participants, especially Dr. El Khalil and Dr. Hamadeh acknowledge that it is essential to be socially satisfied before passing to another level. Another argument was presented by Dr. Shlouk placing primary importance to the Economic factor, in this sequence: production, wealth, equitable distribution of the added value. Only Prof. Al Sayyed Hussein argued that it is true that the social level is basic, but insisted that all levels are equally complementary.
5. Fostering sustainability in organizations has a positive impact on their performance. Eccles, Ioannou, and Serafeim [36] investigated a sample of U.S. companies and compared "high sustainability companies" with "low sustainability companies". The findings were remarkable as high sustainability companies demonstrated a high level of stakeholder engagement... but more importantly, those companies financially outperformed the others in the long term [36]. This outperformance is of interest to all organizations, from any industry, if organizations aim to ensure continuity and financial efficiency. Needless to say that this point is crucial because it creates the motive for the private sector to cooperate with universities to support sustainability and form a coalition to convince the Higher Education Ministry to adopt the sustainability in its strategic plans.
6. Within cultural resistance to implementing sustainability concepts, the role of Lebanese universities is to create a counter culture of sustainability for today's students and tomorrow's leaders. In providing examples of social, financial, and environmental successes, universities can inspire change, innovation and creative actions.
7. Contributors acknowledged the importance of sustainability projects that address renewable energy or safe water, because such projects can increase innovation, and may be even life-saving when addressing sanitation and hygiene. To procure funding for such projects is challenging, but they can still be the way forward in bringing innovation and synergy to an eco-friendly environment and general sustainability in the short and long terms.
8. Surfing the internet helped us find which universities are presenting themselves as leaders in the domain of sustainability. Communication is key. Being able to factually prove and expose excellent performances in this domain, through the internet and social media, can have a positive impact on the reputation of the university.
9. Even though LAU does not have a basic unit for sustainability, LAU is applying sustainable measures to both social and environmental levels. In fact, the university is committed to introduce Green curricula in relevant majors and to adopt a university culture that contributes to environmental sustainability. The same goes

for the Lebanese University, which is intensively working and promoting sustainability through its partnership with EU, Tempus, and European Universities. Projects and assignments related to sustainability, energy efficiency and biodiversity reinforce the current curriculum.

To wrap up this section, note that simply benchmarking with European and American universities shows that a lot is to be done in this context to reach higher levels of performance. "Starting seeds of sustainability are there, under the umbrella of a perseverant Lebanese Higher Education, represented by Dr. Ali El Jammal, who is always reaching for more, as quoted by the Head of LU, Prof. Al Sayyed Hussein, yet we still have a long way to run. Our universities should be built on determination, added Prof. Al Sayyed Hussein, to value and promote a climate of civility and the conditions for sustained knowledge-based."

6 Conclusion and Limitations

To conclude, we can say that historically prominent Lebanese universities are consistent in providing the best education to Lebanese students. The topic of sustainability enthused all contributors. It is a new subject that should be integrated in all courses and curricula. Therefore, projects should be adapted to increase innovation with the participation of the private sector. Implementing Change should represent the bridge between current models and the new models required by the new environment. However, change can be a challenge since it is fundamentally about people, and "most people are reluctant to alter their habits" [37]. Creating a relevant vision and establishing a sense of urgency, "calls for sacrifice and self-discipline and will be met with cynicism, skepticism, and knee-jerk resistance" [37]. In addition, the lack of a contextual, comprehensive model towards which change can be geared presents a limitation to this work. Another obstacle is the lack of government incentives to support sustainability in general. A higher engagement at the government level—and especially at the ministry of Education level—is to be observed in order to reap the best harvest out of higher-quality seeds of sustainability that should be planted in Lebanese universities. Investigating the latitude of governmental involvement is beyond this study, and consequently limits it. Lastly, this study was restricted to historically prominent universities with the valid assumption that they play a leadership role in higher education, however, more universities should be investigated in order to further validate the findings, to complement this project, and to allow for generalizability and comparison with initial findings.

Appendix: Survey on Sustainability

1- How urgent do you think the issue of sustainability is? Explain

- o Very urgent
- o Moderately urgent
- o Not urgent

2- Is sustainability addressed in your curriculum? YES? NO? Explain

3- Enroll the university in one of these four Models. Explain your choice Model.
Which statement suits the university best?

A-The University has a comprehensive strategy to adopt sustainable practices; high profile issue with strong leadership.

B-The University has taken many significant measures to adopt sustainable practices but still lacks a comprehensive strategy.

C-The University has taken only limited measures to adopt sustainable practices

D-The University has taken no significant measures to adopt sustainable practices

4- What are the university management policies for:

Management Policy

Materials

Waste

Recycling

Purchasing

Energy Use

Building

5- Do you promote ecological literacy? YES? NO? Explain

6- Are there any initiatives of cooperation with other organizations –such as NGOs, syndicates, enterprises, government, etc.) Regarding sustainability? Yes? No? Explain

7- What are the main obstacles for not fully adopting and integrating sustainability practices?

	YES	NO
Funds		
Human resources		
The will		
The curriculum is old but no need to change		
The fear of Change		
It demands a lot of work		
No one guided us		
Mentality		
Lack of quality educator training		

8- Do you think you should be integrating sustainable development courses and practices in a new curriculum? YES? NO? Explain

References

1. Brundtland, G. (1987). *Our common future: Report of the 1987 world commission on environment and development*. Oxford: Oxford University Press.
2. European Commission. (2015). *Environment: Sustainable development* [online]. Accessed May 20, 2015, from http://www.ec.europa.eu/environment/eussd/
3. Tbilisi Report. (1977). UNESCO Intergovernmental conference on environmental education, in co-operation with UNEP [online]. Tbilisi: UNESCO. Accessed May 16, 2015, from http://www.gdrc.org/uem/ee/EE-Tbilisi_1977.pdf
4. Reid, A., & Petocz, P. (2006). University lecturers' understanding of sustainability. *Higher Education, 51*(1), 105–123.
5. Cotton, D., Bailey, I., Warren, M., & Bissell, S. (2009). Revolutions and second-best solutions: Education for sustainable development in higher education. *Studies in Higher Education, 34* (7), 719–733.
6. Cotton, D., Warren, I., Maiboroda, M. F., & Bailey, I. (2007). Sustainable development, higher education and pedagogy: Lecturers' beliefs and attitudes. *Environmental Education Research, 13*(5), 579–597.
7. Wyatt, M. (2014). Academics' conceptions of teaching sustainability. *Australian Journal of Environmental Education, 30*(2), 278–279.
8. ULSF Programs. (1990). *The talloires declaration* [online]. Gland: UNESCO. Accessed May 15, 2015 from http://www.ulsf.org/programs_tallories.html
9. Halifax Declaration. (1991). *Creating a common future: University action for sustainable development* [online]. Accessed May 16, 2015 from http://www.iisd.org/educate/declarat/halifax.htm
10. Kyoto Declaration on sustainable development. (1993). [online]. Accessed May 15, 2015, from http://www.iau-aiu.net/sd/sd_dkyoto.html
11. Copernicus Charter. (1994, May). *The university charter for sustainable development, Geneva* [online]. Accessed May 16, 2015, from http://www.iisd.org/educate/declarat/coper.htm
12. Wright, T. (2002). Definitions and frameworks for environmental sustainability in higher education. *International Journal of Sustainability in Higher Education, 14*(2), 209–227.
13. Gray, B., & Stites, J. P. (2013). *Sustainability through partnerships: Capitalizing on collaboration. Network for business sustainability* [online]. Accessed May 28, 2015, from http://www.nbs.net/knowledge
14. Borrell-Damian, L. (2015). *Universities crucial in fight against climate change* (Issue No. 368). University World News.
15. Argyris, C., & Schon, D. A. (1987). *Organizational learning: A theory of action perspective*. Reading, MA: Addison-Wesley Publishing Company.
16. Senge, P. (1990). *The fifth discipline: The art and practice of the learning organization*. New York, NY: Currency/Doubleday.
17. Gilley, A. (2005). *The manager as a change leader*. Westport, CT: Prager.
18. Kotter, J. P. (1996). *Leading change*. Boston: Harvard Business School Press.
19. Orr, D. W. (1999). Education, careers, and callings: The practice of conservation biology. *Conservation Biology, 13*(6), 1242–1245.
20. Penn State Indicators Report. (2000). *Steps towards a sustainable university. Pennsylvania State University*. University Park, PA: The Council.
21. Mc Millin, J., & Dyball, R. (2009). Developing a whole-of-university approach to educating for sustainability. Linking curriculum, research and sustainable campus operations. *Journal of Education for Sustainable Development, 3*, 55–64.
22. Shriberg, M. (2002). *Sustainability in U.S. higher education: Organizational factors influencing campus environmental performance and leadership* (Doctoral dissertation). Ann Arbor, MI: The University of Michigan.
23. Petocz, O. S., Reid, A., & Taylor, P. (2009). Thinking outside the square: Business students' conceptions of creativity. *Creativity Research Journal, 21*(4), 409–416.

24. Shriberg, M., & Harris, K. (2012). Building sustainability change management and leadership skills in students: Lessons learned from 'Sustainability and the Campus' at the University of Michigan. *Journal of Environmental Studies and Sciences, 2*(2), 154–164.
25. Zhou, N.-Z. (2011). *Four 'Pillars of learning' for the reorientation and reorganization of curriculum: Reflections and discussions*. UNESCO-Bangkok-IBE, Report on Basic Education Curriculum. Bangkok: UNESCO PROAP.
26. Burns, H. (2011). Teaching for transformation: (Re) Designing sustainability courses based on ecological principles. *Journal of Sustainability Education, 2*, 1–15.
27. HRSA II. (1996). *Développement des Ressources humaines—Phase II*. Le système d'enseignement supérieur et l'université Libanaise- Eléments de diagnostic.
28. Lebanon Higher Education—The National Tempus Office of Education. (2010). [online]. Accessed April 23, 2015, from http://www.tempus-lb.org/sites/default/files/lebanon_review_of_higher_education.pdf
29. The Ministry of Education and Higher Education Achievements. (2010). [online]. Accessed April 24, 2015, from http://www.mehe.gov.lb/uploads/file/Reports/2011/Progress_Report_of_Ministry_of_Education_18_5_2011_(Repaired).pdf
30. National Educational strategy in Lebanon. (2006). *Vision document. Lebanese association for educational studies (LAES)* [online]. Accessed April 29, 2015, from http://www.laes.org/upload/editor_upload/file/Vision%20Document%20%20English.pdf
31. Kabbanji, J. (2012, June). Heurs et malheurs du système universitaire libanais à l'heure de l'homogénéisation et de la marchandisation de l'enseignement supérieur. *Revue des Mondes Musulmans et de la Méditerranée, 131*, 127–145.
32. UNESCO. (2015, October 14). *Higher education sustainability initiative: Higher education for climate change action, from Rio to Paris: Higher education for climate change action*. Paris: UNESCO Headquarters. [online]. Accessed April 23, 2015, from https://sustainabledevelopment.un.org/sdinaction/hesi/climatechangeaction
33. University of Edinburgh. (2015). *University and NUSA win NUS sustainability and social responsibility awards* [online]. Accessed June 9, 2015, from http://www.ed.ac.uk/about/sustainability/news/archived-news/2015/university-and-eusa-win-nus-srs-awards
34. Oldenburg University. (2015). *Adaptation to climate change, survey—department für* [online]. Accessed June 9, 2015, from https://www.uni-oldenburg.de/en/wire/innovation/research/former-projects/nordwest2050/adaptation-to-climate-change-survey/
35. Orlitzky, M., Schmidt, F. L., & Rynes, S. L. (2003). Corporate social and financial performance: A meta-analysis. *Organization Studies, 24*(3), 403–441.
36. Eccles, R., Ioannou, I., & Serafeim, G. (2014). The impact of corporate sustainability on organizational processes and performance. *Management Science, 60*(11), 2835–2857.
37. Garvin, D. A., & Roberto, M. A. (2005). Change through persuasion. *Harvard Business Review, 83*(2), 104–112.

Supply and Demand for Information System (IS) Core Knowledge in Non-IS Business Occupations: Fresh Graduates' and Professionals' Perceptions and Perspectives

Marie K. Aboujaoude and Khalil Feghali

Abstract The Information Technology continues to infiltrate our business and change every aspect of our work from where we do it to how we do it. More and more, Information Systems are becoming the cornerstone for leading modern organizations. The result is translated into a high demand and genuine need for individuals who can use these Information Systems efficiently and effectively to achieve strategic business goals and develop a sustainable competitive advantage.

On the other hand, the Information Systems programs provided by today's universities, offer a blend of information, technology and business skills required by managers and team leaders in the modern business organizations. Yet, the enrollment in these programs remains considerably low.

The research investigated why business students deter from majoring in Information Systems (IS) disciplines and provided perceptions from Lebanese business professionals on what IS core knowledge and skills are currently required by non-IS new graduates to succeed in their jobs. Simultaneously, the research elaborated students' perceptions of their IS knowledge and skills. Findings indicated a disparity between the IS knowledge and skills supply and demand.

The results of this study can be effective in helping to bridge the identified gap and to better align the business curriculum and more specifically the contents of Management Information Systems (MIS) introductory course with the current labor market needs.

This latter is a core course for all business majors at almost every business school and provides a unique opportunity to equip all business students with IS core knowledge. The insights obtained from this research will also be valuable for other universities offering MIS Introductory course.

M.K. Aboujaoude (✉) • K. Feghali
Faculty of Economics and Business Administration, Lebanese University, Achrafieh, Beirut, Lebanon
e-mail: maboujaoude@ul.edu.lb; khfeghali@ul.edu.lb

J. Marx Gómez et al. (eds.), *Modernizing Academic Teaching and Research in Business and Economics*, Springer Proceedings in Business and Economics,
DOI 10.1007/978-3-319-54419-9_2

Moreover, this research suggested further exploration of reasons students chose Information Systems as a field of study; this will help developing a strategy for promoting the Business Information Systems (BIS) major.

Keywords Information System (IS) • IS core knowledge • IS concepts and skills • Labor market demand • Management Information Systems (MIS) course • Student major selection

1 Introduction

Information Technology is constantly evolving leading to a high demand for qualified people who can translate business needs into technology solutions.

According to the Bureau of Labor Statistics (bls), the employment of computer and information technology occupations is projected to grow 12% from 2014 to 2024, faster than the average for all occupations, (Bureau of Labor Statistics, Occupational Outlook Handbook, (www.bls.gov/ooh), accessed on March 3rd, 2016).

This high demand is imbalanced with the supply of IS graduates where several recent studies indicated a consistent low enrollment in (IS) even with seemingly expedient opportunities available to IS majors.

Information System (IS) degree program is also known across the academia by other names such as Management Information Systems (MIS), Business Information Systems (BIS), Computer Information Systems (CIS) or Business Informatics.

The program is designed to equip the students with the skills to develop and maintain Information Systems that align with the strategic needs of any organization.

When talking about Information System, many people think that it is only about programming or just technology. Information Systems are much more than that. Information Systems development and usage involves organization, technology, and management dimensions.

Gone are the days where Information System is the sole domain of IS specialist. Business professionals can no longer count exclusively on IT experts to make decisions on development, purchasing, and deployment of Information Systems.

Regardless of their major, new graduates who have the appropriate IS knowledge and skills, stand a better opportunity of receiving lucrative employment offers and raises.

According to Kroenke [1], "if we are saying that we are finance, (or accounting, or marketing) major, not an Information Systems major, and we don't need to know how to put together information systems then we are like a lamb headed for fleecing". We need to take an active role in order to align Information Technology (IT) with business needs.

The ultimate aim of this study, is to attract more business students to the IS discipline, and equip non-BIS business students with the knowledge needed to stay in-line with the technology changes.

Therefore in order to not presume or make assumptions on how students or professionals are thinking, we conducted a study, looking for current and fresh data.

This study investigated four main research questions through the lens of Lebanese University business graduates and Lebanese business professionals:

1. Why students select (or not) Business Information Systems (BIS) as a major?
2. How do Lebanese University non-BIS business graduates perceive their levels in IS knowledge and skills after studying the MIS course?
3. What Information Systems (IS) core knowledge and skills does a non-BIS freshly graduate need to have in order to succeed in today's modern business environment?
4. What important topics should be covered in an ideal (MIS) introductory course in order to answer the demand of the labor market needs?

The rest of the paper is organized as follows:

Part II—describes the literature review and recapitulates related studies in the subject area.
Part III—describes the research methodology with a spotlight on respondents profile and instruments of the data collection.
Part IV—provides demographic information with descriptive statistics of survey respondents.
Part V—presents major findings with analysis of the collected data. Finally,
Part VI—summarizes findings and answers to research questions. This part also covers the conclusion, limitation of the study, implications and suggestions for further research and educational practice.

2 Literature Review

Before examining the past research, it was worthy to have a fresh look into some national and regional universities in order to get evidence about the recent enrollments in Information System programs. This investigation was followed by a systemic literature review with the aim of building a conceptual framework, identifying the related patterns and formulating hypotheses.

2.1 Factual Data and Evidence

As a preliminary and pre-study step, we gathered data from Lebanese and Syrian universities in order to get factual answers on the percentage of student majoring in

Table 1 Percentage of enrollment in IS programs in Lebanese and Syrian Universities

	University type	Enrollments in IS programs (%)
1.	Large-size Public University in Lebanon	3.5
2.	Large-size Public University in Syria	≈1.5
3-1.	i-Large-size Private University in Lebanon	6.7
3-2.	ii-Large-size Private University in Lebanon	4.2
4.	Small-size Private University in Lebanon	5
5.	Small-size Private University in Syria	5

IS (from the total enrollment in business program, including finance, accounting and audit, marketing and management). Table 1 provides recent evidence about the enrollment in BIS program (academic year 2015–2016).

These latest data failed to dispel concerns about the low enrollment in Information Systems (IS) program and it became critical to us to understand what hinder and what prompt a student to choose IS as a major.

2.2 *Related Studies: Reasons for Not Majoring in IS*

Several previous studies have examined the factors that impact business students' choice of major either in a broad perspective or for a specific major. Moreover, given the steady decline in the student enrollment in Information Systems, many researchers have examined reasons that deterred student to opt a career in IS. Table 2 summarizes the findings of studies conducted by researchers on factors impacting the selection of majors.

Based on the preceding literature review, eight factors were considered to investigate why business students deter from majoring in Information Systems. These factors are: "Not what they wanted to do for a career, career opportunities, lack of employment security, financial considerations—salary, benefits, lack of Job availability, parents influenced choice of major, friends or teachers influenced choice of major, subject matter too hard, difficulty of curriculum".

Moreover, the above listed studies conducted in western universities revealed that the top two salient reasons that impacted respondents' choice of majors were: "personal interest in the subject matter and career related factors such as salary and job security" while the influence of friends, counselors, teachers and family was irrelevant.

To notice that the purpose of our study was to conduct a survey on the influencing factors among Lebanese University Faculty of Economics and Business Administration, a large and unique public university in a country located in the middle-east region thus most probably students in different culture and beliefs may have different motives and influences in their choices of major.

Table 2 Several previous studies toward student choice of business major

Study toward student choice of business major	Salient reasons for Not majoring in IS	Salient reasons for selecting their current Non-IS major	Salient reasons for selecting IS as a major	Minor reasons (irrelevant)
Burns, Gao, Sherman, Vengerov, and Klein [2]	Personal Interest—(Lack of interest in IS or greater interest in another major), IS is too hard			Counselors, teachers
Snyder and Slauson [3]	Not their Career Choice, not interesting, too hard			Friends/ teachers, parents
Hogan and Li [4]		The job prospects for the major are promising		The major seems easy to study and graduate
Li, Zhang, and Zheng [5]		Personal interest in the subject matter		Friends and family Members
Downey [6]		Job-Security (Long term) and availability (after graduation)		Counselors, teachers, friends
Kuechler, McLeod, and Simkin [7]			Genuine interest in IS. Job salary and availability is not an issue	Job security and availability
Walstrom, Schambach, Jones, and Crampton [8]	Career related, not what they want to do, Subject not of interest			Teachers, counselors
Crampton, Walstrom, and Schambach [9]		Personal Interest in the subject matter		Counselors, friends
Pollacia and Lomerson [10]	Too hard, too technical students are not receiving adequate information about IS careers during their high school			

2.3 *Identifying Pattern for IS System Core Knowledge (Concepts and Skills)*

To address the remaining research questions, the first step was to identify the Information Systems (IS) core knowledge, concepts and terms. Thus, we extended the literature review conducted by He & Guo [11]. According to them, "the content analysis of most popular MIS textbooks selected by most MIS educators will reflect the needs of the dynamic business environment as well as the competitive job market". In this context, we reviewed and replaced the list of sampled textbooks appeared in He & Guo's [11] paper with a new one. Table 3 reflects the new references considered in our study (as of March 7th 2016).

Based on the content analysis of the new sampled textbooks, we identified 31 main topics categorized between 17 concepts/terms and 14 skills as research patterns described in Table 4.

In addition, several studies underlined the special knowledge requirements of Information Systems workforce [28–31]. McMurtrey et al. [32] found that the

Table 3 Sampled MIS textbooks

	MIS textbook—author/s—year	Title
1.	Laudon, Laudon, and Elragal [12]	*Management Information Systems: Managing the Digital Firm*
2.	Kroenke and Boyle [1]	*Experiencing MIS*
3.	O'Brien and Marakas [13]	*Management Information Systems*
4.	Valacich and Schneider [14]	*Information Systems Today: Managing in Digital World*
5.	McNurlin, Sprague Jr., and Bui [15]	*Information Systems Management*
6.	Pearlson and Saunders [16]	*Managing and Using Information Systems: A Strategic Approach*
7.	Laudon and Laudon [17]	*Essentials of MIS*
8.	DeHayes, Hoffer, Wainright, and Perkins [18]	*Managing Information Technology: What Managers Need to Know*
9.	Rainer Jr., Prince, and Cegielski [19]	*Introduction to Information Systems*
10.	Marakas and O'Brien [20]	*Introduction to Information Systems*
11.	Post and Anderson [21]	*Management Information Systems: Solving Business Problems with Information Technology*
12.	Baltzan [22]	*Business Driven Information Systems*
13.	Kroenke and Boyle [23]	*Using MIS*
14.	McKinney and Kroenke [24]	*Processes, Systems, and Information: An Introduction to MIS (2nd Edition)*
15.	Oz [25]	*Management Information Systems*
16.	Bidgoli [26]	*MIS2*
17.	Haag and Cummings [27]	*Management Information Systems for the Information Age*

Table 4 Research patterns: emphasis in MIS course textbooks

Research patterns—(IS) core knowledge
Concepts and terms
1. Strategic uses of Information Systems (IS)
2. Reengineering using Information Technology (IT)
3. Hardware components to consider when buying a computer
4. Open Source Software
5. The process of IS design and development
6. IS/IT Outsourcing
7. Database design, development and applications
8. Telecommunication networks
9. How the Internet works
10. Governance and Auditing of Information Systems
11. Electronic commerce
12. Privacy in the information age
13. Information Systems (IS) security
14. Enterprise Application—ERP/SAP
15. Business Intelligence
16. Cloud Computing
17. Big Data
Skills
1. Use Word Processing (such as Word)
2. Use Spreadsheet (such as Excel)
3. Use Presentation tools (such as PowerPoint)
4. Use Collaboration tools (such as Outlook, Google Docs...)
5. Use Database skills (such as Access)
6. Search for information via WWW search engines
7. Write (English/Business context)
8. Think in system's perspective and understand the relationships among functional units
9. Use software tools and techniques for communication of information
10. Use IT tools for communication between business departments
11. Use Business Intelligence tools to analyze organizational problems and create reports
12. Use software tools to predict financial performance
13. Model business processes using IT tools
14. Translate business needs into IT systems requirements

employers rate business skills and soft-skills as crucial as technical skills for IT Professionals. Aasheim et al. [33] focused on critical skill sets of Entry-Level IT Professionals. Their study indicated that the core skills and knowledge areas in an IT were, operating systems, security, hardware, networking, and database. However the study highlighted the low ranking of programming in relation to other technical skills listed on the survey.

According to Peslak and Davis [34], "IT/IS educators should emphasize general technical skills (as opposed to specific technology skills) first and foremost in IT/IS curricula". The findings of their study also suggest that "IT/IS educators should emphasize general business skills in their curricula". Wilkerson [35] found that skills in the non-technical categories are more important to MIS career success than those in technical categories.

According to Ehie [36], "employers are looking for individuals with a strong systems orientation and a good understanding of an integrative business value-chain".

Lee and Fang [37] surveyed students and recruiters to determine what IT/IS skills are needed by industry and what perception gaps exist between industry and graduating seniors in IT/IS degree programs. They found, as in various other studies, that employers are seeking team skills, communication skills, and critical thinking skills in candidates for IS/IT positions.

Moreover, several studies highlight the existence of gaps between industry and academic perception regarding the importance of various skills and attributes such as [33, 38–41].

To conclude, numerous studies had identified main skills or general knowledge that employers anticipate of business graduates, however little attention has been given to the core IS knowledge and skills that are vital for other business professions. Most of the researchers in this field pinpointed what skills are required from IS graduates. The majority of them did not provide what IS knowledge and skills are required from non-IS business freshly graduates neither what critical topics should be addressed in MIS Introductory course in order to tailoring business educational supply according to the demand of modern industry. Hence, a conceptual framework was compulsory to serve as a guiding map that steers our study's activities and shapes our research processes and approaches.

2.4 *Research Framework and Hypothesis Development*

We conducted a four-phase study to investigate the IS core Knowledge supply and demand:

In phase one, we studied why students select (or not) Business Information Systems (BIS) as a major. In Phase two, we identified IS core Knowledge as pattern to assess students' perceived degree of knowledge as well as the need of IS knowledge and skills from the perspective of business professionals.

In phase three, we compared students' perceptions with business professionals' perceptions and identified disparity that need to be addressed in details in further research. In phase four, we summarized findings and provided conclusion and implication for educational practice. The research framework is illustrated in Fig. 1.

The hypotheses were formulated as follows:

H1 The education in Lebanon at Lebanese University, faculty of Economics and Business Administration, does equip the business graduates with necessary Information Systems knowledge and skills to ensure their success in job market.

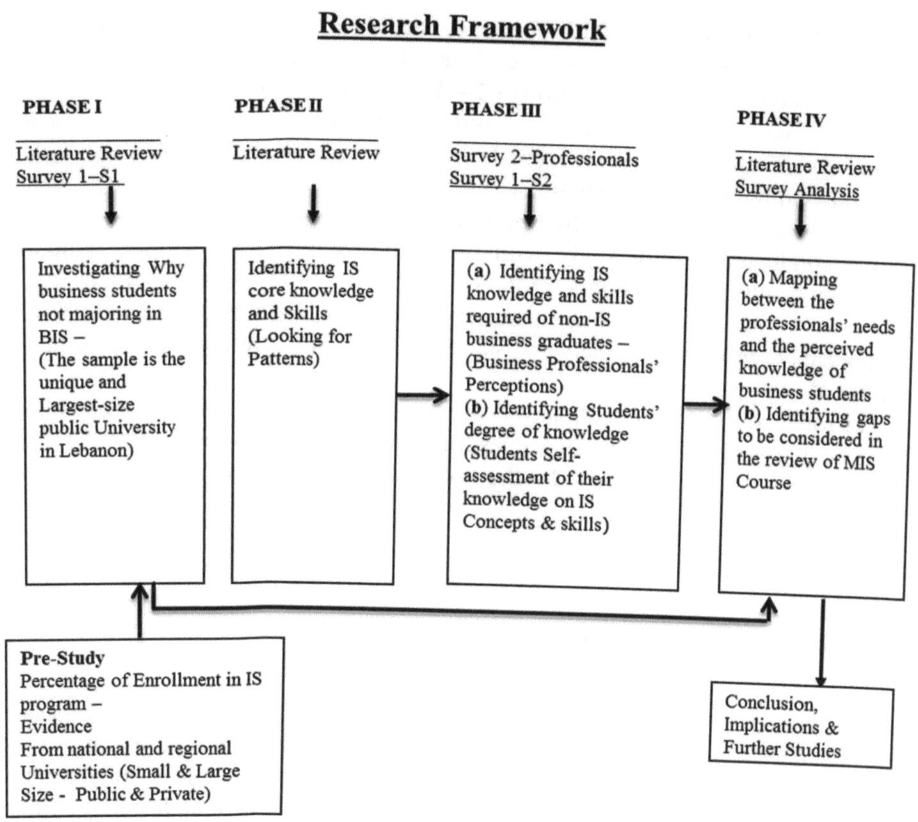

Fig. 1 Research framework (**Survey 1—S1** Questionnaire #1: Section 1: Student Survey on Selection Major, **Survey 1—S2** Questionnaire #1: Section 2: Students perceived IS core Knowledge and Skills, **Survey 2—P** Questionnaire #2: Business Professionals' perceptions on required IS knowledge and Skills.)

H2 Students do not opt for Business Information Systems as a career due to the difficulty of the curriculum.

In order to test these hypotheses, we used a quantitative method described in the following section.

2.5 Methodology

The primary purpose of this study was to identify the IS core knowledge including concepts and skills that business professionals want and new business graduates lack. To this end and based on the results of the literature, we carried out two questionnaires:

The first questionnaire (**Survey 1—S**) was mainly divided into two sections:

The first one (**Survey 1—S1**) was designed to investigate reasons why business students are not selecting Information Systems as a major. The second section

(Survey 1—S2) consisted of 17 IS core concepts and 14 skills that students were asked to rate following their perceived level of knowledge.

In the second questionnaire **(Survey 2—P)**, business professionals were asked to rate the same IS core concepts and skills in terms of importance for non-BIS business graduates (how much these IS core concepts and skills are important to be possessed by non-BIS graduate).

Both questionnaires used a five-point Likert-type scale.

We conducted a pilot study with the participation of 30 people, including students, faculty and business professionals. The feedback contributed in the release of an improved version of the survey that was used in the data collection. In this paper, descriptive means and standard deviation were used as the principal statistical method.

A Cronbach's coefficient alpha was used to calculate the reliability of questions. It was equal to 0.777 for the first questionnaire **(Survey 1—S)** and 0.914 for the second questionnaire **(Survey 2—P)**; both had an acceptable degree of internal consistency.

2.6 *Profile of Respondents (Survey 1—S)*

We conducted a voluntary and anonymous survey during winter 2016 end semester. The first questionnaire was administered among business students in their master final year at Lebanese University, Faculty of Economics and Business Administration. This university has the largest size and it is the sole public institution of higher education in Lebanon where its students represent about 39% of the total students distributed between 52 private universities.

A total of 139 respondents returned the questionnaire. Seven were removed due to incomplete data or incorrectly coded responses, resulting in a total of 132 valid surveys.

As illustrated in Fig. 2, respondents were a predominantly female student (76.52%) which indicates that women were more interested than men in earning a business degree.

The majors of respondents were distributed as follows: 6.1% Business Informatics, 9.8% marketing, 17.4% Management, 30.3% Accounting and Audit and The largest percentage of respondents 36.4% were Finance.

As demonstrated in Fig. 3, our sample was dominated with students majoring in finance, accounting and audit which represents around 67% of the total participants.

In the following section, the profile of business professionals was described along with their related business activities.

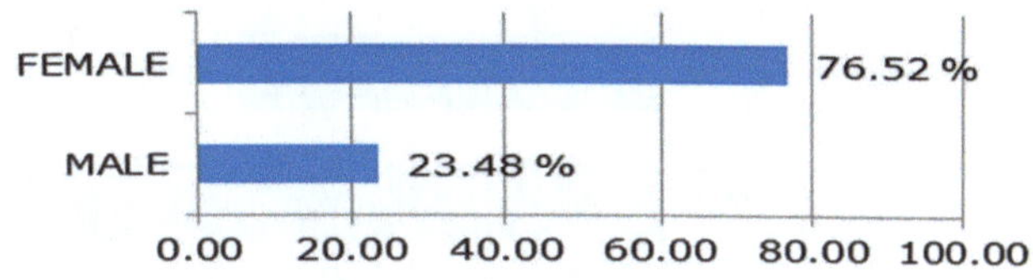

Fig. 2 Gender representation among students

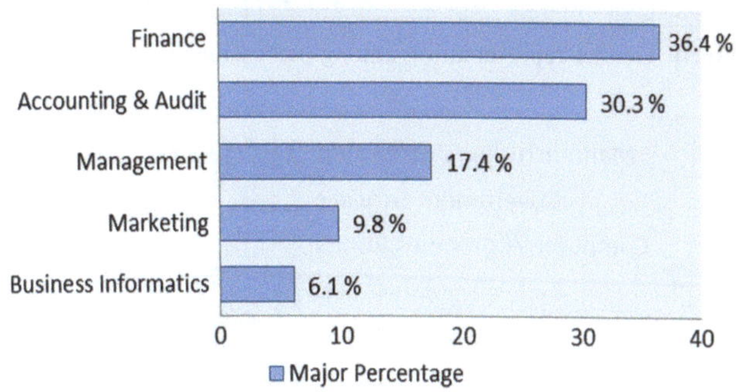

Fig. 3 The distribution of students by major

2.7 *Profile of Respondents (Survey 2—P)*

The second questionnaire was addressed to business professionals from diverse industries. A total of 93 surveys were collected, five of which were excluded due to missing information. This resulted in 88 for this study, with 39.80% females and 60.20% males as shown in Fig. 4.

The gender of business professionals was dominated by male which indicates that in the past, men were more interested than women in earning a business degree, but in the past few years, the trend was reversed.

The percentage of the industries represented by the respondents is illustrated in Fig. 5.

This figure demonstrates that (43%) of the respondents work for financial services, 14.77% for miscellaneous services, 12.50% for retail/wholesale, 10.23% for education, 7.95% for computer/Communications, 6.82% for Government services and 4.55% for Manufacturing/Distribution. This delineation is characterized by the highest proportion of financial Services.

3 Research Findings

The results are divided into four sections; the first section (Sect. 3.1) handles the reasons why business students are not majoring in Information System program. The second section (Sect. 3.2), describes the students' perceptions on their level of knowledge in Information Systems. The third section (Sect. 3.3) identifies the IS core knowledge and skills required of non-BIS graduates and the last section

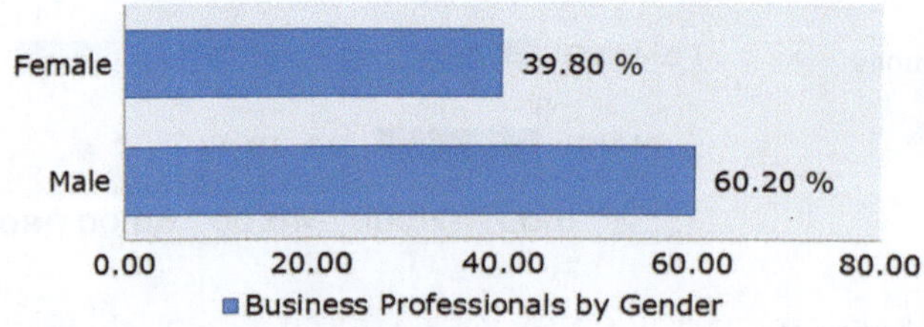

Fig. 4 Gender representation among professionals

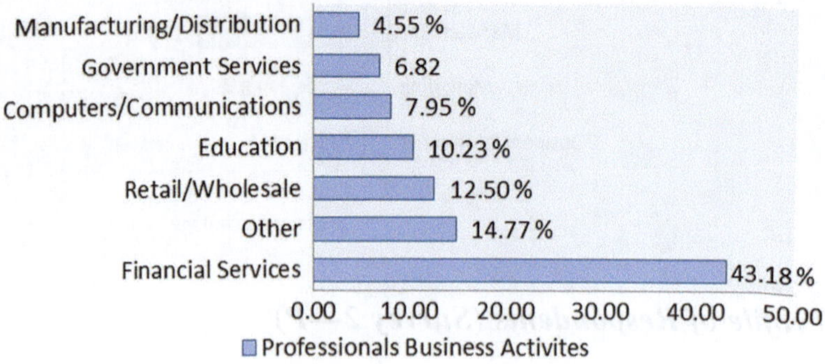

Fig. 5 Percentage of industries represented by the respondents

(Sect. 4) consists of mapping between IS core knowledge and skills supply (Students' perceptions) and demand (Business Professionals' perceptions).

3.1 *Survey 1—S1 (Importance of MIS Course and Reasons for Not Majoring in IS)*

The following section outlines the summary answers of the main questions from the first survey instrument. 73.5% of non-BIS business graduates believe that MIS course can make them more competitive in the job market.

Figure 6 depicts the responses to the question: "I am not a BIS (Business Information Systems) student, but MIS (Management Information Systems) introductory course can make me more competitive in the job market".

Moreover from 132 students, 77 are working and 55 are unemployed.

98.7% from the working students are always/often using the computer for their business activity.

The main question in this section is related to the choice of major. We listed eight main reasons that may impact the student's choice of major and for each one, we asked the participant to rate the degree of its importance using a five-point scale ranging from"1—not important" to "5—very important". The most important

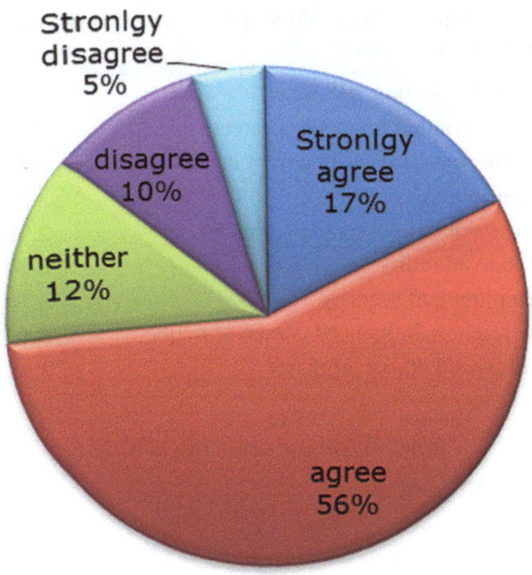

Fig. 6 MIS (Management Information Systems) introductory course can make me more competitive in the job market

reasons were: "not what they want" and "difficulty of curriculum" that seem equally in importance, followed by "career opportunity". However the reasons rated as the least important were: "influence of parents" and "influence of friends or teachers". The statistical means of the responses from the participants are reported consequently in Table 5 and Fig. 7 with higher rated reasons at the top.

This result with—"subject matter too hard, difficulty of curriculum" ranked as the top reason that deters students from majoring in IS—, confirms our hypothesis H2 stating that: "students do not opt for Business Information Systems as a career due to the difficulty of the curriculum".

3.2 Survey 1—S2 (Level of Proficiency in IS Core Knowledge and Skills)

Based on the literature including He and Guo's [11] study and the content analysis of 17 sampled MIS textbooks, we identified a range of Information Systems (IS) Concepts/terms and skills, and for each one, we asked students to self-rate their perceived level of knowledge using a five-point scale, as described in Table 6.

For the purpose of this research, a self-rating of 1 or 2 was considered as low, a 3 was considered an average, and a 4 or 5 were considered as a high.

This question was divided into two parts: the first part handled the perceived level of familiarity with IS concepts/terms and the second the perceived skills level.

Table 5 Importance of reasons in "why" do you think students do not major in BIS (sorted in order of importance, from most to least)

Rank	Reason for not selecting BIS major	Mean	Std. deviation
1	Not what they wanted to do for a career	**3.17**	**1.45**
2	Subject matter too hard, difficulty of curriculum	**3.17**	**1.37**
3	Career opportunities	3.08	1.30
4	Financial considerations—salary, benefits	2.98	1.35
5	Lack of Job availability	2.94	1.44
6	Lack of employment security	2.76	1.28
7	Friends or teachers influenced choice of majors	2.48	1.16
8	Parents influenced choice of major	2.31	1.28

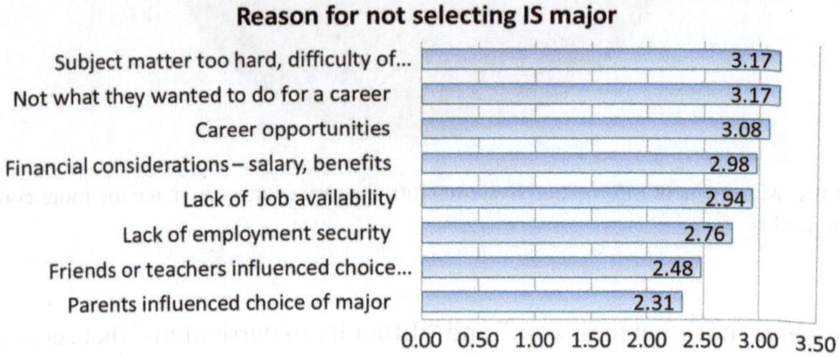

Fig. 7 Respondents were asked to rate the reason their peers do not major in (BIS)—"Why students do not select IS or (BIS) as a major?"

Table 6 Self-assessment five-point Likert-type scale

1. I have no knowledge about the concept/term/skill
2. I have heard about concept/term/skill but could not discuss or demonstrate the concept/term/skill
3. I could discuss or demonstrate the concept/term/skill in a superficial way with someone else
4. I could discuss or demonstrate the concept/term/skill in detail with someone else
5. I consider myself a true expert with regard to this concept/term/skill

For the first part, most of the 17 concepts/terms had low average scores that ranged between 1 and 2. The average self-perceived knowledge level/overall mean was 2.54, with "How the Internet work" scoring the highest at 2.88 and "Reengineering using information technology" scoring the lowest at 2.11.

The second part of this question was related to self-perceived skills level.

Most of the 14 IS skills had average scores that ranged between 2 and 3. The overall mean was 3.17, with "Use Word Processing (such as Word)" scoring the highest at 3.99 and "Model business processes using IT tools" scoring the lowest at 2.33.

The scores for mean and standard deviation are reported in the summary Table 7.

Table 7 Summary table—IS core knowledge: supply versus demand (perceptions and perspectives)

IS core knowledge						
IS Concept	Demand			Supply		
	Rank	Mean	Std. Dev.	Rank	Mean	Std. Dev.
Information Systems (IS) security	1	4.18	0.98	12	2.46	1.09
How the Internet works	2	4.14	1.05	1	2.88	1.15
Privacy in the information age	3	3.92	1.05	10	2.54	1.12
Governance and Auditing of IS	4	3.90	1.17	8	2.58	1.16
Business Intelligence	5	3.90	0.95	4	2.72	1.17
Strategic uses of IS	6	3.83	0.93	16	2.27	1.02
Telecommunication networks	7	3.78	1.08	2	2.85	1.18
Enterprise Application—ERP/SAP	8	3.77	1.07	14	2.50	1.09
Hardware comp. to consider when buying a computer	9	3.66	1.00	3	2.76	2.85
Big Data	10	3.56	1.13	13	2.41	1.18
Electronic commerce	11	3.49	1.14	5	2.64	1.15
Cloud Computing	12	3.47	1.10	7	2.61	1.23
Open Source Software	13	3.44	1.05	9	2.54	2.86
The process of IS design and development	14	3.42	1.04	6	2.62	3.92
Database design, development and applications	15	3.42	1.29	14	2.39	1.13
Reengineering using Information Technology(IT)	16	3.38	1.10	17	2.11	1.00
IS/IT Outsourcing	17	3.33	1.21	15	2.28	1.00
Overall mean		3.68			2.50	
IS Skills						
Use Spreadsheet (such as Excel)	1	4.64	0.76	3	3.89	1.07
Write (English /Business context)	2	4.51	0.74	6	3.54	1.16
Use Collaboration tools (such as Outlook, Google Docs...)	3	4.42	0.78	4	3.77	1.12
Use Word Processing (such as Word)	4	4.33	0.81	1	3.99	1.23
Search for information via WWW search engines	5	4.26	0.86	5	3.77	1.17
Use Business Intelligence tools	6	4.02	0.95	11	2.58	1.11
Use software tools and techniques for comm. of info.	7	3.98	0.86	9	2.77	1.13
Use IT tools for communication between business dept.	8	3.98	0.97	10	2.62	1.13
Use software tools to predict financial performance	9	3.98	0.98	12	2.55	1.13
Use Presentation tools (such as PowerPoint)	10	3.92	1.09	2	3.99	1.06
Think in system's perspective	11	3.89	1.00	8	2.97	2.86
Translate business needs into IT systems requirements	12	3.88	1.01	13	2.36	1.12
Use Database Skills (such as Access)	13	3.72	1.03	7	3.19	1.17
Model business processes using IT tools	14	3.72	1.03	14	2.33	1.12
Overall Mean		4.09			3.17	

3.3 (Survey 2—P): IS Core Knowledge and Skills Required of Non-BIS Graduates

In the first part of this survey, we investigated the level of importance that business professionals place on the IS concepts for non-BIS graduates to possess. A five-points scale was used: 1 = Not Important At All, 2 = Of Little Importance, 3 = Of Average Importance, 4 = Very Important, 5 = Absolutely Essential.

Almost all concepts listed in the survey were considered by business professionals to be important or rather very important.

The 17 concepts/terms had an average scores that ranged between 3.66 and 4.18. The overall mean was 3.68, with "Information Systems (IS) Security" scoring the highest at 4.18 and "IS/IT Outsourcing" scoring the lowest at 3.33. Thus we concluded that this Information System Core Knowledge is considered by business professionals (participants) to be a must-to-have and not only a nice-to-have.

In the second part of this question, we investigated the level of importance that business professionals place on the IS skills. The results indicated that almost all skills listed in the survey were considered to be very important and tend to be absolutely essential as shown in the summary Table 7.

The 14 skills had an average score that ranged between 3.72 and 4.64. The overall mean was 4.09, with "Use Spreadsheet (such as Excel)" scoring the highest at 4.64, followed by "write (English/Business context)" and "Use collaboration tools". Therefore, the majority of business professionals perceived the importance of these skills not only very significant but a necessity for non-BIS business graduates. Although the "Model business processes using IT tools" skill was ranked the lowest, however even with this position, the participants considered it as important with a score equal to 3.72.

4 Mapping Between IS Knowledge and Skills Supply and Demand

When mapping between the new graduates' and professionals' perceptions, we identified a mismatch between the supply and demand as shown in Fig. 8.

The students considered themselves reasonably capable in each of the 14 skills with an average level, whereas they rated their knowledge in IS concepts below the average, which means that they have only heard about these concepts but could not discuss or demonstrate any idea related to the subject matter. This shortage of IS knowledge is faced with strong demand across industries, where our findings indicated that business professionals rated almost all IS concepts listed in the survey as important or very important for non-BIS graduates. As shown in Table 7, the top six IS Concepts emphasized were: "Information Security", "How the Internet works", "Privacy in the information age", "Governance and Auditing of IS", "Business Intelligence" and "Strategic uses of IS".

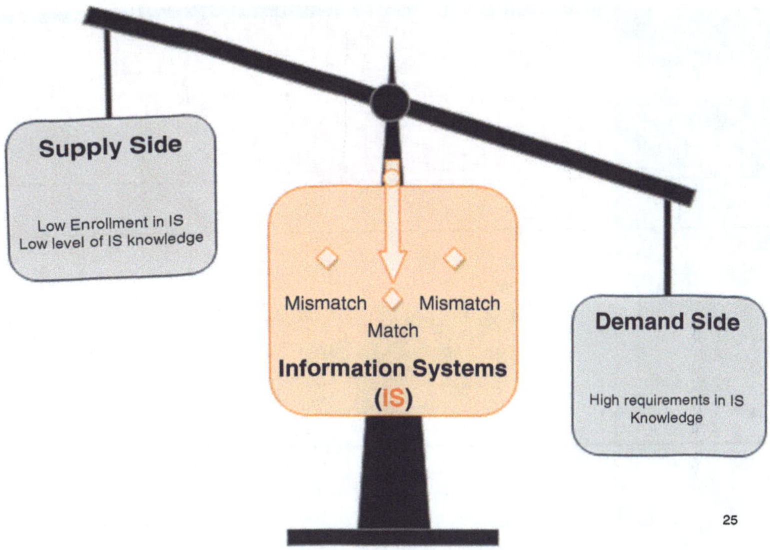

Fig. 8 Demand and supply for the Information Systems core Knowledge are out of balance

The study identified a significant gap in five main areas: "1—Information Security", "2—Strategic Use of IS", "3—Privacy in the information age", "4—Governance and Auditing of IS" and "5—Enterprise Application—ERP/SAP". Figures 9, 10, and 11 highlight the disparity between the IS knowledge and skills supply and demand.

Hypothesis H1 predicted that a majority of students will perceive a knowledge level in IS concepts at least score at 3 which means that they can at least discuss or demonstrate the concept/term/in a superficial way with someone else, however this was not true when examining the students' answers as described in the summary Table 7.

Based on the findings synthetized in the summary Table 7, and after comparing the level of proficiency perceived by the students with the industries' requirements, it became obvious to us that what the job market wants, the new business graduates lack. This fact falsified our hypothesis H1 stating that "The education in Lebanon at Lebanese University, Faculty of Economics and Business Administration, does equip the business graduates with necessary IS knowledge and skills to ensure their success in job market".

5 Conclusion and Limitations

Compared with past studies, our research contributed in providing an analysis of factors that impacting student's choice of major in a university located in Middle-East region. Additionally, our study tackled the Information Systems core knowledge and skills

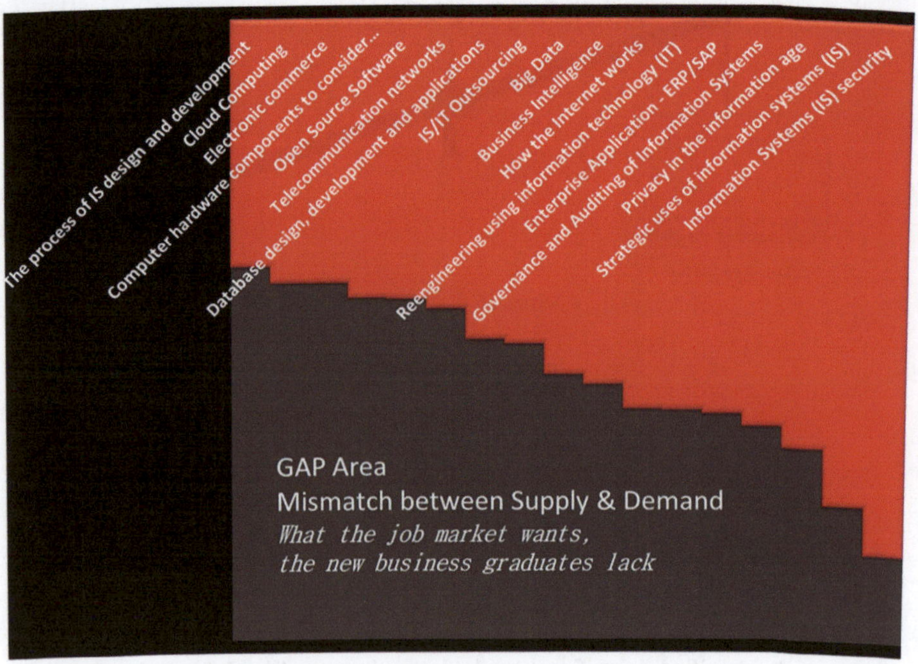

Fig. 9 Significant gaps between what business needs and what fresh graduates have. The discrepancy is highlighted from smallest to largest

required from non-BIS graduates which is quite different from other studies where the focus was given on general skills requirement or the skills required from Information Systems (IS) graduates.

Furthermore, our study extended the research conducted by [11] and identified Information Systems (IS) core knowledge and skills that have been used to compare and contrast between students' overall perception of their knowledge level with what is effectively required in the business job market by experienced professionals. The findings demonstrated a significant discrepancy that needs to be addressed by business faculty; thus the results are crucial.

Educators can consider our findings to review and enhance not only the MIS Introductory course but also to infuse Information Systems into core business curricula with a new integrated approach in order to meet the updated view of market demand. Information Systems should be an integral part not an add-on.

Our survey indicated that the top two reasons for not majoring in Information Systems (IS) were the personal interest "not what they wanted to do for a career" and the difficulty of curriculum "subject matter too hard/difficulty of curriculum". These findings are consistent with the result of several past studies undertaken in western universities such as [2, 3, 10].

Moreover, our research can be extended to scrutinize the content of core introductory courses that are usually taught to business students in their first

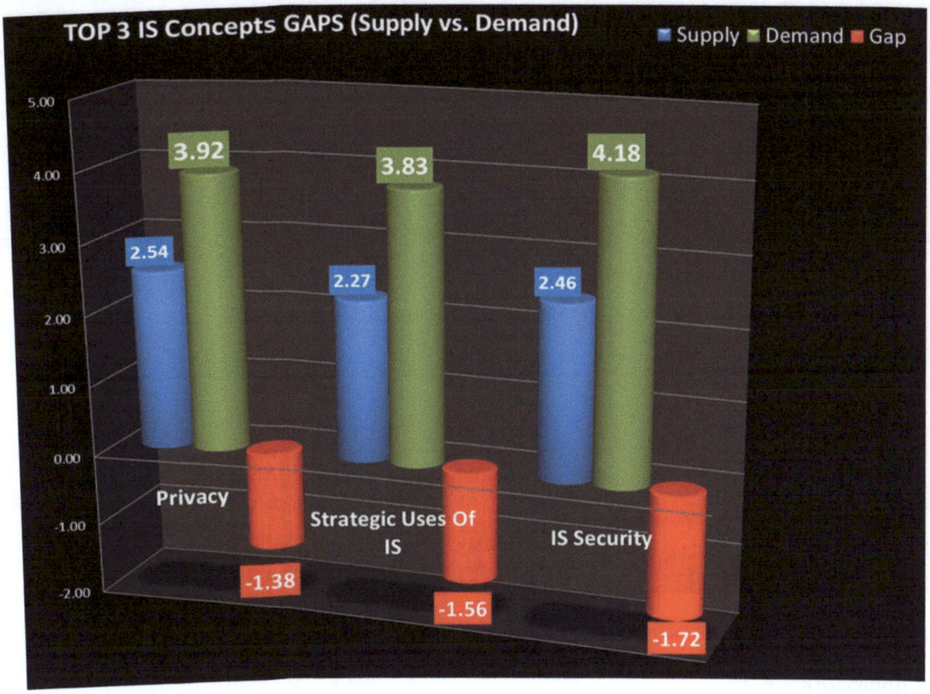

Fig. 10 Top three information system concepts gaps (IS security, strategic use of IS and privacy in the information age)

undergraduate year. A previous investigation conducted by [42] assessed the usefulness of these courses in undergraduate curriculum. However further research is needed to explore the contents of these introductory courses. Topics included may stipulate an opportunity to promote interest in Information Systems programs at a time when business students have not picked a major. In addition, given the perceived difficulty of IS curriculum raised throughout the survey, a study for assessing the coherence of the Information Systems program and its agility to attract more students, is imperative.

Our final suggestion is to put more emphasis on concepts rather than skills since this latter can change rapidly with the advancement of technology. Another potential solution for non-BIS graduate to increase their knowledge and marketability is through an option to have double majors. Further research is possible to gather information about the business students' interest in this subject.

The limitations of our study mostly pertain to the following subjects:

- The students participating in this study came from one Lebanese university which obviously limits generalizability.
- Statistical methods were limited to average mean and standard deviation. Further study using factorial analysis and clustering methods will be of great importance.

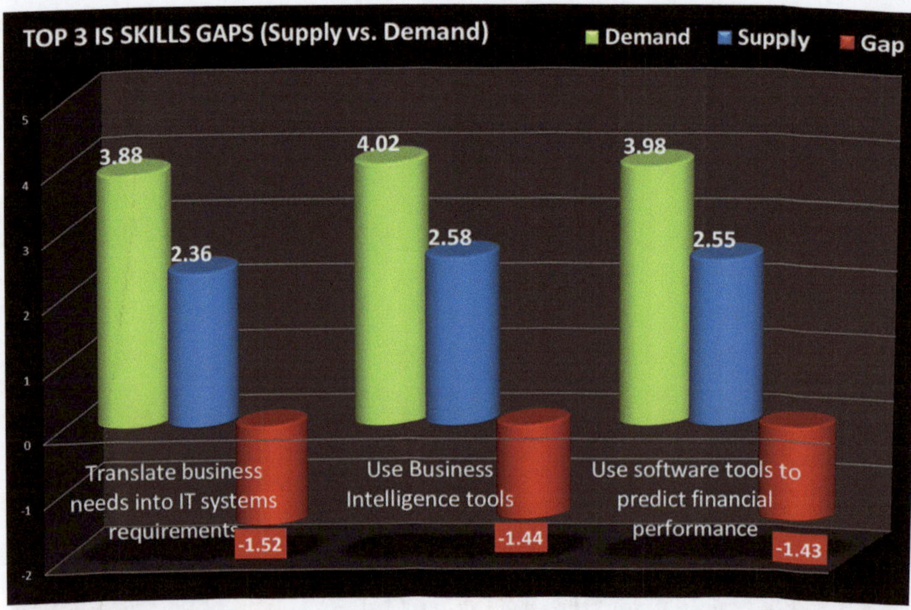

Fig. 11 Top Three Information System Skills gaps (Translate business needs into IT systems requirements, Use Business Intelligence tools and Use software tools to predict financial performance)

– Using the "Self-perception" technique, students may over estimate their self-assessed knowledge level as noted by several studies such as [43–45], however even with such self-overestimation, the participants indicated a low level of Information Systems (IS) knowledge. Further research is required to consider students' performance in addition to their self-perceptions in order to be mapped with the market IS demands.

References

1. Kroenke, D. M., & Boyle, R. J. (2015). *Experiencing MIS* (6th ed.). Harlow: Pearson Education.
2. Burns, T., Gao, Y., Sherman, C., Vengerov, A., & Klein, S. (2014). Investigating a 21st century paradox: As the demand for technology jobs increases why are fewer students majoring in information systems? *Information Systems Education Journal (ISEDJ), 12*(4), 4–16.
3. Snyder, J., & Slauson, G. J. (2014). Majoring in information systems: Reasons why students select (or not) information systems as a major. *Information Systems Education Journal (ISEDJ), 12*(3), 59–66.
4. Hogan, P., & Li, L. (2011). The perceptions of business students regarding management information systems (MIS) programs. *Journal of Technology Research, 2*(1), 1–6.
5. Li, L., Zhang, C., & Zheng, G. (2014). Promoting information systems major to undergraduate students—A comprehensive investigation. *Journal of Information Systems Education, 25*(3), 211–220.

6. Downey, J. (2011). An empirical examination of the composition of vocational interest in business colleges: MIS vs. other majors. *Journal of Information Systems Education, 22*(2), 147–148.
7. Kuechler, W. L., McLeod, A., & Simkin, M. G. (2009). Empirical research, why don't more students major in IS? *Decision Sciences Journal of Innovative Education, 7*(2), 463–488.
8. Walstrom, K. A., Schambach, T. P., Jones, K. T., & Crampton, W. J. (2006). Why are students not majoring in information systems? *Journal of Information Systems Education, 19*(1), 43–54.
9. Crampton, W. J., Walstrom, K. A., & Schambach, T. P. (2006). Factors influencing major selection by college of business students. *Issues in Information Systems, VII*(1), 226–230.
10. Pollacia, L., & Lomerson, W. L. (2006). Analysis of factors affecting declining CIS enrollment. *Issues in Information Systems, 7*(1), 220–225.
11. He, J., & Guo, Y. M. (2014). Should I take more MIS courses? Implications from interviews with business recruiters. *Journal of Higher Education Theory and Practice, 14*(1), 11–25.
12. Laudon, K. C., Laudon, J. P., & Elragal, A. A. (2013). *Management information systems: Managing the digital firm* (Arab Word ed.). Pearson Education Limited: Harlow.
13. O'Brien, J. A., & Marakas, G. (2010). *Management information systems* (10th ed.). New York: McGraw-Hill Education.
14. Valacich, J. A., & Schneider, C. (2015). *Information systems today: Managing in the digital world* (7th ed.). Boston, MA: Pearson Education.
15. McNurlin, B. C., Sprague Jr., R. H., & Bui, T. (2008). *Information systems management* (8th ed.). Upper Saddle River, NJ: Prentice Hall.
16. Pearlson, K. E., & Saunders, C. S. (2012). *Managing and using information systems: A strategic approach* (5th ed.). New York: Wiley.
17. Laudon, K. C., & Laudon, J. P. (2016). *Essentials of MIS* (12th ed.). Upper Saddle River, NJ: Prentice Hall.
18. DeHayes, D. W., Hoffer, J. A., Wainright, M. E., & Perkins, W. C. (2008). *Managing information technology: What managers need to know* (6th ed.). Upper Saddle River, NJ: Prentice Hall.
19. Rainer Jr., R. K., Prince, B., & Cegielski, C. (2015). *Introduction to information systems* (5th ed.). Hoboken, NJ: Wiley.
20. Marakas, G., & O'Brien, J. (2012). *Introduction to information systems* (16th ed.). Boston, MA: McGraw-Hill Education.
21. Post, G. V., & Anderson, D. L. (2005). *Management information systems: Solving business problems with information technology* (4 Rev ed.). New York: McGraw-Hill Education.
22. Baltzan, P. (2014). *Business driven information systems* (4th ed.). Boston, MA: McGraw-Hill.
23. Kroenke, D. M., & Boyle, R. J. (2015). *Using MIS* (8th ed.). Upper Saddle River, NJ: Prentice Hall.
24. McKinney, E., & Kroenke, D. M. (2014). *Processes, systems, and information: An introduction to MIS* (2nd ed.). Boston, MA: Prentice Hall.
25. Oz, E. (2008). *Management information systems* (6th ed.). Boston, MA: Course Technology.
26. Bidgoli, H. (2011). *MIS2* (2nd ed.). Mason, OH: Cengage Learning.
27. Haag, S., & Cummings, M. (2012). *Management information systems for the information age* (9th ed.). Boston, MA: McGraw-Hill Education.
28. Grant, D. M., Malloy, A. D. D., & Murphy, M. C. (2009). A comparison of student perceptions of their computer skills to their actual abilities. *Journal of Information Technology Education, 8*, 141–150.
29. Turban, E., Volonio, L., & Wood, G. R. (2015). *Information technology for management: Advancing sustainable, profitable business growth* (10th ed.). Hoboken, NJ: Wiley.
30. Auken, S. V., Chrysler, E., Wells, L. G., & Simkin, M. (2011). Relating gap analysis results to information systems program attitudes: The identification of gap priorities and implications. *Journal of Education for Business, 86*, 346–351.
31. Walstrom, K. A., & Schambach, T. P. (2012). Impacting student perceptions about careers in information systems. *Journal of Information Technology Education: Research, 11*, 235–248.

32. McMurtrey, M. E., Downey, J. P., Zeltmann, S. M., & Friedman, W. H. (2008). Critical skill sets of entry-level IT professionals: An empirical examination of perceptions from field personnel. *Journal of Information Technology Education, 7*, 101–120.
33. Aasheim, C. L., Li, L., Shropshire, J. D., & Kadlec, C. A. (2011). *IT program curriculum recommendations based on a survey of knowledge and skill requirements for entry-level IT workers*. Department of Information Technology Faculty Research and Publications, Paper 1.
34. Peslak, A. R., & Davis, G. A. (2009). An empirical study of the relative importance of specific technology skills, general business skills, and general technology skills. *Issues in Information Systems, X*(12), 430–438.
35. Wilkerson, J. W. (2012). An alumni assessment of MIS related job skill importance and skill gaps. *Journal of Information Systems Education, 23*(1), 85–99.
36. Ehie, I. C. (2012). Developing a management information systems (MIS) curriculum: Perspectives from MIS practitioners. *Journal of Education for Business, 77*(3), 151–156.
37. Lee, S., & Fang, X. (2008). Perception gaps about skills requirement for entry-level is professionals between recruiters and students: An exploratory study. *Information Resources Management Journal, 21*(3), 39–63.
38. Lee, S., Koh, S., Yen, D., & Tang, H.-L. (2002). Perception gaps between IS academics and IS practioners: An exploratory study. *Information and Management, 40*(1), 51–61.
39. Kim, Y., Hsu, J., & Stern, M. (2006). An update on the IS/IT skills gap. *Journal of Information Systems Education, 17*(4), 395–402.
40. Lee, C. K., & Han, H.-J. (2008). Analysis of skills requirement for entry-level programmer/analysts in fortune 500 corporations. *Journal of Information Systems Education, 19*(1), 17–27.
41. Aasheim, L. C., Li, L., & Williams, S. R. (2009). Knowledge and skill requirements for information technology graduates: A comparison of industry and academia. *Journal of Information Systems Education, 20*(3), 349–356.
42. Mishra, S., Cellante, D., & Kavanaugh, L. (2015). Assessing the usefulness of a core introductory information. *Issues in Information Systems, 16*(1), 31–40.
43. Beverley, O. (2008). Commencing undergraduates' self-efficacy and ability in finding academic resources: Are they improving? *Studies in Learning, Evaluation, Innovation and Development, 5*(3), 1–8.
44. Gross, M., & Latham, D. (2012). What's skill got to do with it?: Information literacy skills and self-views of ability among first-year college students. *Journal of the American Society for Information Science and Technology, 63*(3), 574–583.
45. Hodgens, C., Sendall, M., & Evans, L. (2012). Post-graduate health promotion students assess their information literacy. *Reference Services Review, 40*(3), 408–422.

Higher Education and Employability: Building Student's Self-confidence and Efficacy

Claude Chammaa

Abstract Globalization and ICT revolution have changed the parameters of employability. Skills required become very specific to many fields like HR, Project Management and Engineer. . . All these changes have driven higher education to become a global industry. During the past 10–15 years, the mobility of Lebanese people increased considerably to foreign neighboring countries. It started in the 1980s with the Lebanese civil war and progressed until today. One of the reasons remains that young fresh graduated hardly find jobs in Lebanon and prefer Arab countries that can grant more wealth and secure wage. Some of the most significant challenges that society faces today are matching education and labor market requirement. This article describes student's actual perception of education as well as the influence of learning and experience on their self-confidence and its impact on employability. The methodology used is quantitative based on questionnaire conducted using a convenience sampling without pre-test. It will seek to offer some suggestions for enhancing the support of learning in the Lebanese public universities.

Keywords Higher Education • Modernization • Employability • Self Confidence

1 Introduction

Since the first appearance of the oldest university in Lebanon and the region (American University of Beirut, 1866) followed by the Saint Joseph University (1875), the creation of universities in Lebanon continued over time until reaching 32 universities and 10 institutes in 2016. Among these universities, there is one public university and 41 private universities.

Lebanese university contains almost 40% of the total number of Lebanese students (MHE report, 2011) (Table 1).

The Lebanese academic curriculum follows two systems (French or American) both offering diplomas accredited by Lebanese ministry of education.

C. Chammaa (✉)
Department of Business Administration, Lebanese University, Achrafieh, Lebanon
e-mail: Claude.chammaa@hotmail.com

J. Marx Gómez et al. (eds.), *Modernizing Academic Teaching and Research in Business and Economics*, Springer Proceedings in Business and Economics,
DOI 10.1007/978-3-319-54419-9_3

Table 1 Total number of students, their distribution, between the private and public higher education institutions for 3 academic years

Year	Total number of students	Enrolled in the Lebanese university	Enrolled in the private universities
2006–2007	160,364	72,961	87,403
2007–2008	167,165	74,176	92,989
2009–2010	180,850	72,813	108,037

If we take a look at the Lebanese culture and its effect on the choice of careers by university students, we notice that there is a constant anxiety related to the future (Uncertainty avoidance, Hofstede). Lebanese students are always looking for having better future. As we all know, Lebanese people don't contribute over time to their retirement, so they always aspire to have quick results. This situation motivates the students to have the highest diploma in order to have a better profession. On the other hand, they aspire to generate quick results so they can quickly improve in their career. Hofstede, in his pragmatic dimension, describes how every society has to maintain some links with its own past while dealing with the challenges of the present and future, and societies priorities these two existential goals differently. Normative societies. Which score low on this dimension, for example, prefer to maintain time-honored traditions and norms while viewing societal change with suspicion. Those with a culture which scores high encourage thrift and efforts in modern education as a way to prepare for the future. The very low score on the pragmatic dimension shows that Lebanese culture is normative. People in such societies have a strong concern with establishing the absolute Truth; they exhibit great respect for traditions and a focus on achieving quick results.

In a society that gives great respect to traditions and simultaneously lives in a constant political and economic instability, how can future graduates deal with all requirements of the labor market? Do curriculum and experience impact on their future? The purpose of the study is to observe the possible effect of experience, learning and choice of the university on self-confidence and self-efficacy related to the students at the Lebanese university. Results should bring more light on the student's perception of the actual curriculum.

The overall research question for this paper is:

How can learning and experience motivate students to apply to high-level jobs in Lebanon or abroad?

The sub-research questions include:

Does learning have an effect on the self-confidence of the students? What perception students have about modernizing of higher education? Can we conclude that they are satisfied with the curriculum followed by their university? Do modernizing curriculum and teaching promote self-confidence which can enhance significantly their future?

If we go back to the main question of this research, we notice that theoretically, from teacher's perspective, the main purpose of a course is to be well understood by students whom will be tested at the end of each semester. From the students perspective, the most important goal is to pass exams one after the other to complete the BA diploma and have a master degree after 5 years. But where is the employability in all perspectives? It seems as if everyone should complete step by step all stages and the question of jobs should be reported.

2 Motivation

University teachers have stated that sometimes they are frustrated about attendance in class, uncompleted assignments, and student focusing on grades and results of tests rather than learning. On the other hand, students claim that courses are not interesting, that they fail to recognize the value of what they are learning. In this situation, the gap should be removed from both parties. How can we improve and modernize higher education in order to reduce the gap between teachers and students and to increase the self-confidence of the students that can encourage them to have gain entrance to a well-paid career?

Recent research found that although university participants view technology as having a largely positive impact on their campuses, they acknowledge several challenges. The biggest of these may well be cost, a factor that close to 70% of university respondents cite as their greatest concern [1]. This fact puts universities into different challenges: how can they modernize the higher education with existing resources especially in public universities where budget is too low comparing to private ones?

A constructive association should be forged between the employability and pedagogic reform. To understand how to reform pedagogic curriculum we should understand:

What employers are looking for: In recruiting to specific graduate-level jobs, employers are looking for graduates and diplomats who possess high-level skills, knowledge, and appropriate personal attributes, and who can 'grow' the job or help transform the organization [2].

How students react with learning in addition to their experience and how can we increase the value of these concepts in order to ensure for them a better future?

Our study will be concentrating on the second part: understanding students and their perception of knowledge, learning experience, self-efficacy, self-confidence and their impact on employability.

3 Conceptual Foundations

Research about higher education decision-making [3] and outcomes [4] have focused on the higher education undergraduate population and the significance of demographic characteristics for choices made and career paths followed.

In conducting career choice, [5] had proposed that "Social cognitive career theory (SCCT) represents a relatively new effort to understand the processes through which people form interests, make choices, and achieve varying levels of success in educational and occupational pursuits". They developed a model that shows relationships between personal inputs, background, learning, experiences, interest, actions and much more (Fig. 1).

Based on learning experiences, self-efficacy expectations we developed a conceptual model that shows relationships between experience, learnings, faculty choice, self-efficacy expected self-confidence and professional choice. The model proposed would test the possible relationship between experiences, learnings, faculty choice with mediator variables which leads to employability (local or international).

Conceptual Model and Hypotheses

Grounded in the literature, we developed the conceptual model (Fig. 2).

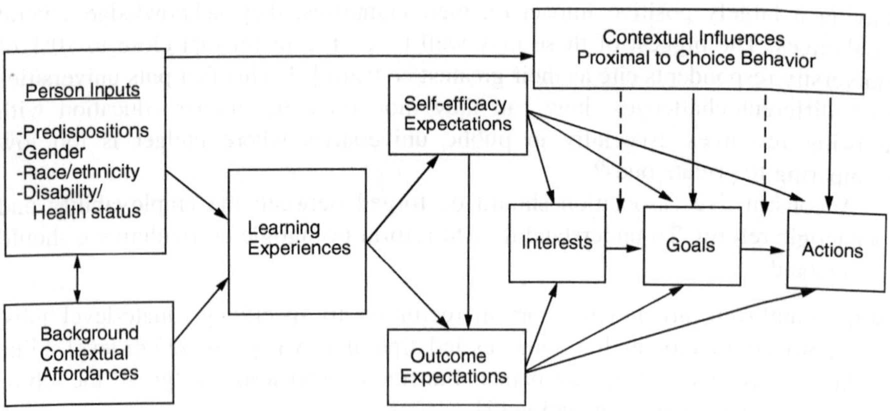

Fig. 1 The social cognitive career model

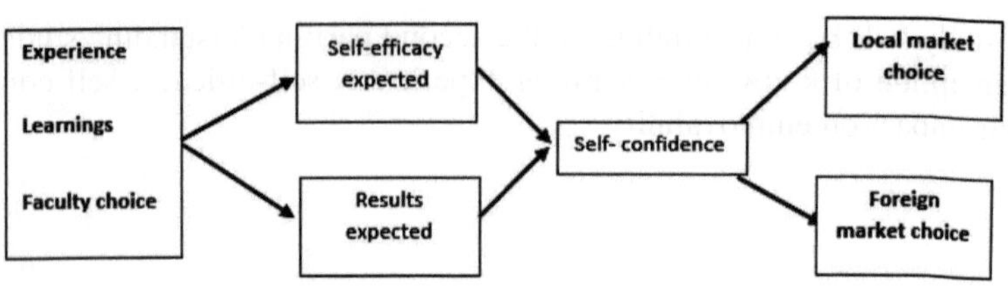

Fig. 2 The conceptual model

As we can see at the cognitive model, mediator variable is: "experience learnings". In our paper, we modified it and separate the two concepts.

3.1 Experience

When students are able to look at an experience from several perspectives, their understanding increased. In this process, they are forced to develop dialogue and multiple perspectives on available resources [6]. This situation can lead them to develop a more viable model of their learning and social experiences [7].

Dewey [8] expresses that "the principle of the continuity of experience may operate so as to leave a person arrested on a low plane of development, in a way, which limits later capacity for growth." Later in his famous paper, he continues that "The greater maturity of experience which should belong to the adult as educator puts him in a position to evaluate each experience of the young in a way in which the one having the less mature experience cannot do."

Griffin [9] claims: we are witnessing the transformation of experiential learning from a progressive educational movement towards reconstruction as an object of institutional policy and professional good practice. As such, it is being incorporated or absorbed into the formal system of educational provision.

Saddington [10] works on the roots of experiential learning while exploring three of the five traditional philosophical roots of adult education:

The Progressive tradition sees education as life-long and therefore "learning how to learn" is important for learners.

The humanistic tradition: is based on the belief that human beings are inherently good. In this tradition, the teacher acts as a "facilitator" and "enabler" of the learner's growth. Learning occurs through group interaction, participation, experimentation, and discovery.

The radical tradition: For this tradition, education is not neutral. It can only be understood by locating it in its structural and historical context.

Finally, [11] compares four theoretical orientations addressing experiential learning and cognition: psychoanalytic perspectives that illuminates desires and resistance, situative perspectives that emphasizes the connection between individual and their communities, critical cultural perspectives that focuses on how power and inequity structure experience and promote social transformation and finally enactivist perspective uphold an ecological systems understanding.

3.2 Learning

There have been requests for new types of learning from many different parts of society [12]. The aim of this divided concept is to know the perception of the students of the methods and learning through time.

Hull [13] states that Accountability in public education is necessary and vital, but relying on the rewards and penalties of old-style standardized tests will not, and cannot, significantly improve schools.

Most of the studies focuses on the teachers' collaborative efforts [14–18]. These studies reinforce the importance of persistently pursuing an instructional focus as teachers engage in their work in learning communities [19].

Learning capacity facilitate the creation of dynamic capacities [20] depending on repetition and experimentation [21]. Ko et al. [22] propose that transfer of knowledge depends on antecedent of communication and motivation.

According to [23], students simply fail to learn much of the material presented to them and they pass exams even they demonstrate misconceptions about fundamental concepts. Marton [24] categorize conception of learning into five classes:

Increasing knowledge
Memorization
Fast acquisition for utilization
Abstraction of meaning
Understanding reality

The first three conceptions explain one aspect of learning which is external to the learner in contrast to the 4th and 5th conceptions.

Many 'types' of learning that are often used and discussed in higher education, including experiential learning, student autonomy, and self-directed learning, belong in or derive from the tradition of adult education [25].

Learning and Employability

Purcell [26], maintains that subjects studied have an effect on the speed with which students fresh graduated obtain their first graduate-level job.

Curriculum and Employability

As noticed by [27], for many, progression to higher education was an unquestioned next step, as automatic and progression from primary to secondary school whereas for others it was a step into the unknown for them and their families. Some other research focus on the fact that student's motivation for entering higher education are not only to study subjects that suits them but to have a professional career, improve job prospects and to gain entrance to a well-paid career [3].

Good teaching activities that provide good learning also promote employability in general. Employability and subject-specific learning are not oppositional but they complete each other. What the 'employability agenda' does is to encourage teachers to use pedagogic approaches that are likely to enhance general employability whilst dealing with the specifics of the subject [28].

3.3 Self-confidence

Students should be entitled to provision that contributes to their employability in three broad ways: fostering a continuing willingness to learn;

- developing a range of employability-related capabilities and attributes;
- promoting confidence in reflecting on and articulating these capabilities and attributes in a range of recruitment situations [28].

Supovitz [18] links employability to capability. "Capable people have confidence in their ability to:

Take effective and appropriate action;
Explain what they are seeking to achieve;
Live and work effectively with others, and
Continue to learn from their experiences both as individuals and in association with others in a diverse and changing society."

More general research has highlighted the employment 'gains' for many groups of students in higher education proposes that confidence raising, and self-esteem might be as important if not more than skills and competences in acquiring good employment for all students, including those from lower socio-economic backgrounds [29].

As observed by [30], Self-assessment refers to the involvement of learners in making judgments about their own learning' [31]. Monitoring their own performance can allow students a chance to gain more confidence.

3.4 Self-efficacy

The concept of self-efficacy is grounded in [32] Social Cognitive Theory. In Social Cognitive Theory, Self-efficacy is best defined as the "beliefs in one's capabilities to organize and execute the courses of action required to produce given attainments" [32]. People have to believe that they have control over what they can do in order to have high self-efficacy. According to [33], Self-efficacy is how a person acquires beliefs about his or her ability to do something.

In their study, [24] exposed some statements from the Self-Efficacy subscale from the Motivated Strategies for Learning Questionnaire:

I believe I will receive an excellent grade in this class.
I'm certain I can understand the most difficult material presented in the readings for this course.
I'm confident I can learn the basic concepts taught in this course.
I'm confident I can understand the most complex material presented by the instructor in this course.
I'm confident I can do an excellent job on the assignments and tests in this course.

I expect to do well in this class.
I'm certain I can master the skills being taught in this class.

Considering the difficulty of this course, the teacher, and my skills, I think I will do well in this class.

Some researchers have concentrated their studies on the hypothesized "sources" of self-efficacy (experience, emotional states, vicarious experience and social persuasion), which are important to construct an individual's self-efficacy [34].

3.5 *Self-efficacy and Results*

In recent work on the possible relationship between self-efficacy and results, some authors have advanced many arguments about the positive relationships between academic self-efficacy and academic achievement [5, 35–39].

Experience and Self-efficacy
It is essential for individuals to have success with their experiences. If the individual experiences success over a period of time, then they are more likely to maintain a high self-efficacy. The occasional failure will not have much negative effect on the self-efficacy of the individual if they have experienced success [32].

Eleven hypotheses formulated for the main effects mode as follows:

The first hypothesis states the relationships (direct effects) between the LEARN construct and SATISFACTION (SATIS) is positive.

H1 There is a positive relationship between LEARN construct and SATIS.

The second hypothesis states the relationships (direct effects) between EXPER construct and the SATIS is positive.

H2 There is a positive relationship between EXPERIENCE construct and SATISFACTION.

The third hypothesis states that there is a direct effect between the choice of the university construct (CHOICE) and the satisfaction construct (SATIS).

H3 CHOICE has a direct positive effect on SATISFACTION.

For the interaction effects model, the fourth hypothesis states that there is a positive effect between the self-efficacy construct (SELF EFFIC) and self-confidence construct (SELF CONFID).

H4 SELF EFFIC had a direct effect on SELF-CONF.

The fifth hypothesis states that there is an indirect effect between LEARN construct and the work in local companies (LOCAL) through SELF CONFID.

H5 LEARN has an indirect effect on LOCAL through SELF CONFID.

The sixth hypothesis states that there is an indirect effect between LEARN construct and the work in international companies (INTER) through SELF CONFID.

H6 LEARN has an indirect effect on INTER through SELF CONFID.

The seventh hypothesis states that there is an indirect effect between EXPER construct and the work in local companies (LOCAL) through SELF CONFID.

H7 EXPER has an indirect effect on LOCAL through SELF CONFID.

The eighth hypothesis states that there is an indirect effect between EXPER construct and the work in international companies (INTER) through SELF CONFID.

H8 EXPER has an indirect effect on INTER through SELF CONFID.

The ninth hypothesis states that there is an indirect effect between Experience construct and the Self-confidence construct (SELF CONFID) through SELF EFFIC.

H9 EXPER has an indirect effect on SELF CONFID through SELF EFFIC.

The tenth hypothesis states that there is a direct effect between learning construct (LEARN) and the international construct (INTER).

H10 LEARN has a direct positive effect on INTER.

The eleventh hypothesis states that there is a direct effect between experience construct (EXPER) and the international construct (INTER).

H11 EXPER has a direct positive effect on INTER.

4 Methodology of Research

As illustrated by [40], "Research is a viable approach to a problem only when there are data to support it".

Data Collection and Analysis

Participants to the survey were students of the third year (BA) and first and second year of master. The first and second year were excluded because of the experience variable that was supposed to test the experience of students in university with a minimum of 3 years learning. The survey took place from late December 2015 to late February 2016. Questionnaires were printed in two versions (English and Arabic). 215 questionnaires were administrated and only 150 were completed. The participants responded to the survey anonymously and are registered in the following majors (Table 2).

Table 2 Distribution of students according to majors

Major	No. of stud.
Audit	71
Finance	46
Management	22
Marketing	2
Economics	9

Gender: 24% males (36); 76% females (114)
Age group: [20–24]

Questions were prepared and administrated by the researcher in French and English (according to the different sections in the university). They were also divided into two types:

Demographic: Age, Year, major, gender

Twenty questions that represents indicators of all variables used in the study. The scale used is likert scale (1—Strongly disagree, 2—disagree, 3—Undecided, 4—Agree, 5—Strongly Agree)

Participant Selection

All participants were selected by availability by administrating the survey before or after classes while they remained with the cooperating teacher. All participants were informed of the aim and requirements of the study.

Responses to the survey were processed in a spreadsheet (Excel) and transferred to a professional statistical software (Smartpls).

Variables and Measures: Variables used in the survey are summarized in Tables 3, 4 and 5.

Table 3 Independent variables

Perceived effect of learnings		
Capacity of analyzing situations	Course content help me to analyze situations	ANALY
Flexibility of contents	Subject content is flexible	SUBCONT
Modernity of learning methods	Learning methods are modern	LEARMETH
Learning new techniques	I feel I am learning new techniques	NEWTECH
Experience		
Perception of education	My perception of education changes over time positively	PERCEDUC
Effect of experience on confidence	My experience makes me more confident when selecting professional choices	EXPER
Choice of university		
I chose the LU because of its reputation	CF1	
I chose the LU because of its financial accessibility	CF2	
I chose the LU because of proximity	CF3	
I chose the LU because I trust the learning methods	CF4	
Satisfaction		
I am satisfied with the courses offered	SATIS	

Table 4 Mediator variables

Self-efficacy	My self-efficacy increases with time	SELF EFFIC
Self-confidence	I feel that my self-confidence increases gradually as I succeed in courses	SELF CONFID

Table 5 Dependent variables

Local employability	I feel that I would be able to work in large local companies	LOCAL
Foreign employability	I feel that I would be able to work in international companies	INTER

Table 6 Descriptive statistics

	ANAL	SUBCONT	LEARMETH	MEDIAUSE
DISAGREE (1,2)	14	33	67	63
UNDECIDED (3)	27	34	36	45
AGREE (4,5)	109	83	47	42

5 Data Analysis

The Table 6 summarizes the distribution of student's opinion concerning their perception of course content, flexibility and learning methods.

We found as a result, that most of the students agree that course content is flexible and help them to analyze situation. In contrary, the number of students that disagree the affirmation of learning methods and media used are modern is much higher than in both previous affirmations. This situation can affect the satisfaction of the students during their whole curriculum at the university.

5.1 Introduction to PLS

"PLS is a family of alternating least squares algorithms, which extend principal component and canonical correlation analysis. The method was designed by Wold [41–46] for the analysis of high- dimensional data in a low-structure environment and has undergone various extensions and modifications. PLS path models are formally defined by two sets of linear equations: the inner model and the outer model. The inner model specifies the relations between unobserved or latent variables while the outer model specifies the relations between a latent variable and its observed indicators or manifest variables" [47] (Fig. 3).

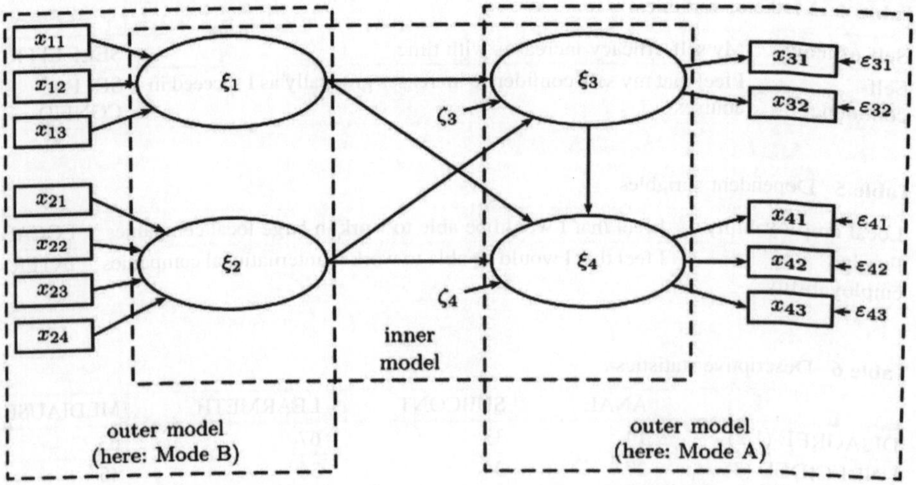

Fig. 3 A simple PLS path model

5.2 *Analysis: PLS-SEM Results*

Our first model included the CF3 indicator (I chose the UL because of proximity) and the variable RESULTS linked by the indicator RESULTS (I often reach the expected results in my studies). After running the model, we noticed that the indicator CF3 is not reliable (less than 0.1). In addition, we also found that the variable result has no effect on other variables but a positive relationship with self-efficacy). This situation led us to exclude indicator CF3 and variable RESULTS from the study in order to avoid complexity. Thus, we continued our model as shown below (Fig. 4).

Target Endogenous Variable Variance

The coefficient of determination, R2 is 0.455 for the SATIS endogenous latent variable. It means that the three latent variables (LEARN, EXPER, and CHOICE) moderately explain 45.5% of the variance in SATIS while they explain 31.4% of the variance in SELF EFFIC.

LEARN, CHOICE explain only 3.8% of the variance in RESULT. For this reason, we decided to omit this variable from our model.

SELF EFFIC, LEARN, EXPER, and CHOICE explain 38.2 of the variance in SELF CONFID. All these variables explain 29.1% of LOCAL and 20.9% of INTER.

Inner model path coefficient sizes and significance:

The inner model suggests that LEARN has the strongest effect on SATIS (0.521), followed by CHOICE (0.156) and EXPER (0.103). It also shows that SELF EFFIC has the strongest effect on SELF CONFID (0.314), followed EXPER (0.325) and LEARN (0.108). All values are summarized in Table 7.

Because the indicators cause the latent variable and are formative, they can have positive, negative, or even no correlations among each other [48, 49] (Table 8).

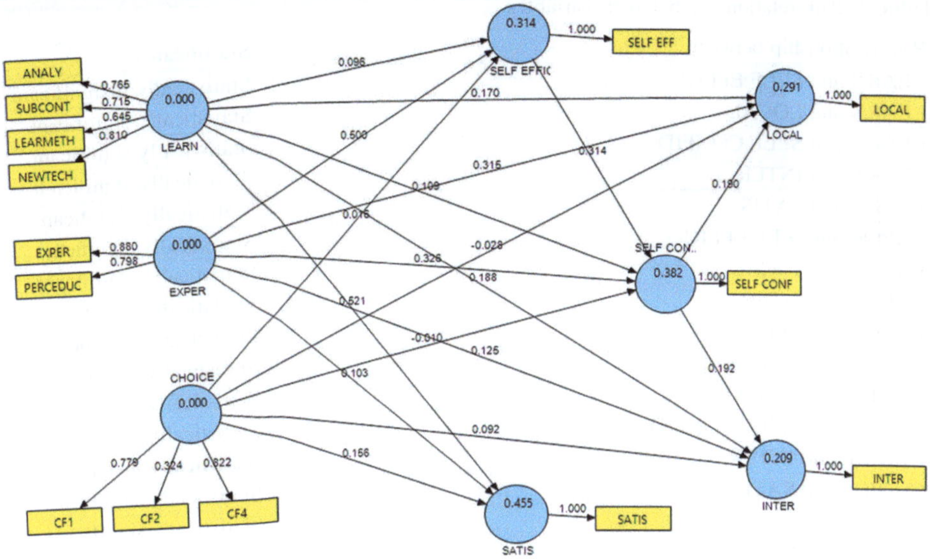

Fig. 4 PLS algorithm

Table 7 Path coefficient

	INTER	LOCAL	SATIS	SELF CONFID
CHOICE	0.092157	−0.027752	0.155648	−0.009698
EXPER	0.124751	0.314575	0.102932	0.325604
INTER				
LEARN	0.188480	0.169974	0.520758	0.108975
LOCAL				
SATIS				
SELF CONFID	0.192152	0.189977		

We can conclude that SELF CONFID is moderately predictors on the dependent variables LOCAL and INTER. We need to make sure of this result by running bootstrapping after the following analysis.

Checking Reliability and Validity

Indicator Reliability: since 0.4 (or higher for an exploratory research) is the composite reliability, the PLS algorithm model shows that all variables (but the CF2, 0.323) are greater than 0.4 which means that all indicators but the CF2 indicator are reliable [50].

Convergent validity: when AVE numbers are 0.5 or higher (other than moderator variable), so convergent validity is confirmed [51]. In our study, we noticed that indicator CF3 has no reliability since it gives a score of 0.044, we deleted this item and Calculate the PLS again. The new report of Quality Criteria gives a score of 0.46 for the AVE of the CHOICE, which can lead us to conclude that all numbers

Table 8 Path relationship between variables

Path relationship between	Significance
LEARN and SELF EFFIC	Statistically insignificant
LEARN and LOCAL	Statistically significant
LEARN and SELF CONFID	Statistically significant
LEARN and INTER	Statistically significant
LEARN and SATIS	Statistically significant
EXPER and SELF EFFIC	Statistically significant
EXPER and LOCAL	Statistically significant
EXPER and INTER	Statistically significant
EXPER and SATIS	Statistically significant
CHOICE and SELF EFFIC	Statistically insignificant
CHOICE and LOCAL	Statistically insignificant
CHOICE and SELF CONFID	Statistically insignificant
CHOICE and INTER	Statistically insignificant
CHOICE and SATIS	Statistically significant
SELF EFFIC and SELF CONFID	Statistically significant
SELF CONFID and LOCAL	Statistically significant
SELF CONFID and INTER	Statistically significant

are convergent. Since deleting the CF3 will not have any major effect on all scores we decided to continue the study without deleting this indicator (Fig. 4).

Discriminant validity: Square root of AVE of each latent variable (manually calculated) should be greater than the correlations among the latent variables [52]. Table 9 shows that the latent variables are larger than the correlation values. This shows that the discriminant validity is well established.

Discussion

The aim of the study is to test possible relationships between learning, experience, choice of university and satisfaction followed by the impact of self-efficacy, self-confidence on employability.

Does self-confidence have impact on the employability? What are the factors that might affect the future career of those students? Where is the role of teachers in increasing self-confidence? In this research the loadings of Learnings explain good indicators (ANALY, 0.765; SUBCONT, 0.715; LEARNMETH, 0.645 and NEWTECH, 0.810). This means that the indicator NEWTECH affects LEARN variable better than the three other variables.

The model also reveals that loadings of the variable EXPERIENCE are significant (0.880 and 0.798). With loadings of 0.779, 0.323 and 0.822 respectively, students are guided by many factors for the choice of the university (Reputation, financial accessibility and trust) while proximity indicator doesn't affect their choice of the university. The analysis of the model shows that SELF EFFIC (1.00) is good indicator of the SELF EFFIC variable which have strong effect on

Table 9 Quality criteria

	AVE	Comp Reliab	R Square	Cronba Alpha	Comm	Redund
CHOICE	0.462	0.6966		0.476744	0.4624	
EXPER	0.705	0.8268		0.586985	0.7053	
INTER	1.000	1.0000	0.2088	1.000000	1.0000	0.04522
LEARN	0.542	0.8246		0.718510	0.5421	
LOCAL	1.000	1.0000	0.2906	1.000000	1.0000	−0.0140
SATIS	1.000	1.0000	0.4547	1.000000	1.0000	0.12141
SELF CONFID	1.000	1.0000	0.3821	1.000000	1.0000	−0.0052
SELF EFFIC	1.000	1.0000	0.3142	1.000000	1.0000	0.00857

the SELF CONFID (0.314). We can also find that LEARN (0.521) have strong effect on SATIS which have a good effect on SELF CONFID.

Finally, SELF CONFID has also an effect on both dependent variables: LOCAL and INTER. This means that more students have self-confidence, the more it will affect their choice of local or international market.

5.3 *Bootstrapping (T-Statistics)*

Bootstrapping is a nonparametric procedure that can be applied to test whether coefficients such as outer weights, outer loadings and path coefficients are significant by estimating standard errors for the estimates. In this procedure, a large number of subsamples (e.g., 5000) are taken from the original sample with replacement to give bootstrap standard errors, which in turn gives approximate T-values for significance testing of the structural path (Fig. 5, Tables 10 and 11).

According to [53], "No need for an effect to be mediated". Furthermore, identify three patterns consistent with mediation and two with nonmediation:

1. Complementary mediation: Mediated effect (a # b) and direct effect (c) both exist and point at the same direction.
2. Competitive mediation: Mediated effect (a # b) and direct effect (c) both exist and point in opposite directions.
3. Indirect-only mediation: Mediated effect (a # b) exists, but no direct effect.
4. Direct-only nonmediation: Direct effect (c) exists, but no indirect effect.
5. No-effect nonmediation: Neither direct effect nor in-direct effect exists.

In Table 12, we will test (Sobel test) mediating power of SELF CONFID on all independent and dependent variables also the mediating power of SELF EFFIC on SELF CONFID variable. To confirm the possible mediating power, we will complete two steps for a test of mediation.

The Sobel test tells whether a mediator variable significantly carries the influence of an independent variable to a dependent variable; whether the indirect

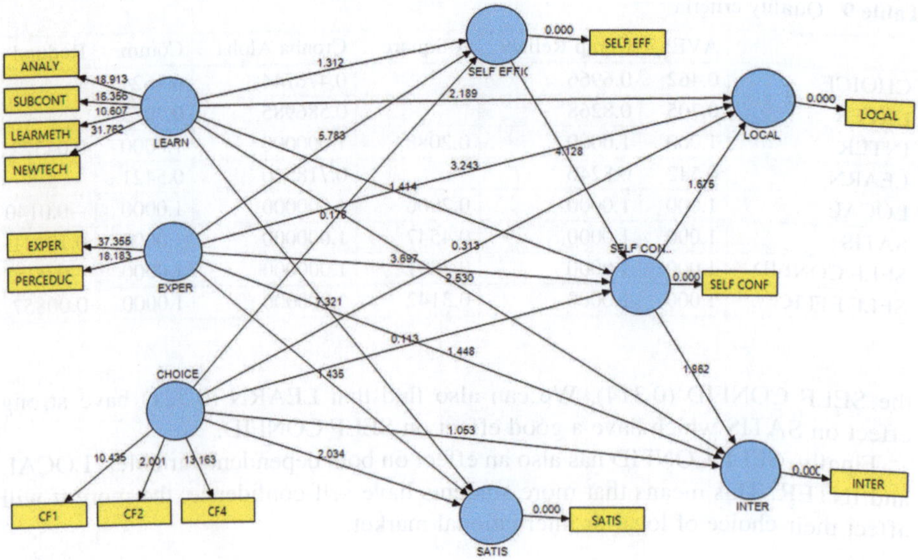

Fig. 5 PLS algorithm

effect of the independent variable on the dependent variable through the mediator variable is significant.

Conclusion of the Hypotheses There is a positive relationship between LEARN and SATIS. The more learning methods are modern, flexible and help students analyze situations, the more students are satisfied.

There is a positive relationship between the choice of the university and satisfaction. The more university has a good reputation, financial accessibility and good learning methods, the more students are satisfied.

The mediator SELF EFFIC mediate the effect between EXPER and SELF CONFID (Complementary mediation because both effect exists and point in the same direction.).

The mediator SELF CONFID did not mediate any effect between LEARN, EXPER and LOCAL, INTER (Direct-only non-mediation). However both variables (LEARN, EXPER) have direct effect on both dependent variables (LOCAL, INTER).

The results provide support for H1, H3, H4, H10, and H11.

Table 10 Path coefficients

	Original sample (O)	Sample mean (M)	Standard deviation (STDEV)	Standard error (STERR)	T statistics (|O/STERR|)
CHOICE -> INTER	0.091283	0.09199	0.08846	0.088466	1.031847
CHOICE -> LOCAL	−0.028616	−0.0209	0.08827	0.088276	0.324160
CHOICE -> SATIS	0.155648	0.15822	0.07650	0.076509	2.034380
CHOICE -> SELF CONFID	−0.004548	0.00909	0.09269	0.092691	0.049063
CHOICE -> SELF EFFIC	0.016398	0.02759	0.09236	0.092365	0.177538
EXPER -> INTER	0.217503	0.21129	0.07286	0.072864	2.985055
EXPER -> LOCAL	0.406276	0.39852	0.07562	0.075627	5.372136
EXPER -> SATIS	0.102932	0.09698	0.07172	0.071721	1.435177
EXPER -> SELF CONFID	0.482697	0.47766	0.07930	0.079304	6.086643
EXPER -> SELF EFFIC	0.500151	0.49149	0.08648	0.086481	5.783339
LEARN -> INTER	0.215228	0.21467	0.07458	0.074580	2.885871
LEARN -> LOCAL	0.196419	0.18982	0.08304	0.083045	2.365224
LEARN -> SATIS	0.520758	0.52335	0.07113	0.071135	7.320705
LEARN -> SELF CONFID	0.139204	0.12900	0.08167	0.081674	1.704387
LEARN -> SELF EFFIC	0.096243	0.08793	0.07334	0.073346	1.312173
SELF CONFID -> INTER	0.192152	0.18724	0.09841	0.098413	1.962499
SELF CONFID -> LOCAL	0.189977	0.18302	0.11339	0.113396	1.675343
SELF EFFIC -> INTER	0.060353	0.05604	0.03258	0.032586	1.852121
SELF EFFIC -> LOCAL	0.059670	0.05431	0.03631	0.036314	1.643162
SELF EFFIC -> SELF CONFID	0.314092	0.30108	0.07608	0.07608	4.128055

Table 11 Hypotheses and outcomes

Hypothesis	Findings Inner model path coefficient > 0.1 Bootstrapping > |1.96|	Conclusion
H1: *There is a positive relationship between LEARN and SATIS*	Inner model path coefficient = 0.520758 Bootstrapping = 7.320705	Supported
H2: *There is a positive relationship between EXPER and SATIS*	Inner model path coefficient = 0.102932 Bootstrapping = 1.435177	Refuted
H3: *CHOICE has a direct positive effect on SATIS*	Inner model path coefficient = 0.155648 Bootstrapping = 2.034380	Supported
H4: *SELF EFFIC had a direct effect on SELF-CONF*	Inner model path coefficient = 0.314092 Bootstrapping = 4.128055	Supported
H5: *LEARN has an indirect effect on LOCAL through SELF CONFID*	Inner model path coefficient LEARN/ SELFCONF = 0.108975; SELF CONF/ LOCAL = 0.189977 Bootstrapping = LEARN/ SELFCONF = 1.704387; SELF CONF/ LOCAL = 1.675343	Refuted
H6: *LEARN has an indirect effect on INTER through SELF CONFID*	Inner model path coefficient LEARN/ SELFCONF = 0.108975; SELF CONFID/INTER = 0.192152 Bootstrapping = LEARN/ SELFCONF = 1.704387; SELF CONFID/INTER = 1.962499	Refuted
H7: *EXPER has an indirect effect on LOCAL through SELF CONFID*	Inner model path coefficient EXPER/ SELFCONF = 0.325604; SELFCONF/ LOCAL = 0.189977 Bootstrapping = EXPER/ SELFCONF = 6.086643; SELFCONF/ LOCAL = 1.675343	Refuted
H8: *EXPER has an indirect effect on INTER through SELF CONFID*	Inner model path coefficient = EXPER/ SELFCONF = 0.325604; SELFCONF/ INTER = 0.192152 Bootstrapping = EXPER/ SELFCONF = 6.086643; SELFCONF/ INTER = 1.962499	Supported (to confirm mediation with sober test)
H9: *EXPER has an indirect effect on SELF CONFID through SELF EFFIC*	Inner model path coefficient EXPER/ SELFEFF = 0.500151; SELFEFF/ SELFCONF = 0.314092 Bootstrapping = EXPER/ SELFEFFIC = 5.783339;SELFEFFIC/ SELFCONF = 4.12805	Supported (to confirm mediation with sober test)
H10: *LEARN has a direct positive effect on INTER*	Inner model path coefficient = 0.188480 Bootstrapping = 2.885871	Supported
H11: *EXPER has a direct positive effect on INTER*	Inner model path coefficient = 0.124751 Bootstrapping = 2.985055	Supported

Table 12 Sobel test

Utility mediation for	Sobel test statistic > |1.96|	Two-tailed probability < 0.05
LEARN/LOCAL	1.08078	0.27979
LEARN/INTER	1.14547	0.25201
EXPER/LOCAL	1.52599	0.12701
EXPER/INTER	1.72654	0.08424
EXPER/SELF CONFID	3.36014	0.00077

6 Conclusion

Findings from this research endorse that the experience strongly affects the future career of the students. The more experience they have, the higher it affects their confidence which also affects the possibility to have greater qualifications beneficial to apply to executive local or international jobs.

Since we found that learning have no effect on the self-confidence which has effect on the employability, if we modernize education by integrating many new learning techniques, it will increase self-confidence which can give students better opportunities. The model also shows (Path coefficient: 0.500, Bootsrapping: 5.783) that the more students experience success over time, then they are more likely to maintain a high SELF-EFFICACY [53].

Not forgetting that Faculty support or encouragement has been associated with students' academic performance [54]. What if we start by encourage students and implement reforms conductive to modernize higher education in Lebanon?

Another important question remains regarding student's perception of actual teaching methods (Table 5). What if modern learning might have an effect on self-confidence that increases the number of students who have full background and are more confident to apply to higher posts in big companies in Lebanon or foreign countries?

To begin with [55] that argues that the role of teachers is to "facilitate" the acquisition of knowledge, not "transmit" it. Finally, it is also important to learn how to learn. This includes learning how to diagnose one's own need for learning and how to be a self-learner [56]. This might be the first step in modernization of higher education.

First, by teaching to students to learn how to learn [10], we might be giving them more confidence which can undeniably affect their future career. In addition, they should be more involved [57] and interactive in classrooms [58].

Second, integrate e-Learning in all curriculum similar to foreign European and US countries. Over the last two decades, many higher education institutions have adopted e-Learning tools into their educational processes. In order to answer to new markets and changing needs and expectations of students, higher education institutions have to define clear and comprehensive strategies for the integration of e-Learning in their educational delivery processes [59].

Multi-access learning (Face to face, Synchronous online, Asynchronous Online, Open Learning and the MOOC) can be also used in order to meet students' needs for access to learning experiences and faculty needs for graduate student recruitment [22, 60]. Multi access learning can help reducing the number of students in one class even if large class sizes became a feature of modern higher level institutions due to staffing and funding issues [61].

Higher education institutions must operate in more competitive world. Because of the decline in public funding, higher education institutions must deal with greater market forces by rising expenses, increasingly diverse student and their changing needs and expectations and heightened demand for new and different programs and services [62, 63]. However, there still remain a number of questions around the effectiveness of these propositions. Improving curriculum is one thing, but ensuring progression both within and beyond higher education is another. Students also have to work on their attitudes and participation in classes. They should take learning advantage more seriously by including research in their academic profile.

Limitations of the Research

As with any research, there are limitations associated with the studies. First, the number of students could be enlarged to give more accuracy and the number of universities to give more diversity (public and private ones). Second, the limitation to the business faculty. It would be more interesting to have data from other fields especially engineer and medical ones.

Extension of research: Future research can expand the reliability of the data by using additional sources from different other universities and even other cultures (foreign universities).

References

1. Glenn, M. (2008). *The future of higher education: How technology will shape learning, a report from the economist intelligence unit sponsored by the new media consortium*. London: The Economist Intelligence Unit.
2. Yorke, M. (2006). *Employability in higher education: What it is—What it is not. Learning and employability: Series 1*. York: Higher Education Academy.
3. Connor, H., Burton, R., Pearson, R., Pollard, E., & Regan, J. (1999). *Making the right choice*. London: Universities UK.
4. Purcell, K., Elias, P., Davies, R., & Wilton, N. (2005). *The Class of '99. A study of the early labour market experiences of recent graduates* (DfES Research Report No. 691). Nottingham: DfES Publications.
5. Lent, R. W., Brown, S. D., & Hackett, G. (1994). Toward a unifying social cognitive theory of career and academic interest, choice, and performance. *Journal of Vocational Behavior, 45*, 79–122.
6. Lund, A., & Hauge, T. E. (2011). Changing objects in knowledge-creation practices. In S. Ludvigsen, A. Lund, I. Rasmussen, & R. Säljö (Eds.), *Learning across sites: New tools, infrastructures and practices* (pp. 206–221). London: Routledge.
7. Doolittle, P. E. (1999). Constructivism: The career and technical education perspective. *Journal of Vocational and Technical Education, 16*(1), 23–46.
8. Dewey, J. (2007). *Experience and education*. New York: Simon and Schuster.
9. Griffin, S. (1992). *The mind's staircase: Exploring the conceptual underpinning of children's thoughts and knowledge*. Hillsdale, NJ: Lawrence Erlbaum Associates, Inc.

10. Saddington, T. (1998). Exploring the roots and branches of experiential learning. *Lifelong Learning in Europe, 3*(3), 133–138.
11. Fenwick, J. T. (2001). Experiential learning: A theoretical critique from five perspectives. *ERIC Information, 385*.
12. Fink, L. D. (2003). *Creating significant learning experiences: An integrated approach to designing college courses*. San Francisco, CA: Jossey-Bass.
13. Hull, D. (2005). *Career pathways: Education with a purpose*. Waco, TX: CORD.
14. Berry, A. (2006). Science: Teaching school subjects 11–19. *International Journal of Science Education, 28*(12), 1495–1498.
15. Bolam, R., McMahon, A., Stoll, L., Thomas, S., Wallace, M., Greenwood, A., Hawkey, K., Ingram, M., Atkinson, A., & Smith, M. (2005). *Creating and sustaining effective professional learning communities* (Research Report 637). London: DfES and University of Bristol.
16. Dunne, E., Bennet, N., & Carré, C. (2000). Skill development in higher education and employment. In F. Coffield (Ed.), *Differing visions of a learning society, Research findings* (Vol. I). Bristol: The Policy Press & ESRC.
17. Strahan, D. (2003). Promoting a collaborative professional culture in three elementary schools that have beaten the odds. *The Elementary School Journal, 104*(2), 127–146.
18. Supovitz, J. A., & Christman, J. B. (2003). *Developing communities of instructional practice: Lessons for Cincinnati and Philadelphia* (CPRE Policy Briefs pp. 1–9). Philadelphia, PA: University of Pennsylvania.
19. Vescio, V., Ross, D., & Adams, A. (2008). A review of research on the impact of professional learning communities on teaching practice and student learning. *Teaching and Teacher Education, 24*, 80–91.
20. Eisenhardt, K. M., & Martin, J. A. (2000). Dynamic capabilities: What are they? *Strategic Management Journal, 21*(10/11), 1105–1121.
21. Ambrosini, V., Bowman, C., & Collier, N. (2003). Dynamic capabilities: An exploration of how firms renew their resource base. *British Journal of Management, 20*(S1), 9–24.
22. Ko, C. H., Yen, J. Y., Chen, C. C., Chen, S. H., Wu, K., & Yen, C. F. (2006). Tridimensional personality of adolescents with internet addiction and substance use experience. *Canadian Journal of Psychiatry, 51*, 887–894.
23. Ditcher, A. K. (2001). Effective teaching and learning in higher education, with particular reference to the undergraduate education of professional engineers. *International Journal of Engineering Education, 17*(1), 24–29.
24. Marton, F., Dall'Alba, G., & Beaty, E. (1993). Conceptions of learning. *International Journal of Educational Research, 19*, 277–300.
25. Fry, H., Ketteridge, S., & Marshall, S. (2009). *A handbook for teaching and learning in higher education*. Oxon: Routledge.
26. Purcell, K., & Elias, P. (2002). Seven years on careers in a changing market. *Graduate Recruiter, 22–23*(Autumn).
27. Purcell, K., Elias, P., Ellison, R., Atfield, G., Adam, D., & Livanos, I. (2008). *Findings from the first futuretrack survey of the 'class of 2006' applicants for higher education*. Coventry: Warwick Institution for Employment Research.
28. Yorke, M., & Knight, P. T. (2006). Embedding employability into the curriculum, Learning and Employability. Series 1 No. 3. Higher Education Academy.
29. Brennan, J., & Shah, T. (2003). *Access to what? Analysis of factors determining graduate employability*. London: Centre for Higher Education Research and Information, Open University.
30. Deeley, S. J. (2014). Summative co-assessment: A deep learning approach to enhancing employability skills and attributes. *Active Learning in Higher Education, 15*(1), 39–51.
31. Dochy, F., Segers, M., & Sluijsmans, D. (1999). The use of self-, peer and co-assessment in higher education: A review. *Studies in Higher Education, 24*(3), 331–350.
32. Bandura, A. (1997). *Self-efficacy: The exercise of control*. New York: Freeman.

33. Trujillo, G., & Tanner, K. D. (2013). Considering the role of affect in learning: Monitoring students' self-efficacy, sense of belonging, and science identity. *CBE: Life Sciences Education, 13*, 1–10.
34. Usher, E. L., & Pajares, F. (2008). Sources of self-efficacy in school: Critical review of the literature and future directions. *Review of Educational Research, 78*, 751–796.
35. Caprara, G. T., Fida, R., Vecchione, M., Bove, G. D., Vecchio, G. M., Barbaranelli, C., & Bandura, A. (2008). Longitudinal analysis of the role of perceived self-efficacy for self-regulated learning in academic continuance and achievement. *Journal of Educational Psychology, 100*(3), 525–534.
36. Carroll, A., Houghton, S., Wood, R., Unsworth, K., Hattie, J., Gordon, L., & Bower, J. (2009). Self-efficacy and academic achievement in Australian high school students: 159. The mediating effects of degree aspirations and delinquency. *Journal of Adolescence, 32*, 797–817.
37. Ferla, J., Valcke, M., & Cai, Y. (2009). Academic self-efficacy and academic self-concept: Reconsidering structural relationships. *Learning and Individual Differences, 19*, 499–505.
38. Zajacova, A., Lynch, S. M., & Espenshade, T. (2005). Self-efficacy, stress and academic success in college. *Research in Higher Education, 46*(6), 677–706.
39. Zimmeran, B. J. (1995). Self-efficacy and educational development. In A. Bandura (Ed.), *Self-efficacy in changing societies* (pp. 203–231). New York: Cambridge University Press.
40. Leedy, P., & Ormrod, J. (2001). *Practical research: Planning and design* (7th ed.). Upper Saddle River, NJ/Thousand Oaks, CA: Merrill Prentice Hall/Sage.
41. Wold, H. O. A. (1966). Non-linear estimation by iterative least squares procedures. In F. N. David (Ed.), *Research papers in statistics* (pp. 411–444). London: Wiley.
42. Wold, H. O. A. (1974). Causal flows with latent variables: Partings of the ways in the light of NIPALS modelling. *European Economic Review, 5*(1), 67–86.
43. Wold, H. O. A. (1982). Soft modelling: The basic design and some extensions. In K. G. Jöreskog & W. HOA (Eds.), *Systems under indirect observation. Causality, structure, prediction* (Vol. II, pp. 1–54). North-Holland: Elsevier Science.
44. Wold, H. O. A. (1985). Partial least squares. In S. Kotz & N. L. Johnson (Eds.), *Encyclopaedia of statistical sciences* (Vol. 6, pp. 581–591). New York: Wiley.
45. Wold, H. O. A. (1985). Partial least squares and LISREL models. In P. Nijkamp, H. Leitner, & N. Wrigley (Eds.), *Measuring the unmeasurable* (pp. 220–251). Dordrecht: Nijhoff.
46. Wold, H. O. A. (1989). Introduction to the second generation of multivariate analysis. In H. O. A. Wold (Ed.), *Theoretical empiricism a general rationale for scientific model-building* (pp. VIII–VIXL). New York: Paragon House.
47. Henseler, J. (2010). On the convergence of the partial least squares path modeling algorithm. *Computational Statistics, 25*(1), 107–120.
48. Haenlin, M., & Kaplan, A. M. (2004). A beginner's guide to partial least squares analysis. *Understanding Statistics, 3*(4), 283–297.
49. Petter, S., Detmar, S., & Arun, R. (2007). Specifying formative constructs in information system research. *MIS Quarterly, 31*(4), 623–656.
50. Hulland, J. (1999). Use of partial least squares (PLS) in strategic management research: A review of four recent studies. *Strategic Management Journal, 20*, 195–224.
51. Bagozzi, R. P., & Yi, Y. (1988). On the evaluation of structural equation models. *Journal of the Academy of Marketing Science, 16*(1), 74–94.
52. Fornell, C., & Lacrker, D. F. (1981). Evaluating structural equation models with unobservable and measurement errors. *Journal of Marketing Research, 18*(1), 39–50.
53. Zhao, X., Lynch Jr., J. G., & Chen, Q. (2010). Reconsidering Baron and Kenny: Myths and truths about mediation analysis. *Journal of Consumer Research, 37*, 197–206.
54. Hackett, G., Betz, N., Casas, J. M., & Rocha-Singh, I. A. (1992). Gender, ethnicity, and social cognitive factors predicting the academic achievement of students in engineering. *Journal of Counseling Psychology, 39*, 527–538.
55. Brookfield, S. D. (1986). *Understanding and facilitating adult learning*. San Francisco, CA: Jossey-Bass.

56. Wirth, K., & Perkins, D. (2008). *Learning to learn*. Retrieved from http://www.macalester.edu/geology/wirth/CourseMaterials.html
57. Bippus, A. M., & Young, S. L. (2000). What behaviours reflect involvement in a course? Students' perceptions and differences between high and low communication apprehensive. *Communication Research Reports, 17*(2), 310–319.
58. Siau, K., Sheng, H., & Nah, F. (2006). Use of a classroom response system to enhance classroom interactivity. *IEEE Transactions on Education, 49*(3), 398–403.
59. Boezerooij, P., Van der Wende, M., & Huisman, J. (2007). The need for E-learning strategies: Higher education institutions and their responses to a changing environment. *Tertiary Education and Management, 13*(4), 313–330.
60. Irvine, V. (2009). The emergence of choice in "multi-access" learning environments: Transferring locus of control of course access to the learner. In G. Siemens & C. Fulford (Eds.), *Proceedings of world conference on educational multimedia, hypermedia and telecommunications 2009* (pp. 746–752). Chesapeake, VA: Association for the Advancement of Computing in Education. Available from EdITLib Digital Library (31583).
61. Cullen, J., Hedges, H., & Bone, J. (2011). Planning, "Undertaking and disseminating research in early childhood settings: An ethical framework". In S. Callan & M. Reed (Eds.), *Work-based research in the early years* (pp. 121–134). London: Sage.
62. Eckel, P. D., Couturier, L., & Luu, D. T. (2005). *Peering around the bend: The leadership challenges of privatization, accountability, and market-based state policy*. Washington, DC: American Council of Education.
63. Douglas, J. A. (2005). *All globalization is local: Countervailing forces and the influence on higher education markets* (Paper CSHE). Berkely, CA: eScholarship Repository, University of California.

56. Wirth, K., & Perkins, D. (2008). *Learning to learn*. Retrieved from http://www.macalester.edu/geology/wirth/CourseMaterials.html
57. Lippus, A. M., & Young, S. L. (2000). What behaviours reflect involvement in a course? Students' perceptions and differences between high and low communication apprehensives. *Communication Research Reports, 17*(3), 310–319.
58. Siau, K., Sheng, H., & Nah, F. (2006). Use of a classroom response system to enhance classroom interactivity. *IEEE Transactions on Education, 49*(3), 398–403.
59. Boezerooij, P., Van der Wende, M., & Huisman, J. (2007). The need for E-learning strategies: Higher education institutions and their responses to a changing environment. *Tertiary Education and Management, 13*(4), 313–330.
60. Irvine, V. (2009). The emergence of choice in "multi-access" learning environments: Transferring locus of control of course access to the learner. In G. Siemens & C. Fulford (Eds.), *Proceedings of world conference on educational multimedia, hypermedia and telecommunications 2009* (pp. 746–752). Chesapeake, VA: Association for the Advancement of Computing in Education. Available from EdITLib Digital Library 31583.
61. Cullen, J., Hedges, H., & Bone, J. (2011). Planning, "Undertaking and disseminating research in early childhood settings: An ethical framework". In S. Callan & M. Reed (Eds.), *Work-based research in the early years* (pp. 121–133). London: Sage.
62. Eckel, P. D., Couturier, L., & Luu, D. T. (2005). *Peering around the bend: The leadership challenges of privatization, accountability, and market-based state policy*. Washington, DC: American Council of Education.
63. Douglass, J. A. (2005). *All globalization is local: Countervailing forces and the influence on higher education markets* (Paper CSHE). Berkeley, CA: eScholarship Repository, University of California.

Using Data Mining and Business Intelligence to Develop Decision Support Systems in Arabic Higher Education Institutions

Mohamad Hamed, Tariq Mahmoud, Jorge Marx Gómez, and Georges Kfouri

Abstract The most academic institutions in Arabic countries depend on the centralized or decentralized information systems, operating independently from each other, the decision-makers rely on these systems in generation of the periodic and routine reports, that assist them in building the right decisions and proper responses to the changes in a timely manner.

The data volume in these institutions have become enormous, after applying these systems for several years, the lack of interconnection between different systems caused difficulties to decision-makers in processing such large amounts of data and get an integrated and useful information that reflects the current situation of the institution.

This paper aims at applying data mining and business intelligence concepts in order to address academic problems, specially the problems that related to students and academic advisors in the Arabic academic institutions. Thus this paper truly contributes to the development of academic quality.

Keywords Data Warehouse (DW) • Data Mining (DM) • Business Intelligence (BI) • Databases • Information • Knowledge • Decision Support Systems (DSS) • Operational Systems (OS)

M. Hamed (✉) • T. Mahmoud • J.M. Gómez
Department of Computing Science, Oldenburg University, 26111 Oldenburg, Germany
e-mail: Mohamad.Hamed@uni-oldenburg.de; Tariq.Mahmoud@uni-oldenburg.de; Jorge.Marx.Gomez@uni-oldenburg.de

G. Kfouri
Department of Economics Informatics, Vilnius University, Vilnius 01513, Lithuania
e-mail: GeorgesKF007@hotmail.com

J. Marx Gómez et al. (eds.), *Modernizing Academic Teaching and Research in Business and Economics*, Springer Proceedings in Business and Economics,
DOI 10.1007/978-3-319-54419-9_4

1 Introduction

The current decade is witnessing rapid development in the information technology field. This development leads to an increase in the number of organizations that take advantage of new technologies. Moreover, these organizations increased its stockpile of data as mentioned in [1]: "the amount of data stored in electronic form has increased recently, this amount of data doubling every 20 months and the data volume within databases is increasing at a greater rate also".

Higher education institutions are often under pressure to enhance the quality of educational and management processes but with a number of features dedicated specifically to academics. The university autonomy should be taken into consideration even in financial issues or other forms related to public and academic responsibilities. Therefore, universities seek to rely more on the accumulated data, invest more resources in tools that directly allow to collect and manage information, and involve teaching staff, students and decision-making processes' local communities [2].

These accumulated data are preoccupation of organizations and companies, as these information constitutes a real wealth of the organization if it has been understood and analyzed optimally [3].

Academic organizations (higher education) were chosen as case of research, because this type of organizations suffers from large volume of data without taking the appropriate information that supports right decision in all academic aspects.

This paper will examine the application of data mining mechanisms and business intelligence solutions to the academic system in the Arab International University in Syria by answering to the following questions:

- Can we consider that the currently applicable systems are able to provide us with real knowledge that can support strategic decision making?
- What are the usual difficulties and obstacles that such systems may encounter during the application?
- What is the reflection of applying business intelligence systems in the education development field?
- Is it possible to build decision support systems from the resulting information of analytical methods and data mining algorithms in the education sector?
- What are the methods and tools that may help in getting optimum benefits from applying these systems?

By proposing set of solutions, mechanisms through the application of data mining and business intelligence concepts to the collected data in data warehouse. Then getting the knowledge in short time to help taking the right decision at the right time especially in the academic advising field.

The next part presents the theoretical background of applying data mining methodologies in higher education, in addition to highlight difficulties and boundaries to fruitfully use the educational data mining and learning investigation.

2 Data Mining in Higher Education

Nowadays there is a raising contest in the higher education environments. Therefore, universities intend to adapt new strategies and instruments to enhance the quality of teaching and research activities besides providing the target communities with relevant services and knowledge [2].

One of the significant facts in higher education institution is the massive growth of educational data. These data are rapidly increasing without reflecting its benefit to the management. To deal with such difficult task, new techniques and tools are required to process the massive amount of generated data in academic business processes to extract useful knowledge and information. In this sense, data mining techniques are analytical tools that can be used to extract meaningful knowledge from large data sets [4].

The task of the higher educational institutions is manifested in creating the suitable environment for the creation and development of scientific research. This must be taken into account in order to let this research contributing in the development and upgrading of all educational sectors (medical, economic, cultural, etc.). The lack of deep awareness and enough knowledge in higher education systems prevents the administration staff from achieving their own quality goals and catching up with the advanced educational institutions in the world.

Nowadays, forecasting the paths of students and alumni is considered to be one of the biggest challenges for higher education institutions. Examples for higher education institutions in this regard includes: which students will be enrolled in specific course programs, and which students will require support in order to get graduated, will some students be more likely to graduate than others? etc. Besides this challenge, traditional issues like enrollment management and time-to-degree are still considered as motivations for higher education institutions to apply better solutions [5].

Higher education institutions can perform academic guidance to students by utilizing the concepts of academic analysis and data mining techniques. These techniques can be useful for people who will choose potential scholarship holders by obtaining indicators for their academic situations. Moreover, these tools can generate early warnings for students' poor performance to administration staff and help them to make smarter choices to influence the students' education process. It can also help the academic and teaching staff in the design process of the courses' schedules [6].

The different information resources and data stores have great influence on the education institutions in the evaluation of their academic work. However, the process of getting accurate and useful information is extremely difficult for decision makers. This requires that the educational institutions must search for an effective and accurate decision support system to collect and analyze data to ensure the support of administrative procedures and contribute to the hidden knowledge discovery systems. Therefore, the use of these systems in the development of academic employment sectors will support many aspects starting from marketing and ending up with students' competencies to be distinct in the labor market [7].

2.1 Difficulties and Boundarie

The new digital technologies in higher education institutions have made it possible to embrace the new teaching practices. However, not all institutions view the technologies in the same perspective. In academia, there is the need to have greater support for professional development and sharing of greatest practice [8]. The confidence and capability in digital learning is far important than the actual mapping of the technology into existing practices. The challenge of ensuring that the technology to be implemented fits with the existing practices makes it difficult to successfully implement the technology in higher education systems.

Another major challenge is the cost associated with the implementation of educational data mining applications. This includes the new practices that supposed to be embraced in order to effectively utilize educational data mining and learning investigation for enhancing educating and learning.

Assessment practice in the education sector in institutions of higher education should be integrated in the learning and program accreditation. The incorporation of the practice would aid in narrowing the efforts required to implement changes in policies such as the implementation of the data mining systems [9].

2.2 User Knowledge Modeling

The user knowledge modelling system is normally used in adaptive educational system. The basis of the system is to build on the idea of a domain model that is designed to deal with the vagueness of the high educational institutions regarding their knowledge description. The model makes use of the knowledge representations and linguistic rules for model updating. Studies show that the use of this model in the educational systems is due to its easy-to-use nature which positively affects the knowledge acquisition, therefore leading to effective learning outcomes [10].

2.3 User Behavior Modeling

This model regularly describes the academic activities as on- or off-errand and can be utilized as an intermediary for student engagement. It depends on the same sorts of learning information utilized as a part of foreseeing academic information in addition to different measures, for example, the amount of time an undergraduate student has spent, whether a student has finished a course, recorded changes in the classroom or school connection and participation, etc.

2.4 *User Experience Modeling*

It aims at finding out whether a student is fully satisfied with the learning experience. It can be judged through the students' reactions to the follow-up surveys or questionnaires, their behaviors, their decisions, and retention in consequent learning units or courses [11]. The collected data from academic system in addition to the surveys, questionnaires or observations is combined to create a detailed picture of the students' activities, the institution and the teachers and can be used to improve the academic performance of the institution [11].

2.5 *Adaptation and Personalization*

To adjust guidelines or customize higher education institutions encounters, information as arrangements of student movement, data on issues or steps a student has endeavored, and academic demographic data are frequently gathered and used to make an individual profile for every student in the educational system. Analysts in [12] examined the checking and elucidation of consecutive learning exercises to enhance adjustment and customize instructive situations. They investigated student critical thinking information from a material science mentoring framework [13] by firstly changing over action arrangements in the crude information into chain-like models and secondly bunching successions to recognize critical thinking styles. These models are utilized to adjust the coaching framework to students' favored learning strategies.

2.6 *Implementation Challenges and Considerations*

Specialists pose a scope of usage implementation considerations and potential obstructions to adopting educational data mining, including technical challenges, institutional limit, lawful, and moral issues. Fruitful utilization of educational data mining and learning investigation won't come without exertion, cost, and a change in instructive society to more continuous utilization of information to decide.

3 Stages of Knowledge Discovery Through Data Mining

The basic stages in data mining processes are depicted in Fig. 1 and can be summarized as follows cf. [14, pp. 77–109]:

1. *Objective definition*: The first stage defines objectives based on a predefined problem. Selecting a group of students in a particular faculty in which their failures repeat in a particular course is considered as an example of problems in the academic field. The objective in this specific case is to know the courses that pose obstacles for students and cause bogging in their academic achievement using data mining.
2. *Data gathering and integration*: This process takes more than 50% of the total time of any data mining project. After defining objectives, data are collected within the data warehouse from one or more resources, then the integration process starts after the Extract Transform Load (ETL) process by loading data into different data marts based on predefined criteria.
3. *Exploratory analysis*: This stage merely presents the data cleansing process in which all irrelevant and abnormal attributes (values) are ignored.
4. *Selection of attributes*: The so-called attribute importance is one of the most important stages in data mining. In this stage only the relevant attributes will be considered. Therefore, this is a pre-process for exploration and choosing attribute groups to be used in the following complex stages.
5. *Model development*: Selecting and application of an appropriate algorithm is the main process at this stage after having a ready data warehouse. However, it is

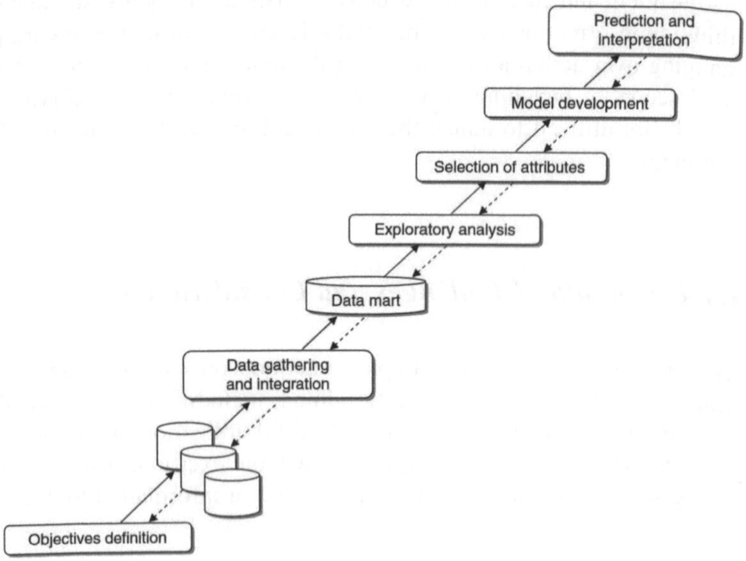

Fig. 1 Data mining stags [14, p. 85]

difficult to choose the best algorithm for each defined objective and therefore more than one algorithm can be checked to get the appropriate one.

6. *Prediction and interpretation*: This is the last stage in the data mining process. The harvested knowledge is coming from applying the appropriate data mining algorithm from the last stage. The easiest way to present this knowledge will be in form of reports. Such reports help managers in the decision-making process.

4 The Proposed System for Higher Education

The following sections show the phases followed to use data mining and business intelligence concepts to develop a decision support system in higher education institutions. It will be then followed by the results of applying the functions of this proposed system on a use case. The phases to develop the proposed system are: using a warehouse builder, building the data mining models and finally building the business intelligence system.

4.1 Using a Warehouse Builder

The builder is used to load data from data sources using the ETL process. The structure of any data warehouse is based on fact and dimension tables as shown in Fig. 2. While dimension tables (colored blue in the figure below) include descriptive attributes for querying constraining and/or filtering, fact tables (colored red in the figure below) include foreign keys refer to dimension tables and historical data used for data analysis process and building reports.

4.2 Building the Data Mining Models

Oracle Data Miner within Oracle SQL Developer had been used to build the following data mining models for each student: The Annual Grade Point Average (AGPA), Course Selection (CS) and Course Result Prediction (CRP) models.

Based on a data mining Algorithm called Support Vector Machine that analyze data used for classification and regression analysis [15], AGPA Model (see Fig. 3) predicts the annual cumulative grade point average based on the different factors namely are: the semester grade point average (GPA), the registered hours (the hours of the whole study lifetime), total finished hours (the achieved ones by student), and the faculty at which the student is enrolled.

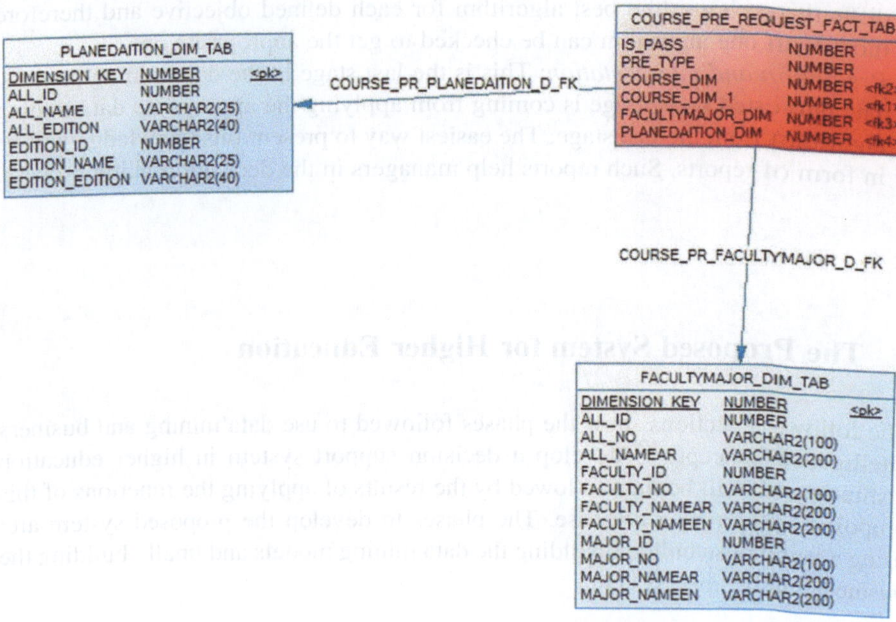

Fig. 2 The correlation scheme between a fact table and dimension tables

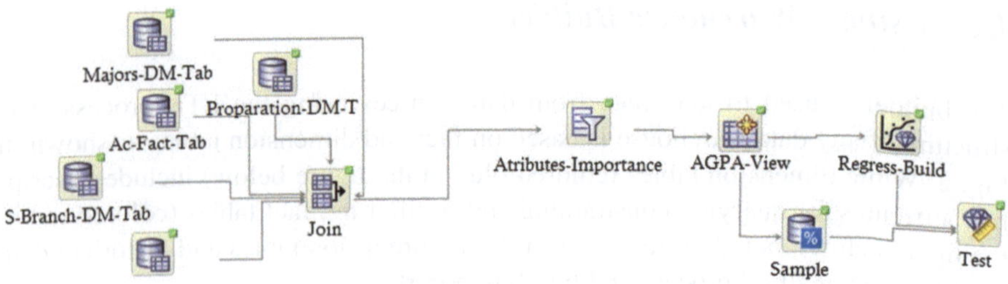

Fig. 3 AGPA model

The CS Model (shown in Fig. 4) identifies the best or worse course selection to be offered for registration for each individual student. This is done by using the association rules within the Oracle data miner.

The CRP Model predicts the final result of particular student in a particular course. The result is either success or failure and this depends on the data mining function called classification. This model is depicted in Fig. 5.

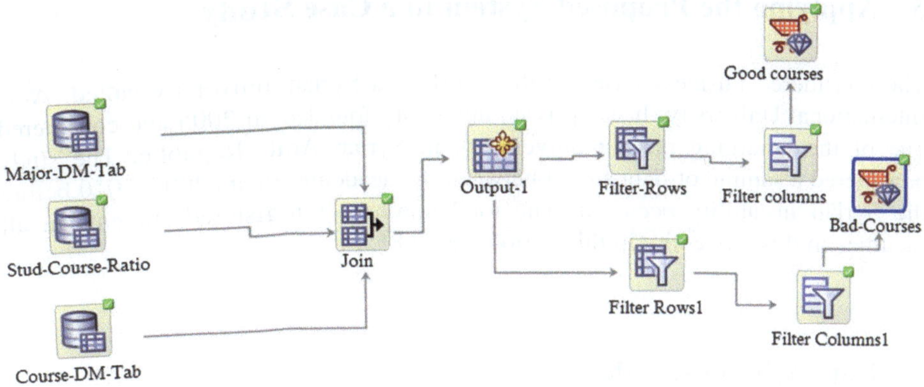

Fig. 4 The CS model

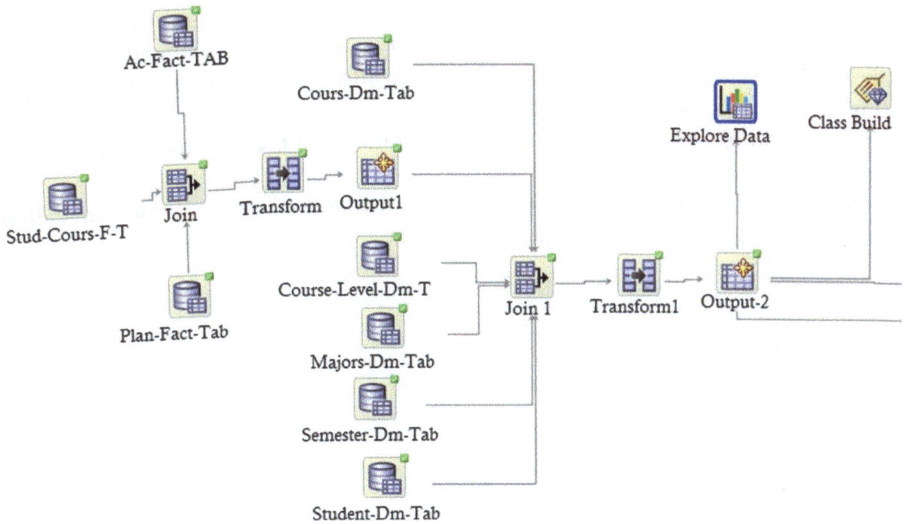

Fig. 5 The CRP model

4.3 *Building the Business Intelligence System*

Oracle Business Intelligence Enterprise Edition (OBIEE) had been used to develop the business intelligence system that consists of a data warehouse that is built using a warehouse builder besides accompanying dashboards. The purpose of having the business intelligence system is to create ad-hoc reports to be shown to the responsible staff to have a holistic overview on the data loaded into the data warehouse. This can be seen as an alternative to the data mining models that had been illustrated in the previous section.

5 Applying the Proposed System to a Case Study

The considered business case for this work is a Syrian university called: Arab International University. It is a private university founded in 2005 and considered one of the emerging private universities in Syrian Arab Republic. The study considered a sample of data stored between the academic years 2005–2010 before the Syrian instability occurred. The total number of registered students in all faculties in this university in this period were 6855.

6 Data Mining Results

This section presents the results of applying the data sample of informatics faculty on two of the three models explained in the data mining models sections.

AGPA had been applied on the sample data by calculating the annual grade point average. Figure 6 shows the importance of the attributes considered while calculating the average for each student.

The most influential attributes are the grade point average then passed hours then finished hours then total registered hours.

AGPA predicts the annual averages for all students using algorithm called "Support Vector Machine". The accuracy of the model's results is 70%.

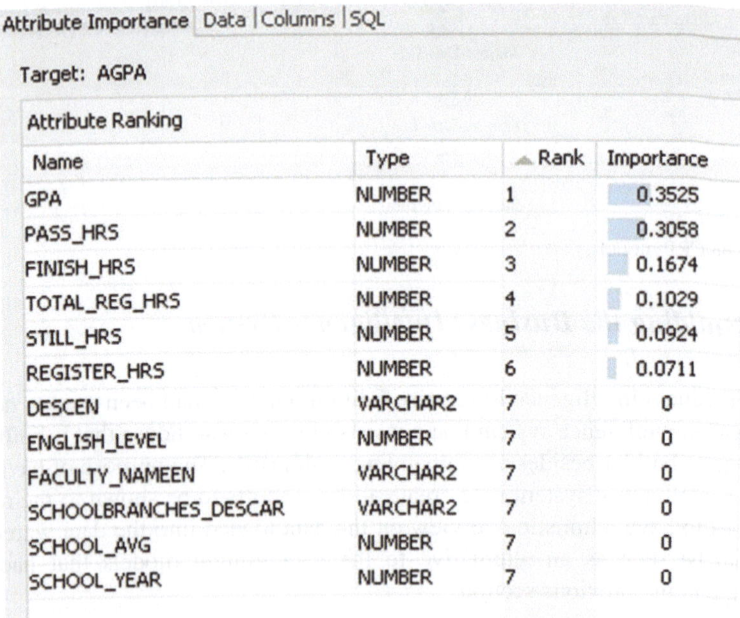
Attribute Importance | Data | Columns | SQL

Target: AGPA

Attribute Ranking

Name	Type	Rank	Importance
GPA	NUMBER	1	0.3525
PASS_HRS	NUMBER	2	0.3058
FINISH_HRS	NUMBER	3	0.1674
TOTAL_REG_HRS	NUMBER	4	0.1029
STILL_HRS	NUMBER	5	0.0924
REGISTER_HRS	NUMBER	6	0.0711
DESCEN	VARCHAR2	7	0
ENGLISH_LEVEL	NUMBER	7	0
FACULTY_NAMEEN	VARCHAR2	7	0
SCHOOLBRANCHES_DESCAR	VARCHAR2	7	0
SCHOOL_AVG	NUMBER	7	0
SCHOOL_YEAR	NUMBER	7	0

Fig. 6 AGPA model results

As for the CS model results, the association algorithm had been applied in this model to sets of available courses for students per semester to provide students with advices on course selection. Figure 7 shows an example that suggests to a student enrolled with matriculation number "487,003" in the computer science faculty to register "Numerical Analysis" course since he passed "Mathematics", "English for Special Purpose", "Discrete Mathematics" and "Computational Theory" courses. This suggestion shows that the confidence value is above 95% whereas this value represents the ratio of the rule support to a specific number of transactions that including previous ones.

7 Business Intelligence System Results

Business intelligence reports are considered as important factors to support decision making process in large companies and institutions. The following sets of dashboards had been built based on the sample data. Figure 8 shows a dashboard that shows courses whose failure rate is more than 15% per semester.

Figure 9 depicts a dashboard that presents the differences in success rate in particular course over semesters. Such a dashboard can help in evaluating the teaching process of a particular course and identifying challenges by comparing the success rates over semesters that can reflect the academic level of the teacher, the levels of students and the scientific content of the considered course.

It is worthy to note here that the considered university had three semesters per academic year. These semesters are winter and summer semesters besides an extra semester to give the students the possibility to go with a faster track in their academic life so that they can graduate in a less time than their counterparts who don't take this extra semester each year. Therefore, this kind of extra semester is optional for the enrolled students. The semesters in Fig. 9 are numbered based on

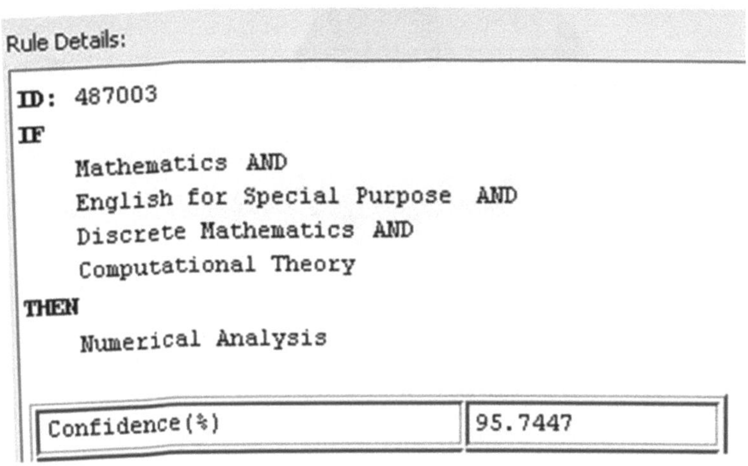

Fig. 7 CS model results

Course order in the semester with the Failure rate above 15%

Semester 20083

Course Name	Full Mark	Passed	Course Registered	Fail Rate
Computer Organization and Assembly Language I	38	6	16	62.50%
Physics (1) I	41	6	12	50.00%
Electronic Circuits (2)	48	7	13	46.15%
Electric Machines I	49	8	13	38.46%
Power Electronics I	51	7	11	36.36%
Algorithms & Data Structures I	51	39	61	36.07%
Discrete Mathematics I	59	9	14	35.71%
Electric Circuits (1)	56	10	14	28.57%
Electric Circuits (2)	52	14	19	26.32%
Logic Circuits I	60	14	19	26.32%
Mathematics (1) I	60	10	13	23.08%
Programming (1) I	58	32	41	21.95%
Programming (2) I	59	23	29	20.69%
Mathematics (2)	63	37	46	19.57%
Signal Processing (I) I	58	25	31	19.35%
Physics (2) I	66	13	16	18.75%
Signal Processing (2) I	61	10	12	16.67%
System Programming I	61	36	43	16.28%

Fig. 8 Dashboard of failure rate in courses per semester

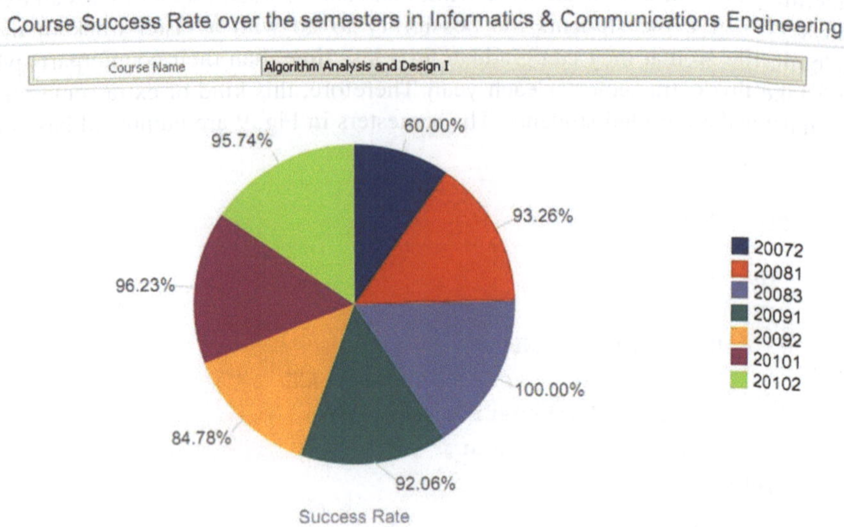

Fig. 9 Dashboard of course success rates over semesters

this semester classification. For example: "20,091" refers to the 1st semester in the year 2009 that is the winter semester, "20,092" refers to the 2nd semester in the year 2009 that is the summer semester, "20,083" refers to the 3rd semester in the year 2008 that is the optional semester, etc.

8 Conclusion

This paper presented how data mining and business intelligence concepts can be used to support decision making in Arabic higher education institutions. The vast amount of data stored in the academic systems in higher education institutions attract attention to the need of taking an advantage of this data to build intelligent systems. Such systems can have a positive impact on the academic level of students by drawing long term strategies that depend on new standards determined by the knowledge extracted from these systems.

The obtained results in the adopted case study can contribute to the re-arrangement of scientific content in the study plan of the targeted university's faculties. Moreover, it can contribute to the development process of academic advising in recommending appropriate courses for registration based on the academic level of each student.

Furthermore, this study has been done due to the lack of research and studies related to data mining and business intelligence concepts at the higher education sector in the Arabic region in general and Syrian Arab Republic in particular. The usage of real database enabled this research to experiment new tools in the proposed data mining models and business intelligence system to infer a new knowledge.

Finally, privacy and ethical issues in such environment must be taken into account. Policy makers bear a moral obligation to explore the legitimacy of any prescient model that is going to be utilized to settle on weighty choices about educational systems. Policy makers must have the capacity to clarify the confirmation for expectations and the moves made by the educational systems that are utilized or going to be utilized on the premise of learning examination.

References

1. Erdoğan, Ş. Z., & Timor, M. (2005). A data mining application in a student database. *Journal of Aeronautics and Space Technologies, 2*(2), 53–57.
2. Bresfelean, V. P., Ghisoiu, N., & Others. (2009). Higher education decision making and decision support systems. *WSEAS Transactions on Advances in Engineering Education, 2*, 43–52.
3. Beikzadeh, M. R., & Delavari, N. (2005). *A new analysis model for data mining processes in higher educational systems*. Proceedings of 6th Information Technology Based Higher Education Training (pp. 7–9).

4. Delavari, N., Phon-Amnuaisuk, S., & Beikzadeh, M. R. (2008). Data mining application in higher learning institutions. *International Journal of Information and Education, 7*, 31–54.
5. Luan, J. (2002). Data mining applications in higher education. *New Dir. Institutional Research, 2002*(113), 17–36.
6. Baepler, P., & Murdoch, C. J. (2010). Academic analytics and data mining in higher education. *International Journal for the Scholarship of Teaching and Learning, 4*(2), 17.
7. Luan, J. (2002). *Data mining and knowledge management in higher education-potential applications*. Paper presented at the Annual Forum for the association, for Institutional Research (42nd, Toronto, Ontario, Canada, June 2–5, 2002).
8. Lynch, C. A. (2003). Institutional repositories: Essential infrastructure for scholarship in the digital age. *Portal: Libraries and the Academy, 3*(2), 327–336.
9. Heywood, J. (2000). *Assessment in higher education: Student learning, teaching, programmes and institutions* (Vol. 56). London: Jessica Kingsley Publishers.
10. Kobsa, A. (2001). *Generic user modeling systems, user modeling and user-adaptived interaction*. Dordrecht: Kluwer Academic Publishers.
11. Black, P., & Wiliam, D. (1998). Assessment and classroom learning. Assessment in education. *International Journal of Medical Education, 5*(1), 7–74.
12. Köck, M., & Paramythis, A. (2011). Activity sequence modelling and dynamic clustering for personalized E-learning. *User Modeling and User-Adapted Interaction, 21*(1–2), 51–97.
13. Vanlehn, K., Lynch, C., Schulze, K., Shapiro, J. A., Shelby, R., Taylor, L., et al. (2005). The Andes physics tutoring system: Lessons learned. *International Journal of Artificial Intelligence Education, 15*(3), 147–204.
14. Vercellis, C. (2009). *Business intelligence: Data mining and optimization for decision making* (1st ed.). New Jersey: Wiley.
15. Cortes, C., & Vapnik, V. (1995). Support-vector networks. *Machine Learning, 20*(3), 273–297.

An Investigation of Students' Social Entrepreneurial Intentions in Syria: An Empirical Test

Olga Medyanik and Farid Al-Jawni

Abstract This paper is a contribution to the developing field of so-called fit models, person—entrepreneurship fit model among them. Such models aim at revealing factors that predict a person's future being involved in social enterprises and his/her success in them. No work of this kind has been conducted in Syria previously. Here, we present our test of Mair and Noboa's model (published in 2006, see J. Mair, J. Robinson, & K. Hockerts (Eds.), Social entrepreneurship. New York: Palgrave MacMillan) recently extended by Hockerts (Entrepreneurship Theory and Practice, 2017) which identifies altogether five antecedents determining young people's SEI: prior experience. empathy, moral obligation, social entrepreneurial self-efficacy and perceived social support. In the test, the empirical data collected from approximately 300 students of Syrian universities business and economics faculties was used.

Several hypotheses were tested in course of the study: those described by K. Hockerts and some other authors. It is well known that, on one hand, social entrepreneurship is a matter of importance especially for women and, on the other hand, that one's understanding of the significance of social activities (as well as one's estimating of own opportunities and preferences) is developing gradually with age. Besides, social as well as business innovative ventures are launched usually by younger people. Our results support the common wisdom that gender and year of studying are important factors affecting students' decision to launch a social venture in future. An important aspect of the study is also comparing the SEI of students of Syrian private and state universities in order to find out if there are any behavioral differences between the two groups. No special teaching courses with a social entrepreneurial profile are being taught yet in Syria neither at private nor at the state universities, so no hypotheses about relation between selecting such

---

O. Medyanik (✉)
Faculty of Business Administration, International University for Science and Technology (IUST), Damascus, Syria
e-mail: oserg.novik@gmail.com

F. Al-Jawni
Faculty of Commerce, Applied Statistics Department, State University of Damascus, Damascus, Syria
e-mail: f.aljaouni@gmail.com

J. Marx Gómez et al. (eds.), *Modernizing Academic Teaching and Research in Business and Economics*, Springer Proceedings in Business and Economics,
DOI 10.1007/978-3-319-54419-9_5

courses and students' SEI is included in the study; but the results of our research call for introducing such teaching courses.

Keywords Social entrepreneurship intentions (SEI) • Person-entrepreneurship fit (PEF) • Measure of fit • Syria

1 Introduction: Conceptualization and Terminology

This paper is devoted to social entrepreneurship (SEP) and to people who bring it to real life—social entrepreneurs (SE). It is a comparatively new field in the vast world of economics and business studies, and it is completely new and uninvestigated in some countries of contemporary world, Syria among them.

SEP has become a separate area of general entrepreneurship studies and is rapidly developing into an independent field of research and practice, capturing a growing attention and interest of policy makers and scholars during the last decades. It is natural that SEP bears many features of general business entrepreneurship, but in an adjusted way. For instance, if business entrepreneurship is a powerful factor of fostering economic growth and increasing competitiveness, then SEP is considered a powerful driver of social change. And in economics as well as in social sphere, there is a growing need for entrepreneurs—people who would accelerate economic and social development through generating new ideas and converting them into profitable ventures. Both business and social entrepreneurial activities provide employment opportunities.

Henderson and Robertson [8] state that "the future working environment will depend on creativity and individuality of the young. However, indeed relatively little is known about young adult views on entrepreneurship". Why some people choose an entrepreneurial career and some do not? Ngugi and Gakure [23] express an opinion that the challenge is that "college graduates are trained to be employment seekers rather than employment creators. Stimulating entrepreneurial interest among students in institutions of higher learning is one way of curbing youth unemployment." All these refers to revealing and developing in young people so-called entrepreneurial intentions (EI) that serve as antecedents of choosing social or business entrepreneurship career in future. EI are usually discussed in close connection with EE—entrepreneurial education, the definition of which is given by F. Liñán in his work "Intention-based models of entrepreneurship education" [16].

Up to now, vast scientific literature exists on EI. To show the scope of this literature resource base, we can mention F. Liñán's "Systematic Literature Review on Entrepreneurial Intentions" [17]. It aimed at systematization and categorization of publications and included the total of 409 papers addressing EI published only between 2004 and 2013. According to the author, his work clarifies a picture of the subfields of EI research by (1) categorizing the main areas of specialization (5 main areas are revealed), SEP among them, and (2) thematic analysis identifying specific themes within each category (25 themes are recognized). "The literature on EI started with Shapero and Sokol, 1982, and Shapero, 1984" [25]. We will return to Shapero's EI model in part 2 of our current paper when we talk about the Method.

Modeling social entrepreneurial intention (SEI) is the subject of our current research.

We believe that it is crucial, at the beginning of the discussion, to make it clear what we here call "social entrepreneurship".

Hockerts [9] states: "The term SEP is used to describe a wide variety of domains ranging from social impacts such as work integration to poverty reduction and sometimes reaching all the way to the protection of environmental resources". Because the area is so broad, different authors still argue about terms and definitions. For example, Bielfield [3] is talking about confusion taking place in modern literature: "Due to relatively recent growth of interest in social enterprise and social entrepreneurship, and with the variety of actors and arenas involved, it is not surprising that terminology is an issue". He indicates that, in some literature, terms SEP and SE are used interchangeably, as the same category, and some authors distinguish them from one another. Nichols [24] discusses substituting in literature terms "nonprofit" and "not-for-profit".

In this paper, we use term SEP to describe behavior aiming at benefiting poor and marginalized people through innovative activities in social and environmental sectors by applying business-inspired strategies.

Speaking of SE, it is not yet exactly defined who social entrepreneurs are themselves. Though, generally, social entrepreneurs don't have to be individuals, but also organizations, in our paper we call entrepreneurs only individual people, namely representatives of young generation who, in very near future, would become enrolled in business enterprises as members of high managing stuff of companies and firms. Those are the people who are going to make decisions and undertake policies that would affect their country's future as a whole.

During past years, the interest to SEP grew rapidly among academicians and practitioners. Numerous research and teaching centers for SEP were being opened worldwide, mostly in the North America and Europe. In 1993, Initiative on Social Enterprise was established at Harvard Business School (University of Alberta, Canada). In March 2004, The First World Forum in SEP was held at the Saïd Business School, University of Oxford, UK—the largest gathering of scholars, practitioners and policymakers involved in SEP that was later called "the Davos of SEP" and has become annual event. Important teaching centers are also such as Columbia Graduate School of Business, USA; Herriot-Watt University, UK; Stern School of Business, New York University, USA etc. A profound description of the emergence of entrepreneurship education is presented in [14].

It is obvious that education and training are most important elements in developing human resources. Adequate education fosters an individual's intentions. Since the education provided by a university inevitably affects the career selection by students, universities are seen as potential sources of future social entrepreneurs. Unfortunately, in the Middle East there has been rather poor knowledge accumulated about SEP so far, no teaching centers exist, no research work is being conducted, and even no specialized courses are offered at teaching institutions. This current article represents its authors' attempt to eliminate this shortcoming.

We decided to try to understand if there are any antecedents for developing SEP in today's Syria, on one side, and any opportunities for developing it—on the other. Because we believe that in SEP, as well as in any other area, the decisive role belongs to the human factor, we chose social entrepreneurial intentions (SEI) of young Syrians as the main object of discussion. Probably at the end of our study it will be possible to figure out if there are any convenient human resources available in Syria to form a basis for developing future social enterprises. We also aimed at contributing to the developing field of so-called fit models, person—entrepreneurship fit model among them. Such models are being built in order to reveal factors that predict a person's future being involved in social enterprises and his/her success in them. No work of this kind has been conducted in Syria previously as well.

The final purpose will be to drive out a conclusion about would it make sense to introduce corresponding teaching courses into syllabus of Syrian private and state universities.

2 Motivation

We see three main reasons why the issue of SEP and SEI represents a matter of particular interest for Syria.

The role of small and medium businesses in Syria. In Syria as well as in any other developing country, small and medium enterprises (SMEs), rooting in the historically strong merchant class, constitute a large and important part of the national economy. According to Asadi [2], in early 2000ths, the Syrian government had to provide almost 200,000 jobs every year, only 90,000 of which were secured in the public sector. According to the International Labor Organization, both private and public SMEs employed 88% of labor force. Previously, because of a centralized nature of Syrian economy, the growth of the private sector was slow. Later on, in the middle of 1990-ies, the country's authorities started decentralizing the economy and, in order to provide smooth transition to a real market, made efforts to encourage small business investors. R. Al Asadi and A. Abdelrahim provide an interesting general review of SME in Syria after 2000 (see work Al Asadi [2]). For our current study, this research seems valuable because it describes organizations where future social entrepreneurs would search for employment and where they are expected to apply their social entrepreneurial abilities. Below, there are the main characteristics of smaller business in Syria given in [2].

The majority of small firms refer to the private service sector. The sample under study was drawn from the population of registered small private businesses located in Damascus such as Car Rental, Travel and Tourism, Hotels, real Estate, Advertising, Restaurant, Coffee Shops, Financial and Engineering offices. Of course, currently some of above-listed (especially Travel and Tourism, Hotel business) are almost in the state of stagnation because of the political situation.

The nature of SMEs requires modest initial capital, with the human element as the main resource. 83.3% of SME consider training of their managerial stuff, while only 16.7% consider training of ordinary employees. 66.7% of firms were ruled and/or owned by individuals less than 41 years in age.

Firms employed not more than 25 employees, with 81.5% of them employing 15 or less people. Firms located in Damascus, privately owned by their management who had all decision making rights.

88.5% of firms relied on self-financing rather than debts and loans in funding their businesses.

Firms have been in business for a minimum of 5 years.

The turbulent state of Syrian economics today. It is generally well known that SEP develops more intensively during periods of economic recession and crisis. During periods of economic growth and stability there is higher demand for labor because large companies offering relatively high salaries distract labor force from small businesses, reducing the rates of starting up small firms and lowering the role of SEP in providing income for certain population groups. At the same time, the share in population of people with low income decreases. On the contrary, when economics of a country is in the state of recession, increase of unemployment emerges due to staff reductions in large companies; as a result, people are forced to launch their own ventures (see Kashina [12]).

There has been a broad discussion of how, under market failure, nonprofit sector balances the shortages of public goods and how, at the same time, it attempts to make up for lost government funding through earned-income ventures. In 1988, Weisbrod [27] proposed the idea of government failure. It states that the government only provides the quantity of public goods demanded by the majority of voters. Any additional quantity is being produced and offered by nonprofits financed through donation and self-financed through their own commercial earned income. Bielfeld [3] reminds how similar events took place in the USA in the early 1980s during the economic slowdown and public service budget cuts by the Reagan administration and in 2000 when the G. W. Bush administration threatened budget cuts. Today's situation in Syrian economy also calls for wide attracting nonprofit enterprises to intensively participate in providing goods and services for population.

The basic objectives of SEP are:

- providing goods and services unavailable in the market or not provided by the public sector;
- developing skills through educating and training;
- creating employment;
- helping socially excluded people to integrate the community;
- poverty alleviation, health care etc.

Therefore, SEP is an instrument for fostering pathways to overcome hardships and difficulties of life in today's Syria.

The gender differences. Syria remains a country with considerable gender segregation in labor market where cultural restrictions form the idea of work which is "relevant" for men and women. There is a strong gender stereotype about most social orientation of a woman that contradicts with modern women's demand for self-fulfillment. In such countries, "for-profit" business and entrepreneurship are "man's" spheres. From this point of view, SEP is a compromising way of women's out-of-family self-realizing. Kashina [12] believes that "It is women with their emotional orientation to the client, care and the responsible relation get advantage before man in realization of the main objectives of social business".

During crisis, usual differences between men's and women's economic situations become more striking, and even performing usual functions of mother and housekeeper becomes more difficult. This makes women search for sources of additional income, and in many cases SEP turns to be the best solution. Even during crisis, men seek for more prestigious and better paid for occupations, while for women, when choosing an occupation, their family's benefits are in the first place. Some research work report of differences in the ways men and women allocate resources, cope with different shocks etc. And some surveys indicate that if men are more successive on the earlier starting-up stage, then women are more successive on the stage of surviving. General questions about who can probably become a social entrepreneur and what qualities such people possess are discussed in [15, 19, 20].

From the statements above, we can derive a triple starting point for our further discussion: in developing countries (a) small and medium enterprises (SME) are important; (b) SME are rapidly developing; (c) SME are responsible for non-profit charity and other social entrepreneurial activities.

For these reasons, it is quite understandable that, in the countries with comparatively low level of economic and social development, academicians as well as practitioners reveal particular concern with different issues of SEP (for example, Yunus [28] and Clarke [4]). In Syria, no research of antecedents and perspectives of SEP development had been conducted yet. And yet there is a growing interest towards such issues.

3 The Method and the Entry Description

As a preface to our model's description, let us give a short review of the theoretical background of entrepreneurial intentions (EI) modeling as a whole.

In his analysis of literature on entrepreneurship, F. Liñán states that "an explosion of research using EI model as a framework" took place in early 1990s (see Liñán [17]). The majority of EI models are similar and compatible and can be divided into two main strands:

- firstly, coming from social psychology with a view to analyzing behaviors in general, shedding light on the mental process leading from attitudes and beliefs to effective action; most important theoretical basis for this approach is constituted by Ajzen's TPB in 1991 (see Ajzen [1]), in which intentions are considered "effective and reliable predictors of behavior";

– secondly, models specific to the field of entrepreneurship, first of all a widely recognized Shapero's model of Entrepreneurial Event, 1982 (see Shapero & Sokol [25]).

All EI models, social as well as business, consider the link between entrepreneurial inclinations on one hand and some so-called genetic personality factors on the other hand. Genetic factors are: self-confidence sometimes called self-efficacy or self-reliance or even self-direction, risk-taking ability, need to achievement, and locus of control. At the same time, an individual is surrounded by a range of cultural, social, economical, political, demographical, and technological factors. This contextual framework also affects entrepreneurship. Genetic and contextual factors should be considered simultaneously and are supposed to be included in EI model as variables.

Shapero's Entrepreneurial Event model points out that the intention to start a business emerges from perception of desirability and feasibility as well as from propensity to act upon opportunity. "Opportunity" supposes that the potential to start a business is prior to the propensity to act. "Perceived feasibility" is the degree to which one feels personally capable of starting a business. "Perceived desirability" in Shapero's model corresponds with Ajzen-Fishbein's "social norms and attitudes". "Propensity to act" variable was added to cover Ajzen's "Perceived behavioral control".

Currently, there is a broad specter of applications and empirical testings of well-known patterns that are constructed upon these principles, though they may have various specific variables included. For example, Turker [26] presents an Entrepreneurial support model that was proposed and empirically tested on a sample of about 300 students in Turkey. The model studies the influence of particular contextual factors on young people's EI. Of these factors, the educational support and the structural support are found to be significant, and the relational support—insignificant. Another example is applying Shapero's model in explaining entrepreneurial inclinations of university students in Kenya by J. K. Ngugi and R.W. Gakure (see study [23]). Numerous models are described by Liñán [16].

The current research is based on person-entrepreneurship fit model first suggested in 2006 by Mair and Noboa (work [18]) who were the first to investigate the antecedents of people's SEI. In its turn, Mair and Noboa's model was also founded on Ajzen's theory of planned behavior TPB and as well included principles of Shapero's EE model (both mentioned above). In work [18], the authors suggested four characteristics of human personality as main antecedents of SEI:

empathy as a proxy for attitudes towards own behavior and behavior of the others;
moral judgment as a proxy for social norms;
self-efficacy as a proxy for internal behavior control;
perceived presence of social support as a proxy for external behavior control.

The listed above qualities' measures constitute four model's main variables. Each variable's value was formed by average 3–4 questions' (or items of the questionnaire) answers, as explained below.

The model was extended by Hockerts [10] in 2016 by adding prior experience with social organizations as a new antecedent of SEI. In his study, the total of 2790 complete answers were grouped according the following facts: gender, nationality (Scandinavian/non Scandinavian), age, racial minority. When analyzing the literature on the subject, the author indicates that very few attempts of empirical verification of Mair and Noboa's model have been provided yet; so, as already stated above, our work offers an empirical test of this model applying Syrian context when retaining Mair and Noboa's variables and hypotheses.

Our research initial data base represent a random sample consisting of approximately 150 observations collected from students of Syrian universities and colleges in urban (Damascus city) and rural (Dera'a governorate) territories. The students were asked to complete a questionnaire (Appendix 1A, 1B) containing 24 questions similar to those suggested in work [10]. In the beginning, a pilot test was conducted at one of private universities in Damascus. The test questionnaire was all written in English; it revealed a difficulty on behalf of the majority of students to understand the meaning of some closely formulated questions (Ex. Questions 7 and 8, 10 and 11). For these reasons, the answers for the pilot test were considered not valid and were not included into analysis. The final version of the questionnaire was presented in two languages—both English and Arabic for surveying private universities with the majority of courses taught in English, and just in Arabic—for the state university colleges. The spaces were provided for gender, year of study, territory, university and faculty. Of 150 final questionnaires, 34 were excluded as not valid, therefore only 116 were taken into consideration.

The questionnaires provided the multiple item scale for measuring five latent variables taken from work [10] and described above. As in [10], each item used a 5-point Lickert-type response format ranging from 1, "strongly disagree", to 5, "strongly agree".

The description of the sample data is shown in Table 1. The complete descriptive statistics for all observations of the sample are presented in 10 tableaus of Appendix 2. The observations were categorized by gender, province and property (state or private).

The set of the questionnaire's 24 items (see Appendix 1A) was divided into 5 subsets characterizing 5 following individual's personal qualities.

Empathy—ability to realize what feelings another person has, or a tendency to generate an emotional respond to another human being's mental and emotional state (see papers [21, 22]). Empathy is the first element of Ajzen's theory of planned behavior (work [1] later developed in [11, 13]) and constitutes a proxy for a person's attitude towards SEP.

Moral obligation—an individual's perceived normative believes about what behavior is expected, accepted and approved by the society (see studies [6, 7]). Moral standards act as important determinants of human behavior within a

Table 1 Description of sample data[a]

	Responds	
	Number	% to the Total
Female	66	57
Private universities	42	36
Territory of Dera'a	58	50
Year of study		
1	27	23
2	39	33
3	35	30
4	15	13
State university colleges		
Accounting	35	30
Law	23	20
Science	10	9
Humanitarian	6	5
Private university colleges		
Business	15	13
Finance	27	23
All respondents: Total	116	100

[a]Description of the sample

community and are also considered important antecedents of SEI because they inspire people help others.

According to Hockerts [10], self-efficacy is an "individual's appreciation of his or her own ability to successfully carry out an intended behavior... Past research (for example [5]) has found self-efficacy to be an important antecedent of social behavior . . . as well as entrepreneurial behavior". It would be reasonable to suppose that the sense of self-efficacy can inspire an individual to attempt take part in solving societal problems.

Perceived social support—beliefs of a person about how he or she, with his or her wishes and intentions, depends on attitudes and opinions prevailing in the community, and what moral support he or she can receive from surrounding people. When talking about social entrepreneurship, these beliefs transform into a person's expectations for funding or some other ways of backing up that can possibly be provided by the environment.

Social entrepreneurial intentions (SEI)—a person's will to start a social venture in future. In this research we are discussing intentions of students—young people who, within a short time, are going to face the challenge of choosing a place for employment. So, the question is how many of them would probably select SEP as occupation.

Described above six personal qualities of an individual correspond with the model's six key variables (see Table 2).

Table 2 Six personal qualities—six model's variables[b]

N	Variable name	Questionnaire Item (Appendix 1A)
1	Prior experience	22, 23, 24
2	Empathy	1, 3, 5
3	Moral obligation	7, 8, 9, 10
4	Social entrepreneurial self-efficacy	11, 12, 13
5	Perceived social support	15, 16, 17
6	Social entrepreneurial intent (SEI)	19, 20, 21

[b]Items and variables

4 Hypotheses and Discussion

We have tested two sets of hypotheses. Hypotheses 1 through 4 allow comparing answers of male and female students, students of private and state universities, rural and urban students and students of different specialities about all five variables. Hypotheses 5 through 8 are about the relationships between each of four independent variables, on one side, and the dependent one—the intent to get involved in social entrepreneurial activities—on the other side.

For all hypotheses and variables the obtained value of Cronbach α is: $\alpha \geq 0.7$ which means that the characteristics of sample reliably describe the whole population.

The results of statistical T-test with "Group Statistics" and summarized "Independent Sample Test" analysis of eight hypotheses are presented in Appendix 3. Generalized ANOVA One-way Analysis is presented in Appendix 4. The latter is followed by Appendix 5 "Post Hoc Analysis" where One-way ANOVA is shown for each of five dependent variables (Empathy, Moral obligation, Self Efficacy, Perceived Social Support, Social Entrepreneurial intentions). In Appendix 5, we also show an example of a Multiple Comparisons table for Empathy variable, although all variables' multiple comparisons were produced during the research work. Appendix 6 (Figs. 1, 2, 3, 4, and 5) presents Means plots for the same five dependent variables' values for different faculties of Syrian private and state universities. Appendix 7 illustrates bilateral correlation between same five variables.

The following is a general verbal interpretation of the model's results.

Hypothesis 1 there is no significant difference ($\alpha = 0.05$) between answers of male and female students for variables 2, 3, 4, 5, 6.

The results of testing H1 are given in Appendix 2 Tables 3 and 4. There is a general strong belief about women having more compassion and empathy for unfortunate people and therefore are more likely to participate in charity projects and social venture. Surprisingly, the test of H1 argue with this belief. It shows approximate equality of answers' means in male and female groups for all independent variables, probably with slightly higher standard deviation value for male students. This is an indicator of lower variance in women's answers. $H1_0$ is accepted. Significance values are high for all five variables varying from 0.171 to 0.969.

Hypothesis 2 there is no significant difference ($\alpha = 0.05$) between answers of students of state and private universities for variables 2, 3, 4, 5, 6.

The results of testing H2 are given in Appendix 2 Tables 5 and 6. Analyzing the effect of a respondent's being a student of a private or the state university is an innovative experiment. The test of H2 shows that the values of variables 2, 4 and 5 (Empathy, Social entrepreneurial self-efficacy, Perceived social support) show considerable differences: the significance level far below 0.05. $H2_0$ is rejected. While for variables 3 (Moral obligation) and especially variable 6 (Social entrepreneurial intent SEI) the differences are not important: accept $H2_0$.

Hypothesis 3 there is no significant difference ($\alpha = 0.05$) between answers of students of rural and urban territories for variables 2, 3, 4, 5, 6.

The outcome of H3 testing are given in Appendix 2 Tables 7 and 8 and they are similar to the previous. Level of empathy to marginalized people, sense of self-efficacy differs and attitudes towards the perceived social support differ considerably from one territory to another ($H3_0$ is rejected), while feelings of moral obligation and intents are similar for two groups ($H3_0$ is accepted).

For hypotheses 1, 2, 3 the extended analysis was conducted by cross-loading gender and the university category (state/private)—see Tables 9, 10, 11, and 12. Here, it is supposed that the link between gender and the survey items' levels is mediated by the fact of the university's being of private or state ownership. It was found out that the mean values of all five independent variables (empathy, moral obligation, social entrepreneurial self-efficacy, perceived social support and social entrepreneurial intent) are considerably higher with the state university students than with those of private ones.

Hypothesis 4 there is no significant difference ($\alpha = 0.05$) between answers of students of different specialities for variables 2, 3, 4, 5, 6.

As shown in Table 1, the data was collected from students of altogether six different colleges of private and state universities in Syria: Accounting, Law, Science, Humanitarian, Business and Finance. Testing H4 is illustrated by Appendix 5 and brought about a conclusion that business students don't have the same feelings, attitudes and intentions as other five groups of respondents: all variables' mean values are considerably lower. Appendix 6 "Means Plots" represents another illustration of testing hypothesis H4, and it proves the same idea. This outcome, unexpected at the first glance, can be explained from the nature of initial data. The reason is that we surveyed business students of only one university, which is private and is situated in Damascus city; consequently, we make a conclusion that this two factors influenced the outcome.

At the beginning of the current section of our paper we have already indicated that the method of next four hypotheses studied in course of our research differ from previous ones by distinguishing a dependent variable from the rest four independent variables. We appointed variable of Social Entrepreneurial intentions as an outcoming dependent one. This repeats Mair and Noboa's and K. Hockerts' approach and corresponds with our final objective—to find out if there are young people in Syria who would, in the nearest future, commit themselves to bringing about social improvement in their country.

The results are demonstrated in Appendix 7 (the correlation analysis was completed for all five variables, in order to provide basis for more conclusions).

Hypothesis 5 Empathy is positively related ($\alpha = 0.05$) to social entrepreneurial intent.

$H5_0$ ("there is no correlation between the two variables") is rejected: Pearson correlation 0.275**, significance level 0.003.

Hypothesis 6 Moral obligations variable is positively related ($\alpha = 0.05$) to social entrepreneurial intent.

$H6_0$ ("there is no correlation between the two variables") is accepted: Pearson correlation 0.179, significance level 0.055.

Hypothesis 7 Social entrepreneurial self-efficacy variable is positively related ($\alpha = 0.05$) to social entrepreneurial intent.

$H7_0$ ("there is no correlation between the two variables") is rejected: Pearson correlation 0.266**, significance level 0.004.

Hypothesis 8 Perceived social support variable is positively related ($\alpha = 0.05$) to social entrepreneurial intent.

$H8_0$ ("there is no correlation between the two variables") is rejected: Pearson correlation 0.243**, significance level 0.009.

From the contents of Appendix 7, we can observe that the strongest link is there between people's empathy and their sense of moral obligation to help marginalized and disabled people: Pearson correlation 0.621**, with significance approaching zero. This is quite natural, from our point of view. The next highest correlation levels can be seen between some other variables and self-efficacy, proving that an individual's self-confidence, his belief about his own capabilities to influence the events of surrounding life and change the world is the most important quality affecting the behavior of people and their decisions.

5 Conclusion

The person-entrepreneurship fit model's empirical testing carried out by the authors of this article brings about the following conclusions.

First, the research outcomes prove, in general, the results described in works [10, 18]. Some contradictions can be explained by certain lack of initial information as well as by obvious cultural peculiarities of the current research content. In other words, in todays' Syria there are people who are able to carry out functions of social entrepreneurs and who experience considerable inclination towards doing so, in spite of serious difficulties existing in modern economic and social situation in Syria.

The second conclusion follows: people who have an intention to fight social problems in contemporary Syria are now in acute need for being systematically taught and trained by specialists and experts in SEP. There is a lot of interest and enthusiasm towards launching social ventures in the country. This was demonstrated when, on the occasion of the World Women's Entrepreneurship Day (WED) celebrated by the UN on November 17, 2015, and under the patronage of the Institute of Human Resource Management (IHRM) and the ENBAT group the First meeting of women entrepreneurs took place in Damascus (3.12.2015). The purpose of the meeting attended by some prominent Syrian businesswomen and academicians was to unite and organize them and allow them share their ideas and experiences. The agenda of the meeting emerged from the necessity of supporting young women of today's Syria in their efforts towards starting up new innovative businesses and encouraging them to participate in future reconstructing the country. Lectures (ex. "Swell Marketing Solutions" by Abeer Akkad, "Seven basic Skills of a Business Leader" by Dr. Mazna Mardini etc.), workshops and exhibitions took place in course of the event in which the participants informed each other about their accomplishments and plans for future business projects.

There is a hope that the meeting would become an annual event ever on. But there is a lack of scientific knowledge on the issue. Therefore, we recommend include subjects with a social entrepreneurial profile in teaching syllabuses of Syrian educational institutions. This can be done by introducing a limited number of corresponding elective courses.

Appendix 1

Appendix 1A

Questionnaire

Entrepreneurial Intentions and Qualities:

Validation Study

Please select one of 5 options. Your answer would reflect your opinion on an ascending scale: 1 – totally disagree (0%); 5 – strongly agree (100%).

Gender

M	***F***

Year of Study

Institution

	Answer	*Code*
Territory		
University/College		
Faculty		

Question	Answer (choose one of five)				
	1	2	3	4	5
1. When thinking about socially disadvantaged people, I try to put myself in their shoes. - عندما افكر بمشاكل الناس الهامشيين (الذين ليس لهم مكانة اجتماعية-فقراء – محرومين من التعليم –محرمين من الخدمات الصحية – السكن الصحي –العمل اللائق والمجزي) أحاول أن أضع نفسي مكانهم.					
2. I don't care how people feel who live on the margins of society. - لا أهتم ولا أعير أهمية لمشاعر الناس الهامشيين في المجتمع.					
3. Seeing socially disadvantaged people triggers an emotional response in me. 3- إن رؤية الناس المحرومين والمعسرين (الهامشيين) يحفز في أعماقي الكثير من المشاعر.					
4. I do not experience much emotion when thinking about socially excluded people. 4- لا تثير الطبقات الاجتماعية الدنيا عندي الكثير من المشاعر عندما أفكر بها.					

5. I feel compassion to socially marginalized people. 5- أشعر بالتعاطف والشفقة مع مشاكل وهموم الطبقات الاجتماعية . الهامشية.					
6. I find it difficult to feel compassionate for people less fortunate than myself.					
7. It is an ethical responsibility to help people less fortunate than ourselves. - من الواجب أخلاقياً مساعدة الناس الذين هم أقل حظاً مني .					
8. We are morally obliged to help socially disadvantaged people. - نحن ملزمين إنسانياً وأدبياً بمساعدة الناس المحرومين من أية مزايا اجتماعية .					
9. Social justice requires that we help those who are less fortunate than ourselves. - من متطلبات العدالة الاجتماعية مساعدة الناس الذين هم أقل حظاً منا .					
10. It is one of the principles of our society that we should help socially disadvantaged people. - إن مساعدة الناس المحرومين والمحتاجين هو من قيم مجتمعنا ومبادئه.					
11. Solving societal problems is something each of us can contribute to. - يستطيع كل واحد منا المساعدة والمساهمة في حل المشاكل الاجتماعية.					
12. I am convinced that I personally can make a contribution to address the societal challenges if I put my mind to it. - أنا على قناعة بأنني أستطيع المساهمة في مواجهة التحديات الاجتماعية إن توفرت النية لدي.					
13. I could figure out a way to help solve the problems that society faces. - لدي القدرة في وضع خطة طريق للمساعدة في حل المشاكل الاجتماعية.					
14. I do not believe that it would be possible for me to bring about a significant social change. - لا أعتقد أنه من الممكن بالنسبة لي إحداث أي تغيير اجتماعي له قيمة.					
15. It is possible to attract investors for an organization that wants to solve social problems. - هناك إمكانية لجذب المستثمرين للمؤسسات أو المنظمات التي ترغب في المساهمة في حل المشاكل الاجتماعية.					
16. People would support me if I wanted to start an organization to help socially marginalized people. - سأحظى بدعم الناس ,ذا بادرت بتأسيس منظمة اجتماعية لمساعدة الفئات الهامشية في المجتمع.					
17. If I planned to address a significant societal problem people would back me up. - سأحظى بدعم الناس , إذا تبنيت قضايا الفئات الاجتماعية الهامشية .					
18. I do not believe that I would receive much support if I were to start a social enterprise.					

- لا أعتقد بأنني ساحظى بكثير من الدعم إن فكرت بتأسيس مشروع اجتماعي.					
19. I believe that at some point in the future I will launch a social enterprise. - أتوقع في المستقبل بأن أكوّن منظمة اجتماعية تعنى بمشاكل الناس الهامشيين.					
20. I have a preliminary idea about what kind of a social enterprise I'm going to launch in the future. - أصبح لدي فكرة بالمنظمة الاجتماعية التي ساعمل معها في المستقبل.					
21. I have no intention of launching a social enterprise. - لا تتوفر لدي النية في الوقت الحاضر في تأسيس منظمة اجتماعية .					

1. المجموعة الثالثة من الأسئلة

اختر واحدة من الإجابات التالية		السؤال
لا	نعم	
		1. I have got some previous experience of dealing with social problems solving. لدي بعض الخبرة في التعامل مع المشاكل الاجتماعية
		2. I have worked for social enterprises as a volunteer or in some other way. عملت بشكل أو اخر مع المنظمات الاجتماعية وقدمت المساعدة لها
		3. I have enough knowledge about social enterprises and their objectives. لدي الثير من المعلومات عن المنظمات الاجتماعية وأهدافها

Thank You!

Appendix 1B

استمارة استبيان

عنوان البحث

"مواصفات الشخصية والنية في إنشاء منظمة اجتماعية خيرية"

الهدف من البحث: يهدف هذا البحث الى الربط بين مواصفات الشخصية ورح المبادرة في إنشاء منظمة اجتماعية خيرية تهدف الى مساعدة الناس الهامشيين في المجتمع وقياس العلاقة بين المتغيرين كمياً.

1. المجموعة الأولى من الأسئلة

النوع

ذكر	أنثى

السنة الدراسية

سنة أولى	سنة ثانية	سنة ثالثة	سنة رابعة

الكلية................ القسم ....

2. المجموعة الثانية من الأسئلة

السؤال	اختر واحدة من الإجابات الخمسة التالية				
	أوافق بشدة	موافق	ليس لدي إجابة	غير موافق	غير موافق بشدة
1- عندما افكر بمشاكل الناس الهامشيين (الذين ليس لهم مكانة اجتماعية-فقراء – محرومين من التعليم –محرومين من الخدمات الصحية – السكن الصحي –العمل اللائق والمجزي) أحاول أن أضع نفسي مكانهم.					
2- لا أهتم ولا أعير أهمية لمشاعر الناس الهامشيين في المجتمع.					
3- إن رؤية الناس المحرومين والمعسرين (الهامشيين) يحفز في أعماقي الكثير من المشاعر.					
4- لا تثير الطبقات الاجتماعية الدنيا عندي الكثير من المشاعر عندما أفكر بها.					
5- أشعر بالتعاطف والشفقة مع مشاكل وهموم الطبقات الاجتماعية . الهامشية.					
7- من الواجب أخلاقياً مساعدة الناس الذين هم أقل حظاً مني .					
8- نحن ملزمين إنسانياً وأدبياً بمساعدة الناس المحرومين من أية مزايا اجتماعية .					
9- من متطلبات العدالة الاجتماعية مساعدة الناس الذين هم أقل حظاً منا .					
10- إن مساعدة الناس المحرومين والمحتاجين هو من قيم مجتمعنا ومبادئه.					
11- يستطيع كل واحد منا المساعدة والمساهمة في حل المشاكل الاجتماعية.					
12- أنا على قناعة بأنني أستطيع المساهمة في مواجهة التحديات الاجتماعية إن توفرت النية لدي.					
13- لدي القدرة في وضع خطة طريق للمساعدة في حل المشاكل الاجتماعية.					
14- لا أعتقد أنه من الممكن بالنسبة لي إحداث أي تغيير اجتماعي له قيمة.					
15- هناك إمكانية لجذب المستثمرين للمؤسسات أو المنظمات التي ترغب في المساهمة في حل المشاكل الاجتماعية.					
16- سأحظى بدعم الناس ,ذا بادرت بتأسيس منظمة اجتماعية لمساعدة الفئات الهامشية في المجتمع.					
17- سأحظى بدعم الناس , إذا تبنيت قضايا الفئات الاجتماعية الهامشية .					
18- لا أعتقد بأنني سأحظى بكثير من الدعم إن فكرت بتأسيس مشروع اجتماعي.					
19- أتوقع في المستقبل بأن أكوّن منظمة اجتماعية تعنى بمشاكل الناس الهامشيين.					
20- أصبح لدي فكرة بالمنظمة الاجتماعية التي سأعمل معها في المستقبل.					
21- لا تتوفر لدي النية في الوقت الحاضر في تأسيس منظمة اجتماعية .					

2. المجموعة الثالثة من الأسئلة

السؤال	اختر واحدة من الإجابات التالية	
	نعم	لا
1-لدي بعض الخبرة في التعامل مع المشاكل الاجتماعية.		
2- عملت بشكل أو اخر مع المنظمات الاجتماعية وقدمت المساعدة لها.		
3- لدي الثير من المعلومات عن المنظمات الاجتماعية وأهدافها.		

Appendix 2: Descriptive Statistics

Table 3 GENDER = Male

Descriptive statistics[a]

	N	Minimum	Maximum	Mean	Std. deviation
25-Questions 1, 3, 5	48	1.67	5.00	4.2257	0.68459
25-Questions 7, 8, 9, 10	48	1.50	5.00	4.1163	0.81952
25-Questions 11, 12, 13	48	2.00	5.00	3.9549	0.67086
25-Questions 15, 16, 17	48	1.00	5.00	3.6007	0.88642
25-Questions 19, 20, 21	48	1.00	4.33	3.2188	0.70221
Valid N (listwise)	48				

[a]GENDER = Male

Table 4 GENDER = Female

Descriptive statistics[a]

	N	Minimum	Maximum	Mean	Std. deviation
25-Questions 1, 3, 5	64	2.67	5.00	4.2474	0.55871
25-Questions 7, 8, 9, 10	64	1.50	5.00	4.3008	0.59920
25-Questions 11, 12, 13	64	1.67	5.00	3.9948	0.57426
25-Questions 15, 16, 17	64	1.33	5.00	3.7161	0.67826
25-Questions 19, 20, 21	64	1.33	4.67	3.2135	0.68652
Valid N (listwise)	64				

[a]GENDER = Female

Table 5 PROVINCE = Dera

Descriptive statistics[a]

	N	Minimum	Maximum	Mean	Std. deviation
25-Questions 1, 3, 5	71	2.67	5.00	4.3803	0.50252
25-Questions 7, 8, 9, 10	71	2.67	5.00	4.3204	0.57055
25-Questions 11, 12, 13	71	2.67	5.00	4.1009	0.53265
25-Questions 15, 16, 17	71	1.33	5.00	3.7606	0.74840
25-Questions 19, 20, 21	71	1.67	4.67	3.2981	0.64113
Valid N (listwise)	71				

[a]PROVINCE = Dera

Table 6 PROVINCE = Damascus

Descriptive statistics[a]	N	Minimum	Maximum	Mean	Std. deviation
25-Questions 1, 3, 5	41	1.67	5.00	4.0000	0.69921
25-Questions 7, 8, 9, 10	41	1.50	5.00	4.0447	0.88958
25-Questions 11, 12, 13	41	1.67	5.00	3.7317	0.73492
25-Questions 15, 16, 17	41	1.00	5.00	3.4309	0.84736
25-Questions 19, 20, 21	41	1.00	4.67	3.0732	0.74354
Valid N (listwise)	41				

[a]PROVINCE = Damascus

Table 7 State/private = Private university

Descriptive statistics[a]	N	Minimum	Maximum	Mean	Std. deviation
25-Questions 1, 3, 5	41	1.67	5.00	4.0000	0.69921
25-Questions 7, 8, 9, 10	41	1.50	5.00	4.0447	0.88958
25-Questions 11, 12, 13	41	1.67	5.00	3.7317	0.73492
25-Questions 15, 16, 17	41	1.00	5.00	3.4309	0.84736
25-Questions 19, 20, 21	41	1.00	4.67	3.0732	0.74354
Valid N (listwise)	41				

[a]state/private = private university

Table 8 State/private = State university

Descriptive statistics[a]	N	Minimum	Maximum	Mean	Std. deviation
25-Questions 1, 3, 5	75	2.67	5.00	4.3600	0.52565
25-Questions 7, 8, 9, 10	75	2.67	5.00	4.3300	0.56394
25-Questions 11, 12, 13	75	2.67	5.00	4.0867	0.52301
25-Questions 15, 16, 17	75	1.33	5.00	3.7556	0.74047
25-Questions 19, 20, 21	75	1.67	4.67	3.2733	0.64296
Valid N (listwise)	75				

[a]state/private = state university

Table 9 GENDER = Male, state/private = private university

Descriptive statistics[a]	N	Minimum	Maximum	Mean	Std. deviation
25-Questions 1, 3, 5	11	1.67	5.00	3.8788	1.06742
25-Questions 7, 8, 9, 10	11	1.50	5.00	3.6364	1.21637
25-Questions 11, 12, 13	11	2.00	5.00	3.5758	0.83121
25-Questions 15, 16, 17	11	1.00	5.00	3.3030	1.06931
25-Questions 19, 20, 21	11	1.00	4.00	2.8788	0.80654
Valid N (listwise)	11				

[a]GENDER = Male, state/private = private university

Table 10 GENDER = Male, state/private = state university

Descriptive statistics[a]					
	N	Minimum	Maximum	Mean	Std. deviation
25-Questions 1, 3, 5	37	3.33	5.00	4.3288	0.49766
25-Questions 7, 8, 9, 10	37	2.67	5.00	4.2590	0.61199
25-Questions 11, 12, 13	37	3.00	5.00	4.0676	0.58196
25-Questions 15, 16, 17	37	1.33	5.00	3.6892	0.82042
25-Questions 19, 20, 21	37	1.67	4.33	3.3198	0.64595
Valid N (listwise)	37				

[a]GENDER = Male, state/private = private university

Table 11 GENDER = Female, state/private = private university

Descriptive statistics[a]					
	N	Minimum	Maximum	Mean	Std. deviation
25-Questions 1, 3, 5	27	3.00	5.00	4.0741	0.52569
25-Questions 7, 8, 9, 10	27	1.50	5.00	4.1883	0.69936
25-Questions 11, 12, 13	27	1.67	4.67	3.8395	0.66904
25-Questions 15, 16, 17	27	1.33	4.67	3.5802	0.68308
25-Questions 19, 20, 21	27	1.33	4.67	3.1852	0.74152
Valid N (listwise)	27				

[a]GENDER = Female, state/private = private university

Table 12 GENDER = Female, state/private = state university

Descriptive statistics[a]					
	N	Minimum	Maximum	Mean	Std. deviation
25-Questions 1, 3, 5	37	2.67	5.00	4.3739	0.55473
25-Questions 7, 8, 9, 10	37	3.00	5.00	4.3829	0.50859
25-Questions 11, 12, 13	37	2.67	5.00	4.1081	0.47176
25-Questions 15, 16, 17	37	2.67	5.00	3.8153	0.66642
25-Questions 19, 20, 21	37	2.00	4.67	3.2342	0.65317
Valid N (listwise)	37				

[a]GENDER = Female, state/private = state university

Appendix 3: T-test

Table 13 Independent samples test—significance levels of a t-test for equality of means

	Significance levels (2-taled) for variable		
	GENDER	STATE/PRIVATE	PROVINCE
Questions 1, 3, 5			
Equal variances assumed	0.854	0.002	0.001
Equal variances not assumed	0.858	0.005	0.003
Questions 7, 8, 9, 10			
Equal variances assumed	0.171	0.037	0.048
Equal variances not assumed	0.191	0.068	0.080
Questions 11, 12, 13			
Equal variances assumed	0.735	0.003	0.003
Equal variances not assumed	0.741	0.008	0.006
Questions 15, 16, 17			
Equal variances assumed	0.436	0.034	0.035
Equal variances not assumed	0.454	0.043	0.042
Questions 19, 20, 21			
Equal variances assumed	0.969	0.132	0.095
Equal variances not assumed	0.969	0.151	0.109

Table 14 T-Test: GENDER

Group statistics					
	GENDER	N	Mean	Std. deviation	Std. error mean
25-Questions 1, 3, 5	Male	48	4.2257	0.68459	0.09881
	Female	64	4.2474	0.55871	0.06984
25-Questions 7, 8, 9, 10	Male	48	4.1163	0.81952	0.11829
	Female	64	4.3008	0.59920	0.07490
25-Questions 11, 12, 13	Male	48	3.9549	0.67086	0.09683
	Female	64	3.9948	0.57426	0.07178
25-Questions 15, 16, 17	Male	48	3.6007	0.88642	0.12794
	Female	64	3.7161	0.67826	0.08478
25-Questions 19, 20, 21	Male	48	3.2188	0.70221	0.10135
	Female	64	3.2135	0.68652	0.08582

Table 15 T-test: STATE/PRIVATE

Group statistics					
	State/private	N	Mean	Std. deviation	Std. error mean
25-Questions 1, 3, 5	Private university	41	4.0000	0.69921	0.10920
	State university	75	4.3600	0.52565	0.06070
25-Questions 7, 8, 9, 10	Private university	41	4.0447	0.88958	0.13893
	State university	75	4.3300	0.56394	0.06512
25-Questions 11, 12, 13	Private university	41	3.7317	0.73492	0.11478
	State university	75	4.0867	0.52301	0.06039

(continued)

Group statistics					
	State/private	N	Mean	Std. deviation	Std. error mean
25-Questions 15, 16, 17	Private university	41	3.4309	0.84736	0.13234
	State university	75	3.7556	0.74047	0.08550
25-Questions 19, 20, 21	Private university	41	3.0732	0.74354	0.11612
	State university	75	3.2733	0.64296	0.07424

Table 16 T-test: PROVINCE

Group statistics					
	PROVINCE	N	Mean	Std. deviation	Std. error mean
25-Questions 1, 3, 5	Dera	71	4.3803	0.50252	0.05964
	Damascus	41	4.0000	0.69921	0.10920
25-Questions 7, 8, 9, 10	Dera	71	4.3204	0.57055	0.06771
	Damascus	41	4.0447	0.88958	0.13893
25-Questions 11, 12, 13	Dera	71	4.1009	0.53265	0.06321
	Damascus	41	3.7317	0.73492	0.11478
25-Questions 15, 16, 17	Dera	71	3.7606	0.74840	0.08882
	Damascus	41	3.4309	0.84736	0.13234
25-Questions 19, 20, 21	Dera	71	3.2981	0.64113	0.07609
	Damascus	41	3.0732	0.74354	0.11612

Appendix 4: Anova One-Way Analysis

ANOVA						
		Sum of squares	df	Mean square	F	Sig.
25-Questions 1, 3, 5	Between groups	5.651	5	1.130	3.390	0.007
	Within groups	35.340	106	0.333		
	Total	40.991	111			
25-Questions 7, 8, 9, 10	Between groups	4.108	5	0.822	1.665	0.149
	Within groups	52.308	106	0.493		
	Total	56.417	111			
25-Questions 11, 12, 13	Between groups	4.953	5	0.991	2.622	0.028
	Within groups	40.054	106	0.378		
	Total	45.008	111			
25-Questions 15, 16, 17	Between groups	6.677	5	1.335	2.209	0.059
	Within groups	64.076	106	0.604		
	Total	70.753	111			

(continued)

ANOVA						
		Sum of squares	df	Mean square	F	Sig.
25-Questions 19, 20, 21	Between groups	5.653	5	1.131	2.575	0.031
	Within groups	46.549	106	0.439		
	Total	52.202	111			

Appendix 5: Post Hoc Tests

Table 17 One-way ANOVA for empathy

ANOVA					
25-Questions 1, 3, 5					
	Sum of squares	df	Mean square	F	Sig.
Between groups	5.651	5	1.130	3.390	0.007
Within groups	35.340	106	0.333		
Total	40.991	111			

Table 18 Multiple comparisons for empathy

Multiple comparisons						
Dependent variable: 25-Questions 1, 3, 5						
LSD						
					95% Confidence interval	
(I) FACULTY	(J) FACULTY	Mean difference (I-J)	Std. error	Sig.	Lower bound	Upper bound
Accounting	Law	0.0740	0.15799	0.641	−0.2392	0.3872
	ط§ Business	0.6588*	0.17897	0.000	0.3040	1.0137
	Sciences	−0.0078	0.20771	0.970	−0.4197	0.4040
	Humanitarian	−0.1412	0.27656	0.611	−0.6895	0.4071
	Finance	0.2383	0.15043	0.116	−0.0599	0.5365
Law	Accounting	−0.0740	0.15799	0.641	−0.3872	0.2392
	ط§Business	0.5848*	0.19334	0.003	0.2015	0.9682
	Sciences	−0.0818	0.22021	0.711	−0.5184	0.3548
	Humanitarian	−0.2152	0.28606	0.454	−0.7823	0.3520
	Finance	0.1643	0.16726	0.328	−0.1673	0.4960
ط§Business	Accounting	−0.6588*	0.17897	0.000	−1.0137	−0.3040
	Law	−0.5848*	0.19334	0.003	−0.9682	−0.2015
	Sciences	−0.6667*	0.23572	0.006	−1.1340	−0.1993
	Humanitarian	−0.8000*	0.29817	0.008	−1.3911	−0.2089
	Finance	−0.4205*	0.18721	0.027	−0.7917	−0.0493

(continued)

Multiple comparisons						
Dependent variable: 25-Questions 1, 3, 5						
LSD						
					95% Confidence interval	
(I) FACULTY	(J) FACULTY	Mean difference (I-J)	Std. error	Sig.	Lower bound	Upper bound
Sciences	Accounting	0.0078	0.20771	0.970	−0.4040	0.4197
	Law	0.0818	0.22021	0.711	−0.3548	0.5184
	ط§Business	0.6667*	0.23572	0.006	0.1993	1.1340
	Humanitarian	−0.1333	0.31626	0.674	−0.7603	0.4937
	Finance	0.2462	0.21485	0.255	−0.1798	0.6721
Humanitarian	Accounting	0.1412	0.27656	0.611	−0.4071	0.6895
	Law	0.2152	0.28606	0.454	−0.3520	0.7823
	§طBusiness	0.8000*	0.29817	0.008	0.2089	1.3911
	Sciences	0.1333	0.31626	0.674	−0.4937	0.7603
	Finance	0.3795	0.28196	0.181	−0.1795	0.9385
Finance	Accounting	−0.2383	0.15043	0.116	−0.5365	0.0599
	Law	−0.1643	0.16726	0.328	−0.4960	0.1673
	ط§Business	0.4205*	0.18721	0.027	0.0493	0.7917
	Sciences	−0.2462	0.21485	0.255	−0.6721	0.1798
	Humanitarian	−0.3795	0.28196	0.181	−0.9385	0.1795

*The mean difference is significant at the 0.05 level

Table 19 One-way ANOVA for moral obligation

ANOVA					
25-Questions 7, 8, 9, 10					
	Sum of squares	df	Mean square	F	Sig.
Between groups	4.108	5	0.822	1.665	0.149
Within groups	52.308	106	0.493		
Total	56.417	111			

Table 20 One-way ANOVA for SE self-efficacy

ANOVA					
25-Questions 11, 12, 13					
	Sum of squares	df	Mean square	F	Sig.
Between groups	4.953	5	0.991	2.622	0.028
Within groups	40.054	106	0.378		
Total	45.008	111			

Table 21 One-way ANOVA for perceived social support

ANOVA					
25-Questions 15, 16, 17					
	Sum of squares	df	Mean square	F	Sig.
Between groups	6.677	5	1.335	2.209	0.059
Within groups	64.076	106	0.604		
Total	70.753	111			

Table 22 One-way ANOVA for social entrepreneurial intentions

ANOVA					
25-Questions 19, 20, 21					
	Sum of squares	df	Mean square	F	Sig.
Between groups	5.653	5	1.131	2.575	0.031
Within groups	46.549	106	0.439		
Total	52.202	111			

Appendix 6: Means Plots

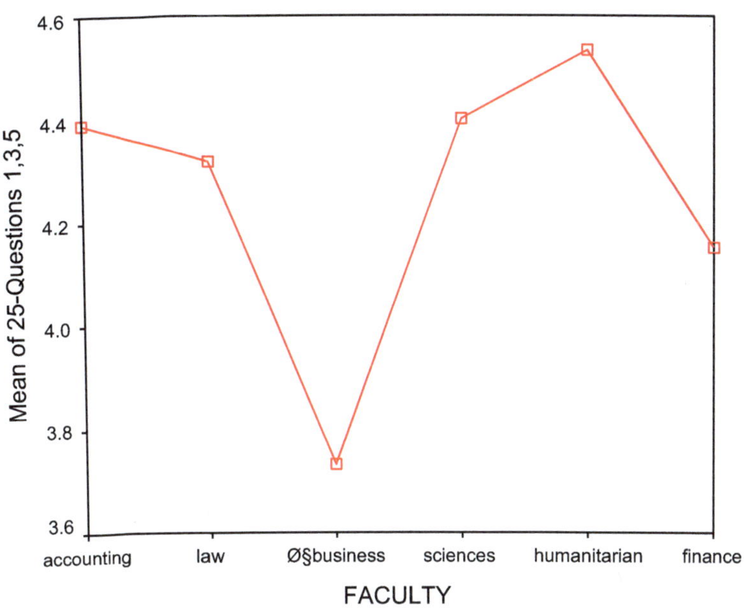

Fig. 1 Mean empathy values for different faculties of Syrian universities

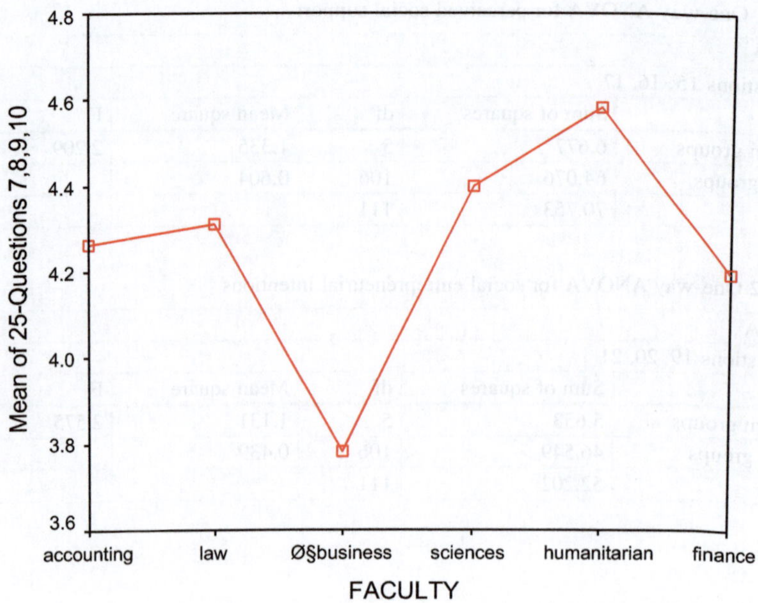

Fig. 2 Mean moral obligation levels for different faculties of Syrian universities

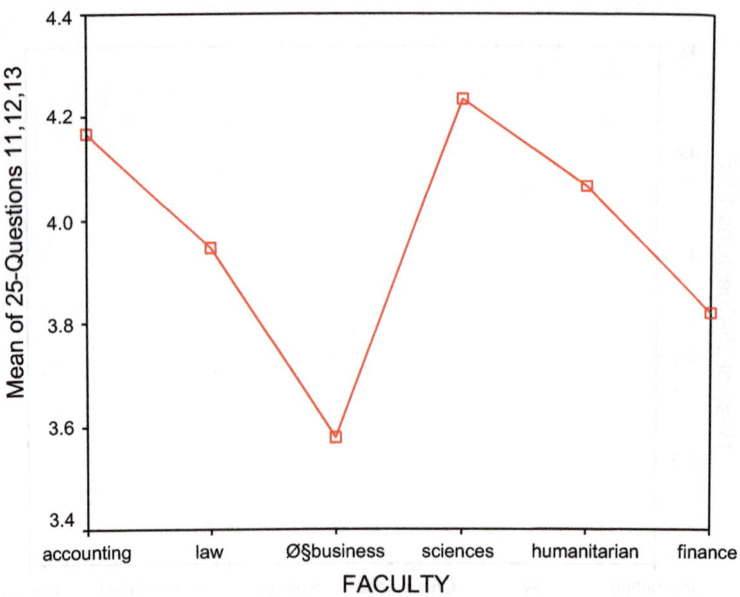

Fig. 3 Mean SE self-efficacy levels for different faculties of Syrian universities

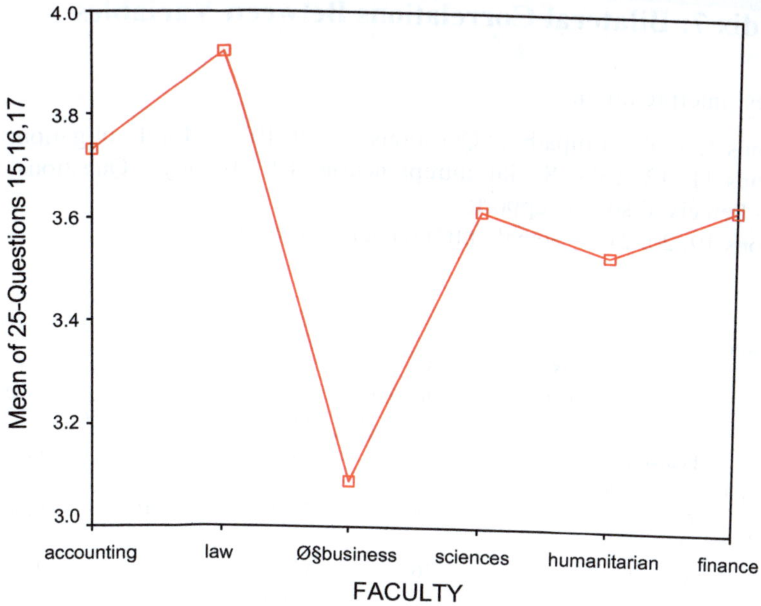

Fig. 4 Mean perceived social support levels for different faculties of Syrian universities

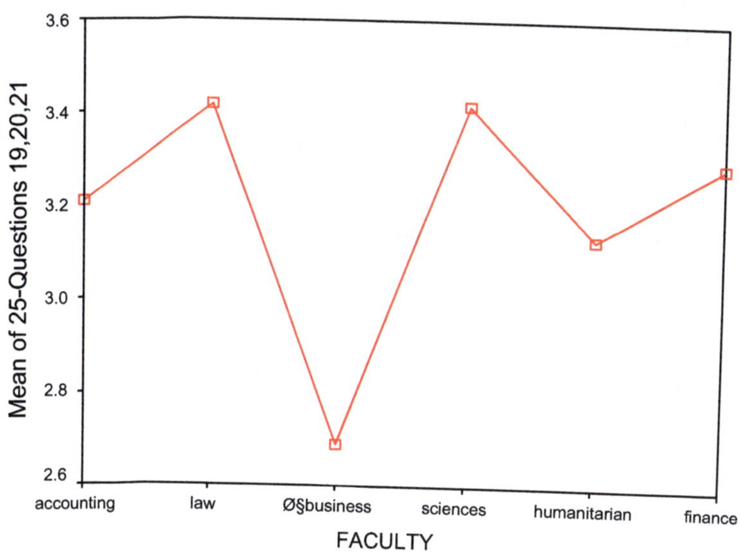

Fig. 5 Mean social entrepreneurial intentions levels for different faculties of Syrian universities

Appendix 7: Bilateral Correlations Between Variables

Variables' interpretation:

"Questions 1, 3, 5"—Empathy; "Questions 7, 8, 9, 10"—Moral obligation;
"Questions 11, 12, 13"—Social entrepreneurial self-efficacy; "Questions 15, 16, 17"—Perceived social support;
"Questions 19, 20, 21"—Social entrepreneurial intentions

Correlation						
		25-Questions 1, 3, 5	25-Questions 7, 8, 9, 10	25-Questions 11, 12, 13	25-Questions 15, 16, 17	25-Questions 19, 20, 21
25-Questions 1, 3, 5	Pearson correlation	1	0.540**	0.528**	0.302**	0.275**
	Sig. (2-tailed)	.	0.000	0.000	0.001	0.003
	N	116	116	116	116	116
25-Questions 7, 8, 9, 10	Pearson correlation	0.540**	1	0.621**	0.383**	0.179
	Sig. (2-tailed)	0.000	.	0.000	0.000	0.055
	N	116	116	116	116	116
25-Questions 11, 12, 13	Pearson correlation	0.528**	0.621**	1	0.339**	0.266**
	Sig. (2-tailed)	0.001	0.000	0.000	.	0.009
	N	116	116	116	116	116
25-Questions 15, 16, 17	Pearson correlation	0.302**	0.383**	0.339**	1	0.243**
	Sig. (2-tailed)	0.001	0.000	0.000	.	0.009
	N	116	116	116	116	116
25-Questions 19, 20, 21	Pearson correlation	0.275**	0.179	0.266**	0.243**	1
	Sig. (2-tailed)	0.003	0.055	0.004	0.009	.
	N	116	116	116	116	116

**Correlation is significant at the 0.01 level (2-tailed)

References

1. Ajzen, I. (1991). The theory of planned behavior. *Organizational Behavior and Human Decision Processes, 50*(2), 179–211.
2. Al Asadi R., & Abdelrahim A. (2007). Critical analysis and modeling of small business performance (Case study: Syria). *Journal of Asia Entrepreneurship and Sustainability, 3*(2), ISSN: 1176-8592.
3. Bielefeld, W. (2015). Issues in social enterprise and social entrepreneurship. *Journal of Public Affairs Education, JPAE, 15*(1), 69–86. Indiana University.
4. Clarke, D., & Kumar, N. (2015). *Microinsurance decisions: Gendered evidence from rural Bangladesh* (Discussion paper 01465). Poverty, Health and nutrition division of International Food Policy Research Institute.
5. Gist, M. E., & Mitchell, T. B. (1992). Self-efficacy: A theoretical analysis of its determinants and malability. *Academy of Management Review, 17*(2), 183–211.
6. Haines, R., Street, M. D., & Haines, D. (2008). The influence of perceived importance of an ethical issue on moral judgment, moral obligation, and moral intent. *Journal of Business Ethics, 81*(2), 387–399.
7. Hemingway, C. A. (2005). Personal values as a catalyst for corporate social entrepreneurship. *Journal of Business Ethics, 60*(3), 233–249.
8. Henderson, A., & Robertson, M. (2000). Who wants to be an entrepreneur? Young adults attitudes to entrepreneurship as a career. *Career Development International, 5*(N6), 279–287.
9. Hockerts, K. (2015). Antecedents of social entrepreneurship intentions: A validation study. *Social Enterprise Journal, 11*(3).
10. Hockerts, K. (2017). Determinants of social entrepreneurial intentions. *Entrepreneurship Theory and Practice, 41*(1), 105–130.
11. Kaiser, F. G. (2006). A moral extention of the theory of planned behavior: Norms and anticipated feelings of regret in conservationism. *Personality and Individual Differences, 41* (1), 71–81.
12. Kashina, M. A., & Utkina, N. Y. (2015). *Social entrepreneurship as the "relevant" business for women*. Available at SSRN: http://ssrn.com/abstract=2671872
13. Kautonenen, T., Van Gelderen, N., & Fink, M. (2013). Robustness of the theory of planned behavior in predicting entrepreneurial intentions and actions. *Entrepreneurship Theory and Practice*. doi: 10.1111/etap.12056.
14. Kuratko, D. (2005). The emergence of entrepreneurship education: Development, trends and challenges. *Entrepreneurship Theory and Practice, 29*(5), 577–597.
15. Light, P. (2005, November). Searching for social entrepreneurs: Who they might be, where they might be found, what they do. Paper presented at the annual meetings of the Association for Research on Nonprofit Organizations and Voluntary Action, Washington, DC, pp. 17–19.
16. Linñán, F. (2004). Intention-based models of entrepreneurship education. *Piccola Impresa/ Small Business, N3*, 11–35.
17. Linñán, F., & Fayolle, A. (2015). *A systematic literature review on entrepreneurial intentions: Citation, thematic analyses, and research agenda*. New York: Springer Science Business Media.
18. Mair, J., & Noboa, E. (2006). Social entrepreneurship: How intentions to create a social venture get formed. In J. Mair, J. Robinson, & K. Hockerts (Eds.), *Social entrepreneurship* (pp. 121–136). New York: Palgrave MacMillan.
19. Markman, G. D., & Baron, R. A. (2003). Person-entrepreneurship fit: Why some people are more successful as entrepreneurs than others. *Human Resource Management Review, 13*, 281–301.
20. Massarsky, S. (2005, November). *Ten characteristics that define social movements in the nonprofit sector*. Handout at the session colloquy: Emerging Issues in Social Entrepreneurship Research, at the annual meetings of the Association for Research on Nonprofit Organizations and Voluntary Action, Washington, DC, pp. 17–19.

21. Miller, T. L., Grimes, M. G., Mcmullen, J. S., & Vogus, T. J. (2012). Venturing for others with heart and head: How compassion encourages cosial entrepreneurship. *Academy of Management Review, 37*(4), 616–640.
22. Naman, J. L., & Slevin, D. P. (1993). Entrepreneurship and the concept of fit: A model and empirical tests. *Strategic Management Journal, 14*, 137–153.
23. Ngugi, J. K., Gakure, R. W., Waithaka, S. M., & Kiwara, A. N. (2010). Application of Shapiro's model in explaining entrepreneurial intentions among university students in Kenya. *International Journal of Business and Social Research*.
24. Nicholls, A. (Ed.). (2004). *Social entrepreneurship: New models of sustainable social change*. Oxford: Oxford University Press.
25. Shapero, A., & Sokol, L. (1982). The social dimentions of entrepreneurship. In C. Kent, D. Sexton, & K. H. Vesper (Eds.), *Encyclopedia of Entrepreneurship* (pp. 72–90). Englewood Cliffs, NJ: Prentice Hall.
26. Turker, D., & Selcuk, S. S. (2009). Which factors affect entrepreneurial intention of university students? *Journal of European Industrial Training, 33*(2).
27. Weisbrod, B. (1988). *The nonprofit economy*. Cambridge, MA: Harward University Press.
28. Yunus, M., Moingeon, B., & Lehmann-Ortega, L. (2010). Building social business models: Lessons from the Grameen experience. *Long Range Planning, 43*(2–3), 308–325.

Review of Leadership Research in Higher Education

Ahmad Zein

Abstract Studies in organizations has generated a massive amount of examples on the way leadership growth can successfully advance employees' performance and work-related attitudes such as obligation or contentment. On the other hand, the higher education sector lacks tremendously such studies on leadership best practices and advancement. Nevertheless, this research proposes that the encouraging effects of leadership advancement in commercial associations also be valid to the academic framework. Thus, the rationale of this theoretical research paper is to scan previous studies and highlight the best practices of leadership in higher education institutes. The study will analyze ten similar studies in the domain and based on focus group practices, recommendations will be proposed.

Keywords Leadership • Higher education • Effectiveness

1 Introduction

Higher education sector necessitates employees who are not influenced with a formal responsibility of leader to achieve leadership but rather it should be part of their daily job description. In higher education institutes, leadership must be applied on a constant basis. Leadership management in higher education is predisposed by amplification in managerial monitoring, marketplace competition, organizational reformation and government examination. The dilemma between fulfilling the industry antagonism and applying the ethics and noble message of higher education will always shape contradiction in the strategic operation of educational institutions. Institutions of higher education are anticipated to be proficient with acceptable fees, resilient in their offerings, and up to the expectation of students in both their needs and demands. The pressure resulted from this predicament generated bitterness and feeling of low independency among faculty members. This study scans best practices in leadership and suggests styles to have

A. Zein (✉)
International School of Business, MUBS, Beirut, Lebanon
e-mail: azein@mubs.edu.lb

J. Marx Gómez et al. (eds.), *Modernizing Academic Teaching and Research in Business and Economics*, Springer Proceedings in Business and Economics,
DOI 10.1007/978-3-319-54419-9_6

an effective outcome with emphasis on staff development. Academic leadership is expected to integrate a central part in academic functions especially teaching, and research without exceeding the line of morality and decency all covered by the sacred message that it is supposed to engender. The motive behind this analysis is the changing nature of higher education institutions influenced by globalization and the increase demand of students to minimize the gap between theoretical learning and real jobs. The higher education industry is evolving like no other business but with more difficulties in the management techniques and lower outcome than before.

2 Literature Review

As mentioned earlier, higher education keep on suffering from noteworthy transformation in responding to features as government regulations, ongoing intensification in demand for superior levels of educational accomplishments and qualifications. Bolden et al. [1] justifies this change to the availability of information, advancement of technologies and globalization effect that are increasing on a daily basis. The sudden surfacing of the perception of the information economy and its significance as a cause of financial expansion has progressively challenged more the higher education industry to offer expert employees that can service such developments [2]. Worldwide universities, even the institutions ranked top on the list of education provider are not immune to this competition in the market and top management of those leading institutions are aware that if they don't keep updated with the current requirements of the industry. Universities worldwide are more aware of the need for faculty development and they are investing large amount of money on hiring top researchers and leaders in their fields as it is more obvious that such scholars are the most valuable asset of any academic association. This approach advocates the crucial need to transform the mentality of higher education institutes to employee satisfaction basis as a concept to amplify student satisfaction. Believing in this starting approach, Garvin [3] believes that the best way to succeed is to handle the management of universities to managers of academic background. This growing revolutionize requires from higher education organizations to find the best practices on how to balance by their mission and the positioning of the university in customers' mind. Jones et al. [4], aligns with previous studies such as Ramsden's [5] which states that leadership is expected to be in the behavior of academics rather than in the legitimate power possessed. To reach this advanced model in managing an organization Bolden et al. [1] outlines a different representation of universities with a extremely self-governing and decentralized procedure of decision making, placing leadership as a public accountability replacing the conventional theories of management and formal powers. This research will emphasize on studies that proposed such model to conclude a well-organized business model through focus group practices.

3 Leadership

Leadership is still a vague concept despite the many attempts to standardize this concept. Who is a leader? What are the true characteristics of true leaders? Why this person is a leader and this person is not? Was Stalin a leader or a war hero?

A lot of questions are being asked by researchers and scholars decades and decades ago. Many definitions have been given to leadership but till this moment no unified definition is agreed on.

Are leaders supposed to have positions or can a normal employee be a leader. How did Steve Jobs converted from being a shy man to a star on stage.

Leadership in ancient times was about power and authority, it was synonym for dictatorship. A leader was a person feared by his followers. Hitler, Mussolini and other war leaders were considered as great figures because of the dread they caused to the surroundings. Few decades ago this concept was deviated into more peaceful characteristics and the pioneers to practice this belief were Martin Luther King, Gandhi and Mandela.

In today's competitive markets, leaders are frequently challenged to uncover pioneering and innovative styles to engage and motivate employees. Leaders are the agents who are responsible for the positive change and stability of the company's bottom line. Each time, your position in an organization increases; more responsibilities will be assigned to you. The more responsibilities you are allocated, the more skills you are urged to have. When we talk about great leaders we are referring to leaders with astounding communication skills. It is unquestionably impracticable to develop into a great leader without being a first-class communicator. Commonly, a savvy leader's achievement is directly tied to his/her skills in communication. Nevertheless, people visualize a skilled communication as a talkative person which is totally misleading. Great communication starts from listening and observing the nonverbal messages of the receiver. The only language a leader must have is communication. Project managers according to the PMBOK spend 90% of their time communicating. So, what is the preeminent technique to be a great communicator? There are seven indispensable tips to communication positively.

1. Listen, listen and Listen: Listening is an elegant art. People tend to talk more than listen. To be a good listener you have to practice and decide on listening. Listening will help you analyze the nonverbal messages of the sender which is normally 65% of the message.
2. Think before you talk: Great communicators analyze the other person's message and think of the most suitable respond. With proper training and practice, this will not take more than 2 s.
3. Change the tone of your voice: Monotone will result in great annoyance on the receiver side. A great communicator will be excellent in changing the tome of his voice to grab the most of the concentration of the receiver.
4. Change your behaviour: No one was born an outstanding communicator. We were all born crying. The paramount means to become a superior communicator is to train and change your habits that don't fit the communication bible.

5. Speak comprehensible language: The secret to deliver the message to your receiver is to understand his decoding metabolism. Hence when you talk understand your receiver and send the message according to his dictionary not your desire.
6. Know what you are talking about: A leader is never shy of saying "I don't know" as long as he doesn't say it frequently. Never say anything you are not skilled in. Try your utmost possibility not to make people correct you. They will lose trust in you.
7. Don't jump into conclusions: One of the barriers for good communication is jumping into conclusions. Ask questions when you are not sure of an information.

All the above skills will be more than beneficial in the leadership style of academics especially when it is related to teaching capabilities.

4 Leadership in Higher Education

This study will adopt the analysis performed by Joyce and O'boyle [6] which scans ten previous studies in Leadership development. The studies period is between 2007 and 2012 and the sample is very much diversified which enriches the study tremendously. The attributes of successful leadership showed a lot of dissimilarity in the outcome (Table 1).

5 Conclusion

Based on a focus group of eight academics in the higher education sector, seven skills were chosen to be required for scholars to be seen as a person leadership character in the higher education industry. The seven traits are:

1. Promoting the group
2. Role model
3. Mentor
4. Providing directions
5. Fostering a supportive and collaborative environment
6. Having personal integrity
7. Academic credibility

On the other hand the negative aspect of an academic were adapted totally from Bryman [12] when he mentions how not to lead:

1. Failing to consult
2. Not respecting existing values
3. Actions that undermine collegiality

Table 1 Key characteristics of successful leadership in higher education

Authors	Successful leadership	Sample
Bolden et al. [1]	Energising Competent Warm Ethical Promoting the group Scholarship	Informal academic leaders
Jones et al. [4]	Trust Respect Recognition Collaboration Commitment to reflective practice	Academic, professional and executive staff
McFarlane [7]	Role model Mentor Advocate Guardian Acquisitor Ambassador	University professors
Ngui et al. [8]	Relating to people Leading change Managing process Producing results	Academic staff (all levels) from 20 Malaysian public universities
Gibbs et al. [9]	Establishing personal credibility and trust Identifying problems, turning them into opportunities Articulating a rationale for change Devolving leadership Building a community of practice Rewarding and recognising teaching Setting teaching expectations Marketing the department as a success Supporting change and innovation Involving	Departmental leadership of teaching in research-intensive environments/
Goodall [10]	Credibility Expert knowledge Standard bearer (arbiter of quality) Signalling commitment to research excellence on behalf of the institution	Vice chancellors (research profiles)
Breakwell and Tyherleigh [11]	Academic credibility Financial awareness Adaptability Confidence Strong persona Sense of mission, strategy and/or vision	Vice chancellors in UK universities
Bryman [12]	Providing direction Creating a structure to support the direction Fostering a supportive and collaborative environment Establishing trustworthiness as a leader Having personal integrity	Literature review and interviews with 14 leadership researchers about effective academic leadership and departmental level

(continued)

Table 1 (continued)

Authors	Successful leadership	Sample
	Having credibility to act as a role model Facilitating participation in decision-making; consultation Providing communication about developments Representing the department/institution to advance its cause(s) and networking on its behalf Respecting existing culture while seeking to instill values through a vision for the department/institution Protecting staff autonomy	
Bryman [12]	A proactive approach to pursuing the university's mission An emphasis on a visionary approach that guides and provides focus for what the leader seeks to achieve for the institution Being internally focused, i.e. in being well connected in the institution, being seen and drawing inspiration from its participants Being externally focused, i.e. networking with a variety of constituencies and reinforcing within those constituencies the direction the university is taking—good understanding of higher education Having personal integrity Introducing changes in a way that entails consultation with others Importance of not sealing leaders off from the university at large Importance of not undermining pre-existing organisational culture Being flexible in approach to leadership Entrepreneurial/risk-taking Influencing the organisational culture and values to support change Designing structures to support change	Literature review in relation to effective leadership at an institutional level
Spendlove [13]	Academic credibility Openness honesty Willingness to consult others Ability to think broadly and strategically ability to engage with others	Pro-vice chancellors in ten UK institutions

Source: Joyce and O'boyle [6]

4. Not promoting the interests of those for who the leader is responsible
5. Being uninvolved in the life of the departments/institution
6. Undermining autonomy
7. Allowing the department/institution to drift.

6 Recommendation for Future Studies

The study suggests future studies to adopt quantitative methodology covering a wider and more diversified sample. Quantitative methodology might generate more reliable results in this case; however, the results of this study showed consistency with the ten mentioned studies. A beneficial recommendation will be for future studies to develop their own validated and reliable scale.

References

1. Bolden, R., Gosling, J., O'Brien, A., Peters, K., Ryan, M., & Haslam, A. (2012, June). *Academic leadership: Changing conceptions, experiences and identities in higher education in UK universities*. Final Report, Research & Development Series. London: Leadership Foundation for Higher Education.
2. Thorp, H., & Goldstein, B. (2010, April). *Engines of innovation: The entrepreneurial university in the twenty-first century*. Chapel Hill, NC: University of North Carolina Press.
3. Garvin, T. (2012, May 1). The bleak future of Irish universities. *The Irish Times*.
4. Jones, S., Lefoe, G., Harvey, M., & Ryland, K. (2012). Distributed leadership: A collaborative framework for academics, executives and professionals in higher education. *Journal of Higher Education Policy and Management, 34*(1), 67–78.
5. Ramsden, P. (1998, February). *Learning to lead in higher education*. London: Routledge.
6. Joyce, P., & O'Boyle, C. (2013). Sustaining academic leadership in higher education. In C. O'Farrell & A. Farrell (Eds.), *Emerging issues in higher education* (Vol. 111, pp. 69–81). Athlone: EDIN.
7. Macfarlane, B. (2011). Professors as intellectual leaders: Formation, identity and role. *Studies in Higher Education, 36*(1), 57–73.
8. Ngui, K. N., Hong, K. S., Gan, S. L., Usop, H. H., & Mustafa, R. (2010). Perceptions of senior executive leadership behaviour and effectiveness in Malaysian public universities. In M. Devlin, J. Nagy, & A. Lichtenberg (Eds.), *Research and development in higher education: Reshaping higher education* (Vol. 33, pp. 515–527). Hammondville: HERDSA.
9. Gibbs, G., Knapper, C., & Piccinin, S. (2009, June). *Departmental leadership of teaching in research intensive environments*. Final Report, Research & Development Series. London: Leadership Foundation for Higher Education.
10. Goodhall, A. (2009, May). *Socrates in the boardroom: Why research universities should be led by top scholars*. Princeton, NJ: Princeton University Press.
11. Breakwell, G., & Tytherleigh, M. (2008, September). *The characteristics, roles and selection of vice chancellors*. London: Leadership Foundation for Higher Education.
12. Bryman, A. (2007, April). *Effective leadership in higher education*. Final Report, Research & Development Series. London: Leadership Foundation for Higher Education.
13. Spendlove, M. (2007). Competencies for effective leadership in higher education. *International Journal of Educational Management, 21*(5), 407–417.

The Determinants of Business Students' Faculty Performance: Evidence from a Private University in Syria

Sulaiman Mouselli, Kinaz Al Aytouni, and Kinan Naddeh

Abstract This study investigates factors that affect students' performance at the Faculty of Business Administration at a private university in the Syrian Arab republic. The impact of four variables; high school GPA, motivation, source of high school certificate, and gender, on student's faculty GPA have been examined using large sample of students for the period from 2005 to 2015. Applying Ordinary Least Squares (OLS) estimates, we find that high school GPA is the main determinants of student's faculty performance. Moreover, the difference in average faculty GPA between males and females is significant with males underperforming females. Furthermore, motivation seems an important determinant of faculty GPA though it is less reliable than high school GPA. Hence, Awareness sessions should be conducted for high school students to raise their awareness of their future careers. Moreover, admission policies need to be reviewed and developed to include motivation element in the admission process.

Keywords Academic performance • Motivation • Source of high school certificate • Gender • Business faculties

1 Introduction

Education is considered as important element of human capital, and thus a great provider to the improvement of the quality of life. Global competitiveness report, published by World Economic Forum (WEF) ranks countries' relative competitiveness in terms of their ability to raise productivity by utilizing their resources

S. Mouselli (✉) • K. Naddeh
Department of Accounting and Finance, Arab International University, Damascus, Syria
e-mail: S-mousele@aiu.edu.sy; k-naddeh@aiu.edu.sy

K. Al Aytouni
Department of Management Information Technology, Arab International University, Damascus, Syria
e-mail: k-aytouni@aiu.edu.sy

J. Marx Gómez et al. (eds.), *Modernizing Academic Teaching and Research in Business and Economics*, Springer Proceedings in Business and Economics,
DOI 10.1007/978-3-319-54419-9_7

based on nine pillars. Higher education and training is the fifth pillar, which takes into account the quality of the educational system [1].

One of the methods that measure the overall effectiveness and the quality of higher educational institutions is student outcomes, which includes persistence, graduation rates, and student attrition [2]. Academic achievement is one of the most common methods for evaluating student persistence [3].

A number of factors have been suggested as potential determinants of students' faculty performance. For example, the previous performance of students as proxied by high school GPA [4, 5] is a dominant factor in explaining faculty performance as it reflects its ability in isolation of any possible faculty influence. Moreover, variation in the performance of students based on their gender is also observable. Furthermore, the source of high school certificate whether it is local or foreign, public or private could reflect different level of facilities and attention allocated to students.

A number of theories also propose motivation in education setting. One of the primary theoretical frameworks is Self-Determination Theory (SDT) [6]. SDT classifies motivation as intrinsic, extrinsic or amotivation [7]. However, Education motivation has three dimensions, individual's beliefs in ability to perform a specific task, reasons and goals of the individual in doing the task, and the emotional response concerning perform the task [8]. Having a choice can be a powerful motivator, which means people would be more likely to engage in an action if they believe they had chosen it. Patall et al. [9] find that providing choice enhanced intrinsic motivation.

Motivation can take two dimensions. First, students with high school GPA, who have alternative study choices beyond business study majors, are considered intrinsically motivated. If a student chooses her major, which is the result of her own choices, she will be in a higher level of motivation. Second, students are extrinsically motivated during their study in the university when they engage in academic tasks and become interested in their major [10]. Unfortunately, given the absence of data on such engagement, this paper will concentrate on the first dimension of motivation.

Investigating the determinants of business students' faculty performance in Syria is an interesting topic for many reasons. First, the admission to university in Syria is based on one method, which is student's high school GPA only. Moreover, the majority of students in Syria lack clear motives in terms of their educational and career goals. The result of such admission system is high percentage of dropouts and consequently huge amount of time and resources are wasted. Furthermore, exploring the main determinants of business students' faculty performance should help faculty administrators to understand factors that have the most influence in order to concentrate on them in their efforts to enhance students' performance.

The rest of the paper is constructed as follow: Sect. 2 reviews the related literature on the variables that affect students' faculty GPA. Section 3 presents the sample, methodology followed, and statistical tools implemented. Results are discussed in Sect. 4. Conclusion is presented in Sect. 5 with a summary of results and recommendations.

2 Literature Review

Researchers have explored many factors affecting student academic achievement, including student characteristics, learning/teaching process and social factors. The high school grade point average (HSGPA), motivation, and gender are amongst the thoroughly investigated variables.

Many researchers report that high school performance has a significant impact on academic performance [11–14], while others view high school performance as less reliable indicator of student academic achievement [15].

For example, Geiser and Santelices [12] argue that high school grade point average (HSGPA) is consistently the strongest predictor with a positive and statistically significant impact with on 4-year College grades for a sample of practically 80,000 students admitted to the University of California. Another study investigates the factors that determine student's performance in introductory economics for a sample of students at the University of Toronto [13]. This study found that the most important factor is the high school achievement, with a positive influence. According to [14] high school GPA is an extremely reliable predictor of college performance. They document a positive relationship between performance in high school and performance in college. Others consider HSGPA as an unreliable predictor of academic success in university. They argue that the reason of the insignificant impact of high school performance on academic performance could be the variations in grading standards across schools [15].

During the last three decades, numerous researchers have highlighted the importance of motivational variables for students' experience and performance in education setting [16]. Motivation is considered as an important factor that influences a learners' ability to learn and the level of their achievement [17]. Breen and Lindsay [18] argue that academic performance is based on motivation and ability. Moreover, a positive and significant correlation between academic motivation and academic achievement among university students has been documented in a number of studies [8, 10, 19].

Kusurkar et al. [20] differentiates between two types of motivation, autonomous motivation and controlled motivation. Autonomous motivation originates within an individual while controlled motivation originates from external sources. They construct a new variable based on a combination of the above two types of motivation. This new variable is positively associated with high study effort and better GPA.

Tessema et al. [2] assess the effect of gender on some education outcomes. Female students tend to have higher GPAs than male students do. Woodfield and Earl-Novell [21] confirm this result finding that female students outperformed male students and attributed this partly to female students being more study-reliable and thus less likely to skip lectures. However, in other countries the fact "female outperform their counterparts" are reversed ([22], p. 1).

3 Sample and Methodology

The data for this study was obtained from the registration system of the Arab International University, a privet university in Syria. The total number of observations is 11,463 enrolled students covering six faculties. Our study is concerned with students from the Faculty of Business Administration. Hence, the sample is reduced to 2267 that includes all students, graduated and enrolled, with complete set of information. The final sample consists of 2267 cases covering 11 year period from 2005 (establishment year) to 2015.

3.1 Variables

The dependent variable that represents academic achievement of students is the student's faculty GPA (FGPA). Four predicting independent variables are included in this non-experimental study; high school GPA (HSGPA), gender (Gender), the source of high school certificate (SHSC), and motivation (BusMotv). The following table defines the set of variables used (Table 1).

Table 1 Variables used in the study

Serial	Variable name	Definition	Variable label	Measurement term	Value labels	
					Value	Value label
1	FGPA	The student's faculty GPA	Faculty GPA	Scale	[0, 4]	
2	HSGPA	High school GPA	High school GPA	Scale	[50, 100]	
3	Gender	Demographic variable	Gender of student	Dichotomous	[1, 0]	1 = Male
4	SHSC	Source of high school certificate	Syrian high school certificate	Dichotomous	[1, 0]	1 = Syrian HS certificate
5	BusMotv	Student has a HSGPA gives him/her a chance to register in another faculty with a higher required grade, but he/she chooses to enroll in the faculty of business administration	Intrinsic motivated students variable	Dichotomous	[1, 0]	1 = HSGPA is equal or higher than 60%

Table 2 Descriptive statistics of the variables for the period 2005–2015

Variable	Minimum	Maximum	Mean	Standard deviation	Skewness	Kurtosis
FGPA	0.17	3.95	2.1225	0.74476	−0.406	−0.139
Gender	0	1	0.73	0.445	−1.027	−0.946
HSGPA	50.00	99.75	65.6948	10.70795	0.797	0.031
SHSC	0	1	0.87	0.339	−2.166	2.693
BusMotv	0	1	0.65	0.477	−0.628	−1.607

3.2 *Descriptive Statistics*

Table 2 provides descriptive statistics for the above-defined variables. It can be noticed that the average faculty GPA is 2.1225 with a standard deviation of 0.74476. This indicates a modest average performance of business students given that the pass GPA is two. However, the standard deviation is quite large. The skewness for FGPA variable is −0.406 means that the data are mildly skewed to the left of the mean. The kurtosis statistics for FGPA is −0.139, which indicates that the variable is flattered (short-tailed than normal).

High school GPA (HSGPA) has a mean of 65.6948, which is higher than the minimum GPA that is required to enroll in the faculty of 50%. However, the standard deviation of HSGPA is 10.70795, which is quite high and indicates that considerable number of students has a HSGPA that is higher than the minimum required by the faculty. The skewness for HSGPA is +0.797 which means that the data of this variable are skewed to the right of the mean. The Kurtosis for HSGPA is +0.031, which indicates that, the distribution has slightly heavier tails and a sharper peak than the normal distribution. The above statistics can be further noticed in Fig. 1, which shows the distribution of HSGPA and FGPA.

3.3 *Frequency Analysis*

Table 3 further shows the frequency information for the three other variables. The number of female students of 616 students constitutes (27.2%) of the total number of students enrolled at the faculty of Business Administration that is considerably lower than those for males with 1651 enrolled students. This table also shows that non-Syrian high school certificate is relatively small with 301 students that represent only 13.3% of the sample. Students with a motivation, as measured by BusMotv, are almost twice (1473 students) the number of students that are not motivated (794 students).

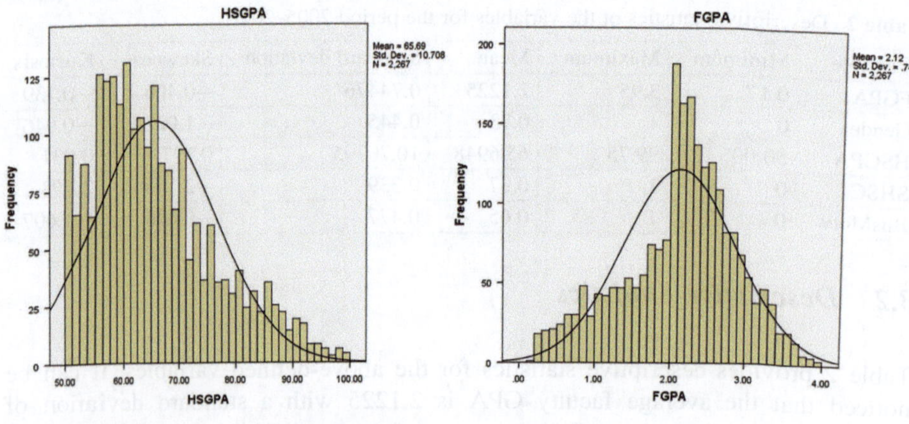

Fig. 1 The distribution of HSGPA and FGPA

Table 3 Frequency distribution for gender, SHSC, and BusMotv

Variable	Distribution	
Gender	Female	Male
	616	1651
SHSC	Not Syrian	Syrian
	301	1966
BusMotv	Not motivated	Motivated
	794	1473

3.4 *Correlation Matrix*

Table 4 shows the Pearson correlation coefficients between the examined variables. The first row indicates significant correlation FGPA and gender of (−0.203) as the negative sign indicate that female is performing better than males. There is also a positive and significant correlation coefficient between FGPA and HSGPA (0.210). This positive correlation is expected given that it represents a higher ability of students should be reflected in a higher FGPA. The correlation between FGPA and SHSC of −0.016 is insignificant which suggests that students who obtained their high school certificate from a foreign country perform no worse than those with Syrian high school certificate do. There is also a positive and significant correlation, though not strong, between motivation and FGPA of 0.110.

3.5 *Regression Analysis*

We apply Ordinary Least Squares (OLS) multiple regression for the whole sample period to investigate the predicting ability of a set of four variables: *motivation,*

Table 4 Pearson correlation coefficients of the tested variables for the period 2005–2015

Variable	FGPA	Gender	HSGPA	SHSC	BusMotv
FGPA	1	−0.203***	0.210***	−0.016	0.110***
Gender		1	−0.157***	0.004	−0.112***
HSGPA			1	−0.335***	0.709***
SHSC				1	−0.181***
BusMotv					1

***indicates significance at the 1% level of significance

grades in high school, source of high school and gender. That is, we run the following regression.

$$FGPA = c + Gender + SHSC + HSGPA + BUSMotv + e \tag{1}$$

We estimate five versions of the above equation including variables in the estimation subsequently in order to clarify the individual impact of each variable on the faculty GPA (FGPA).

4 Results

Table 5 shows the results from all tested models using OLS regressions. All models (1–5) indicate a negative and significant coefficient of Gender on faculty GPA. This indicates that male business students perform worse than female students do. Model 1 suggests that business students with clear business motives perform better than those without business motives by 0.137 point.

Model 3 indicates that high school GPA has a positive and significant impact on faculty GPA with a coefficient of 0.013. This is consistent with [11–14]. The source of high school certificate (SHSC) has positive and significant impact on faculty GPA as suggested by model 3 with a coefficient of 0.113. This suggests that students that hold a Syrian high school certificate perform better in there faculty compared to their non-Syrian high school certificate holders counterparts.

Model 4 indicates a positive and significant impact of high school GPA on Faculty GPA. The coefficient of high school GPA is 0.014 is significant at 1% level of significance. Moreover, Gender factor has a negative and significant impact on faculty GPA. The gender coefficient of −0.287 indicates that female students performs better than males by 0.287. This different performance is also significant at 1% level of significance. This result is consistent with Tessema et al. [2] and Woodfield and Earl-Novell [21].

Model 5, that contains all examined variables, confirms model 3 and 4 results. The only surprising result is that the business motive variable (BusMotv) has changed its sign from positive to negative with a coefficient of 0.135. This contradicting effect is due to the high correlation between HSGPA and BusMotv

Table 5 The results from running OLS regressions on the faculty GPA (dependent variable)

Model	1	2	3	4	5
Constant	2.268***	2.268***	1.498***	1.316***	1.104***
Gender	−0.323***	−0.323***	−0.291***	−0.287***	−0.286***
SHSC		0.001		0.113**	0.125***
HSGPA			0.013***	0.014***	0.018***
BusMotv	0.137***	0.137***			−0.135***
Adj-R2	0.048	0.047	0.073	0.075	0.078

Table 6 Descriptive statistics for the two BusMotv students with tests of equality

	BusMotv	Number	Mean	Standard deviation	Standard error	F-test	T-test
FGPA	1	1473	2.182	0.77356	0.02016	15.2	5.47
	0	794	2.011	0.67464	0.02394	0	0

Note: F-test is Levene's Test for Equality of Variances while t-test is for Equality of Means when Equal variances are not assumed

of 0.709 that is significant at 1% level of significance. Hence, the negative sign of the BusMotv coefficient should be ignored.

To further examine the last result of the impact of business motive on student's faculty performance, we first split our sample into two groups; one with business motive that comprises students with high school GPA of 60% or more, while the other group consists of students with less than 60% high school GPA. Students with High school GPA of equal or more than 60% have the opportunity to enrol in another faculty require higher HSGPA.

Then, we perform an F-test for the equality of variance. The p-value form the F-test indicates that the variances of the faculty GPA of both groups are not equal. Next, we examine if the averages of the faculty GPA of both groups are equal using t-test.

The results from Table 6 indicate that students with business motives (BusMotv = 1) have higher mean FGPA of 2.18 compared to students without business motives (BusMotv = 0) with a mean FGPA of 2.01. The results from testing the equality of variance between two groups: with business motives (BusMotv = 1) and without business motives (BusMotv = 0) suggests rejection of the null hypothesis that variances are equal as indicated by p-value of 0.000. The t-test for equality of means yields a t-value of 4.729, which is significant at 1% level of significance. It indicates that there is a significant difference between the means of both groups of 0.17 and suggests that students with business motives (BusMotv = 1) has significantly higher faculty GPA than students without business motives (BusMotv = 0). Hence, the result of the regression model 5 of negative impact of business motive on faculty performance is merely due to the mutlicollniearity between high school GPA and busMotv variables.

5 Conclusion and Recommendations

We investigate factors that predict student's academic achievement based on a set of variables that cover information about student's prior achievement, gender, source of high school certificate and the degree of motivation. We find that high school GPA is the main determinants of student's faculty performance. Moreover, the difference in average faculty GPA between males and females is significant with males underperforming females. Furthermore, motivation seems an important determinant of faculty GPA though it is less reliable than high school GPA.

The results obtained from this paper have a number of implications. First, high school GPA remains the dominant factor in determining faculty GPA. This suggests that policy makers should continue to use this criteria in admission process. However, special attention needs to be paid to motivation and consequently this factor should be implemented in admission policies. Second, awareness sessions and visits need to be arranged for high school students to a number of faculties to raise their awareness of their future careers in order to avoid any future disappointments and possible dropouts. Third, faculties should encourage students from both genders to work in mixed teams when doing assignments and projects to motivate males for better academic performance. Finally, special attention and academic guidance should be made available for non-Syrian high school certificate holders' students to fit in their new academic and social environment.

Four caveats apply to this research. First, our findings are based on one private university in the Syrian Arab Republic. Hence, expanding the sample to cover other private and public universities should add to our understanding of the factors that affect business students' faculty performance. Second, this study concentrates on business students and do not include students from other disciplines. Expanding this study to include other disciplines will enrich the results and make it better generalized. Third, we measure motivation as a dummy variable, which takes two values only. This raises the issue of multicollinearity between HSGPA and motivation. Another possible way to measure motivation is the number of choices the student has. Finally, this paper investigates the impact of four variables on business students' faculty performance. Other factors such as engagement, learning process, institutions, and social factors could play an important role in determining student performance. Addressing those caveats and investigating such additional factors would constitute a venue for further research.

References

1. Schwab, K. (2010). *The global competitiveness report 2010–2011*. Geneva: World Economic Forum.
2. Tessema, M., Ready, K., & Malone, C. (2012). Effect of gender on college students' satisfaction and achievement: The case of a midsized midwestern public university. *International Journal of Business and Social Science, 3*(10), 1–11.

3. Tross, S. A., Harper, J. P., Osher, L. W., & Kneidinger, L. M. (2000). Not just the usual cast of characteristics: Using personality to predict college performance and retention. *Journal of College Student Development, 41*(3), 323–334.
4. Educational Testing Service, USA, & Zwick, R. (2012). El rol de los exámenes de admisión, de las notas de educación secundaria y de la situación socioeconómica en la predicción del desempeño universitario. *Pensamiento Educativo. Revista de Investigación Educacional Latinoamericana, 49*(2), 23–30.
5. Stewart, S., Lim, D. H., & Kim, J. (2015). Factors influencing college persistence for first-time students. *Journal of Developmental Education, 38*(3), 12–16.
6. Ryan, R. M., & Deci, E. L. (2000). Intrinsic and extrinsic motivations: Classic definitions and new directions. *Contemporary Educational Psychology, 25*(1), 54–67.
7. Abeysekera, L., & Dawson, P. (2015). Motivation and cognitive load in the flipped classroom: Definition, rationale and a call for research. *Higher Education Research and Development, 34*(1), 1–14.
8. Amrai, K., Motlagh, S. E., Zalani, H. A., & Parhon, H. (2011). The relationship between academic motivation and academic achievement students. *Procedia—Social and Behavioral Sciences, 15*, 399–402.
9. Patall, E. A., Cooper, H., & Robinson, J. C. (2008). The effects of choice on intrinsic motivation and related outcomes: A meta-analysis of research findings. *Psychological Bulletin, 134*(2), 270–300.
10. Ibrahim, I. R. A., & AL-Ali, W. A. (2016). The academic intrinsic motivation and its relationship with the emotional intelligence level with a sample of the academic overachievers and underachievers of Najran university. *Journal of Studies in Education, 6*(2), 119.
11. Allen, D. (1999). Desire to finish college: An empirical link between motivation and persistence. *Research in Higher Education, 40*(4), 461–485.
12. Geiser, S., & Santelices, M. V. (2007). *Validity of high-school grades in predicting student success beyond the freshman year: High-school record vs. standardized tests as indicators of four-year college outcomes*. Berkeley, CA: Centre for Studies in Higher Education.
13. Anderson, G., Benjamin, D., & Fuss, M. A. (1994). The determinants of success in university introductory economics courses. *The Journal of Economic Education, 25*(2), 99–119.
14. Belfield, C. R., & Crosta, P. M. (2012). *Predicting success in college: The importance of placement tests and high school transcripts* (CCRC Working Paper No. 42). New York: Community College Research Center, Columbia University.
15. Camara, W., Kimmel, E., Scheuneman, J., & Sawtell, E. (2003). *Whose grades are inflated?* (College Board Research Report No. 2003–2004). New York: College Entrance Examination Board.
16. Katz, I., Kaplan, A., & Buzukashvily, T. (2011). The role of parents' motivation in students' autonomous motivation for doing homework. *Learning and Individual Differences, 21*(4), 376–386.
17. Saeed, S., & Zyngier, D. (2012). How motivation influences student engagement: A qualitative case study. *Journal of Education and Learning, 1*(2), 252–267.
18. Breen, R., & Lindsay, R. (2002). Different disciplines require different motivations for student success. *Research in Higher Education, 43*(6), 693–725.
19. Eymur, G., & Geban, Ö. (2011). An investigation of the relationship between motivation and academic achievement of pre-service chemistry teachers. *Education and Science/Egitim ve Bilim, 36*(161), 246–255.
20. Kusurkar, R. A., Ten Cate, T. J., Vos, C. M. P., Westers, P., & Croiset, G. (2013). How motivation affects academic performance: A structural equation modelling analysis. *Advances in Health Sciences Education, 18*(1), 57–69. Accessed April 11, 2016, from http://link.springer.com/article/10.1007/s10459-012-9354-3/fulltext.html
21. Woodfield, R., & Earl-Novell, S. (2006). An assessment of the extent to which subject variation between the arts and sciences in relation to the award of a first class degree can explain the 'gender gap' in UK universities. *British Journal of Sociology of Education, 27*(3), 355–372.
22. Atinaf, W., & Petros, P. (2016). Socio economic factors affecting female students academic performance at higher education. *Health Care: Current Reviews, 4*(1), 163.

Adopting Mobile Business Solutions in the Modernization of Business Education

Giedrius Cyras and Vita Maryte Janusauskiene

Abstract Inexorable advances of the modern technologies make mobile communication not only popular in society, but most of us cannot imagine life without this tool. At the same time mobility has spread in the field of teaching and learning. Essential changes in learning are initiated by the demand for mobility. The article presents a mobile teaching structure. Structure is intended for the development and simplification of the mobile learning project, to enable the opportunity for different project development related participants' to contribute to the separate levels. Each of them would be able to build on and develop thanks to the other proposed or implemented functions. There's no doubt it can be said that the knowledge management and learning community are the two most important issues in terms of mobile teaching. In fact, they are two structures of changes in the whole learning paradigm.

Keywords Mobile learning • Mobile business • Mobile learning applications • Electronic learning

1 Introduction

With the development of wireless and mobile networks, it does not last long until the mobile learning applications emerge. How should the wireless technology change in order to support this learning style? E-learning phenomenal growth continues, but mainly it's related to the development of wired infrastructure. Due to the rapid development and spread of wireless and mobile networks, it can be said that new application opportunities will emerge in mobile learning too [1, 2]. One of the latest and most significant developments in the study environment is mobility, e.g. mobility requirement. Mobile communication is becoming popular in society and most people can afford to use it. In addition, the exponent development of

G. Cyras (✉) • V.M. Janusauskiene
The Department of Business Technologies, Vilnius Gediminas Technical University (VGTU), Vilnius, Lithuania
e-mail: gcyras@vgtu.lt; vitaj@vgtu.lt

J. Marx Gómez et al. (eds.), *Modernizing Academic Teaching and Research in Business and Economics*, Springer Proceedings in Business and Economics,
DOI 10.1007/978-3-319-54419-9_8

wireless and mobile network has also led to major changes in mobile devices, protocol development, standardization and spread of networks and consumer acceptance.

Mobile learning is primarily linked to the wireless network. It can be adapted quickly and easily, so as to meet the changing needs of the learning mode. Students can receive such a learning method that is most acceptable to them and choose what to study for themselves, what they think is most useful, regardless of the learning space limitations. In order for learning process to be more efficient, mobile students can collaborate with teachers and other students anywhere, anytime. The mobile learning material can be supplied in multiple formats, fast and cost-effective manner. Purpose of the article is to analyze the development of mobile learning opportunities, customization options of various emerging applications, and to create a mobile learning structure.

2 Mobile Learning Structure

It is appropriate to assume that the next level of e-learning development will focus on mobile learning. Mobile learning is an area where the mobile computing and e-learning intercross, which would result in the development of learning skills regardless time or place. Further analysis would suggest a mobile learning structure such as provided in Fig. 1.

This mobile learning structure defines several functional levels, which simplifies the project itself and development so that the different participants (such as customers, suppliers, designers) would be directed to separate individual levels. It is not necessary to create a new purpose in order to create the mobile learning

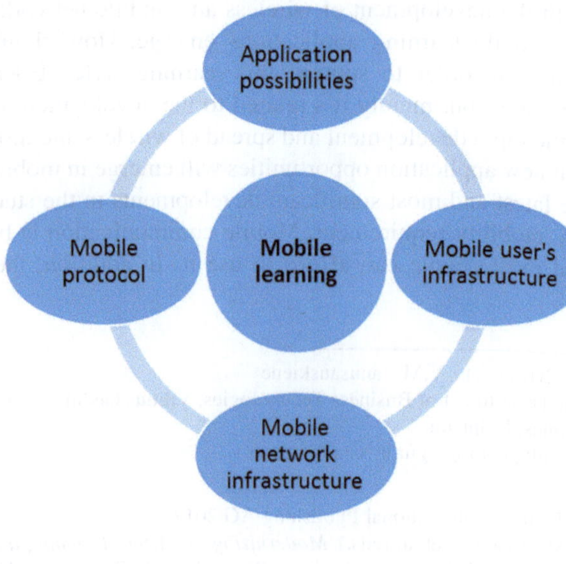

Fig. 1 Mobile learning structure [created by authors]

systems, but it is possible to rely on functionality of vertices of other systems when using this structure. The structure is divided into four levels. In the level of mobile learning application possibilities many new applications become available, but at the same time, many existing e-learning applications can be adapted to mobile environment. The level of mobile user's infrastructure must take into account the fact that the user's mobile devices would support the new forms of mobile learning applications. The main objective of the mobile protocol level is to hide the details of the reference network from applications, providing equal and easy access in the Mobile network infrastructure level, the quality of service would primarily be dependent on network resources and capacity. These four levels will be examined in further research.

2.1 Mobile Learning Application Possibilities

With an unlimited number of potential mobile learning applications, the most interesting areas of research would be the mobile learning performance management and proactive management of learning. There are many types of studies when learning beyond closed classroom limits. For example, students can visit museums in order to know certain exhibits or to collect a variety of samples from the interactive tours. Mobile learning activity management would be able to identify the student's current location and evaluate the student's needs in certain situations in order to achieve the appropriate course material delivery, at the same time thereby improving and enhancing student's learning objectives [2, 3].

For example, when a student is collecting material outside the classroom, it is appropriate to get certain information. Relevant information can be transferred via a mobile device. Mobile learning activity management success depends on the price, reliability of wireless infrastructure and students' comfort level with the use of new technologies.

The system would help students to learn without the participation of another person. In the mobile learning environment students would be faced with certain applications that accompany the user through a series of steps that will help them successfully complete the course. Examples would include a knowledge database, used to solve the typical learning problems and learning flow links that accompany routine activities. The system would be equipped with on-demand support for the implementation and provide all the knowledge required to complete the learning tasks.

The information about students' needs would be collected thanks to the proactive learning management applications. That information would be given to the teaching system in order to enable it to effectively present information and knowledge. It is determined that this teacher controlled process can improve communication efficiency [4, 5]. Teacher can customize the content for the student. This could be done by collecting information on a student when he accesses different mobile devices. Questions could be asked and students could answer them with the help of different programs. This may be done via adaptation of suitable forms of communication and content in real time. This would highlight certain aspects of the educational content which would be of interest to the student who earlier provided his goals and expectations to the system.

For example, the application could gather information about what students did during the course. After a training course students can be instructed in order to carry out certain actions on the basis of this information. Teachers can use this type of information to better manage the lecture content in the future. This detailed information would enable them to assign a training program for those students who may need some kind of skills and knowledge in the following lessons.

2.2 Mobile User's Infrastructure

Mobile devices and wireless networks can provide textual, audio, video material or information services. Students would need proper mobile devices and broadband wireless networks. Permanent login option is important because the disconnection caused during the transmission of the information may seriously affect the quality of information services. In order to implement these applications, students are required to have a number of functional components. First of all, a mobile device with sufficient memory, large enough screen and all the communication functionality is required. In this case, it could be adapted to tablets (PAD) with a wireless modem or smartphones with functions of personal computer with many gadgets, which are invented for mobile business and education learning. All vendors of operating systems have inspired the mobile application developers to provide product for smaller portable devices (such as Android—Samsung, iOS—iPad, etc.) [6].

2.3 Mobile Protocol

Mobile protocol integrates different applications, tools, networks and technologies in order to provide the standard user interface. It is important that the application would become independent of the device and wireless technologies. The protocol is a kind of layer in order for the mobile learning applications to be connected with the different mobile networks and operating systems. Then it becomes possible to adjust to the fluctuations in mobile bandwidth which lead to delays, as well as to the student's location changes. This gives applications an opportunity to provide faster responses and be reliable. A typical optimization technique includes data compression, delayed recognition and combination of several smaller packets into one in order to reduce wireless network traffic.

2.4 *Mobile Network Infrastructure*

In addition to mobile devices and protocols, mobile learning applications must depend on network support. The data transfer rate and network coverage are the two most important factors. Developers now standardize the fourth generation of wireless networks that can support broadband at speed of even dozen megabits per second [7]. Another important factor is the possibility of live communication, when a group of users communicate in real-time with multimedia support. Wireless and mobile networks have to offer an opportunity to provide the multimedia communication [7]. Generally, mobile learning requires quality wireless services, which will affect the effectiveness of mobile learning applications, which could prevent various delays, data loss and other signs of poor quality. Positioning is also required, and it is important part of many mobile learning applications, especially those covering location or searching for the students. Reliable and durable wireless networks are required. Students can access the mobile learning applications even after errors in several levels of network. Roaming across multiple heterogeneous networks can allow students to access mobile learning applications from anywhere, even when coverage of one wireless network is limited.

3 Knowledge Management and Learning Community

It can be said that mobile learning proves that it is becoming more and more useful and powerful, ipso facto arguing and inspiring the development of Internet and mobile networks. These areas include management of content, information and knowledge; creation of educated and modern community; teaching, learning and cooperation; course management systems. Mobile learning has the following properties:

- Mobile learning is dynamic.
- Mobile learning functions in real time. Students get what they need when they need it.
- Mobile learning is a collaborative since people learn from each other. It links students with experts, colleagues and professionals.
- Mobile learning is individual. Each student has the opportunity to choose the next sessions from the menu of personal study options, those which would be most suitable for his determined vision.
- Mobile learning is comprehensive. It provides a wide variety of learning material from a number of sources, giving student the opportunity to choose the privileged format or learning method, or even educational content provider.
- Mobile learning forms modern and leading society.

The power of mobile learning efficiency is its property to transfer the idea or thought to a specific form. It is possible to capture ideas of other people within seconds and share them with the world. It is possible to record comments, updates, thoughts, etc. Also, mobile students can easily be combined to form a learning community. Innovative teachers can encourage students to support their groups and personal mobile websites. Enthusiasm grows because students take over the management of content. They write, proofread, review and publish content. Teachers provide access to articles in the wireless networking medium. In the future students can improve by collecting personal digital "knowledge portfolios".

In general, learning is a social process. In the past, people have encountered some communication barriers during the learning process. Due to the rapid advances of modern technology, mobile learning provides freedom, unimproved time opportunity and encourages to study in this way. New learning styles and multi-faceted knowledge is provided. According to different authors [8–10] learning style differences "challenge the education system, which believes that everyone has to study the same material in the same way". Mobile learning does not impose specific and categorical methods to present a certain lesson for a particular person. However, it definitely gives the probability of development success by providing a multi-faceted learning opportunity. Concentration on student and interlink of students would be the main aim.

Further it would be appropriate to examine the changes in opportunities provided by technology for teaching and learning areas by defining them with paradigm shift. (Fig. 2) When more than 30 years ago a computer, in one form or another, has been used in education, the core idea was to create a class inside the network. Nowadays there are virtual or online courses, modules and tasks. In fact, most of the innovations mimic the methods which they change. However, most of the computer-based learning was late ideas of the traditional teaching and learning. In the past people were faced with technical problems in incompatibility issues. For example, the use of part of educational software which is not suitable to achieve the objectives and comfortable work. But it was never an obstacle for hype, which was always followed by a disappointment. Development of information technologies, encompassing the Internet and wireless networks, has created a single, user-friendly, universally accessible platform and avoided incompatibility problems. Networked learning and mobile learning should not focus solely on the opportunity to provide access to information and competences. The concentration on a teacher model is being replaced by the concentration on a student and it extends beyond the classroom and networked learning borders, including much richer architecture of online resources. In fact, when there is a focus on the information organization anywhere and at any

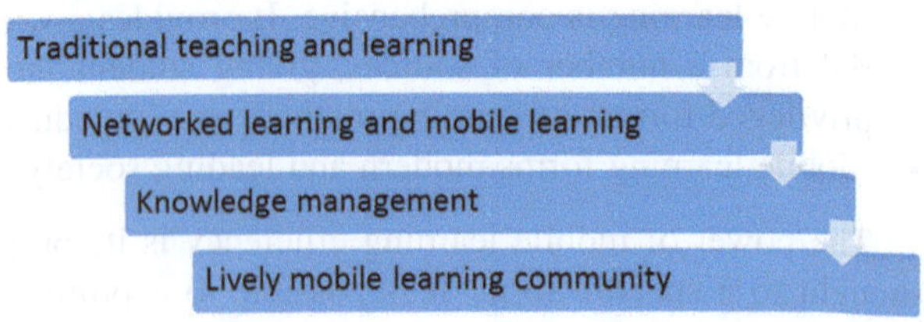

Fig. 2 Changes in teaching and learning opportunities paradigm shift [created by authors]

time, making this knowledge available anywhere and at any time, then you are faced with the knowledge management.

Knowledge management includes the ability to collect, archive, manage, evaluate, and distribute information across a learning community. It uses technologies but the decisive impact for the success of development is given by a person. The transfer of learning in a learning community is to a large extent the function of quality and strength of personal relationships. It is appropriate to give students the opportunity to find each other and constantly be in touch. We learn from each other more often than we do from any other source and it will never change. Mobile learning extends teaching and learning beyond all limitations of any physical classroom and educational resources. Knowledge management provides immediate and real-time information and competencies for anyone, anywhere. Together they define mobile learning in ways that make it preferable and it becomes a part of the learning culture rather than its annex. This is the key to success of mobile learning door.

When a student needs information, he can get it by working together with others in the mobile learning community. When examining from this point of view, learning is not so much a process of acquisition of the new information, but communication with people who help to provide this information with a new context and propose new ways of understanding it. This social aspect is the main way in which people learn in a mobile learning community. In fact, it is the main feature of the learning culture.

Possibilities of the electronic communication caused a displacement from the permanent place based community toward the real-time learning community, where the new "online + mobile" personalities and identities were born. It is likely that the information processing of each person individually is no faster than when working in groups, communicating with each other in person. However, it is appropriate to examine whether it is possible to form groups in the network without personal communication interaction? Is it possible to create a community without it at all? What can be a basis for such community, which appeals on ideals such as ethics, goals, commitments and social norms when it is not possible to see one another? Lack of the mutual support and group participation may inhibit learning in a network. However, such simple humanistic approaches like the discovery of common interests, discussion about personal issues, demonstration of flexibility from the teacher's side and adaptation would provide a basis for more effective online learning experiences. This would be a guide towards stronger and lively mobile learning community.

4 Conclusions

Mobile learning area is constantly faced with changes and the need to develop students with the aid of latest knowledge. People tend to constantly concentrate on the improvement of their skills, thus environment with a comprehensive mobile learning program would be attractive for them. The effectiveness of mobile learning cost is also important. The traditional class-based learning method has a high price if you consider different forms of the meeting sites, while mobile learning would eliminate some of these costs. Mobile learning is considered to be more responsible and more efficient because a student quickly receives program according to his needs and can view his results, which guarantees the successful pursuit of objectives.

However, it would be very short-sighted to believe that the mobile learning is to replace the traditional class-based learning. In the traditional classroom people can get to know each other and find common interests. Mobile communication has provided the opportunity to move the learning environment from fixed to mobile. Since usually to generate the received information more time is spent individually than in a collective, this teaching tool is more attractive for closed, introvertical and concentrated people. But without live communication and leadership, mobile learning can become very modest. Students must be able to communicate with teachers and other students to discuss and obtain further instructions. The ideal average would be achieved if students would share part of their contribution during the course of mobile learning, but also would meet in the traditional classroom setting regarding the decisions on strategic tasks.

The best mobile learning systems must use both, teaching and information methods. It is necessary to focus on the information in the same way as on the instructions, but at the same time look for opportunities to implement the knowledge management perspectives. Technology is the key mobile learning engine, but it is more likely that the most important challenges will be in the field of content, strategy and transformational changes.

References

1. Cheona, J., Leeb, S., Crooksa, S. M., & Song, J. (2012). An investigation of mobile learning readiness in higher education based on the theory of planned behavior. *Computers and Education, 59*(3), 1054–1064.
2. Yeonjeong, P. (2011). A pedagogical framework for mobile learning: Categorizing educational applications of mobile technologies into four types. *The International Review of Research in Open and Distributed Learning, 12*(2), 78–102.
3. Woon Hau, C., Fan, Z., & Haines, R. (2014). Emerging technologies and research challenges for 5G wireless networks. *Wireless Communications, IEEE, 21*(2), 106–112.
4. Kourouthanassis, P. E., & Giaglis, G. M. (2012). Introduction to the special issue mobile commerce: The past, present, and future of mobile commerce research. *International Journal of Electronic Commerce, 16*(4), 5–18.
5. Traxler, J. (2013). *Mobile learning: Shaping the frontiers of learning technologies in global context, Reshaping Learning* (pp. 237–251). Berlin: Springer.

6. Horning, M., Robinson, H. R., & Carroll, J. M. (2014). A scenario-based approach requirements for wireless proximal community networks. *Computers in Human Behavior, 35*, 413–422.
7. Dipankar, R., & Gerla, M. (Eds.). (2011). *Emerging wireless technologies and the future mobile internet*. New York: Cambridge University Press.
8. Cyras, G., & Uturyte-Vrubliauskiene, L. (2010). Differentiation of electronic and mobile business aspects. *Business, Management and Education, 8*, 201–213.
9. Subhankar, D., & Varshney, U. (2011). Challenges and business models for mobile location-based services and advertising. *Communications of the ACM, 54*(5), 121–128.
10. Howard, G. (2011). *Frames of mind: The theory of multiple intelligences*. New York: Basic Books.

Relationship Between Sustainable Leadership and Organizational Trust: Empirical Evidence from Private Higher Education Institutions in Syria

Serene Dalati

Abstract The purpose of this research paper is to develop a theoretical model of sustainable leadership and organizational trust in Higher Education environment in Syria. The model assesses academic and administrative staff perception of outstanding leadership behaviors and examines its relationship with perceived organizational trust in the field of higher education institutions in Syria. A theoretical model is established, clarifying the significance of selection of sustainable leadership behaviors and members' trust in their co-workers. Research Methodology, measurement, empirical testing and application of the theoretical model is investigated. A quantitative approach is employed to design a self-administered questionnaire survey. Back translation is administered to ensure better validity of the scale. Exploratory factor analysis is conducted to examine the validity of sustainable leadership and trust in co-workers scales. Cronbach alpha Reliability test shows strong internal consistency and significance. Higher Education industry is investigated in this research study selecting a convenience sample from Higher Education institutions. A bivariate correlation analysis is conducted to examine the association between the two variables. Results of research study indicates a positive and significant relationship between sustainable leadership and trust in coworkers. However the association is not strong. The managerial implication of the research study recommends application and adoption of sustainable leadership behaviors among functional, mid and senior levels of managers and academics in management positions in higher education institutions. The limitation of research is mainly indicated in the sample size and measurement scales of sustainable leadership and organizational trust.

Keywords Sustainable leadership • Vision in organisations • Teambuilding • Communication in organisations • Organisational trust

---

S. Dalati (✉)
Faculty of Business Administration, Arab International University, Damascus, Syria
e-mail: s-dalati@aiu.edu.sy

J. Marx Gómez et al. (eds.), *Modernizing Academic Teaching and Research in Business and Economics*, Springer Proceedings in Business and Economics,
DOI 10.1007/978-3-319-54419-9_9

1 Introduction

Leadership in Higher Education is becoming a very popular research topic of investigation that requires comprehensive examination. The need for institution and faculty leaders is increasingly growing in Higher Education environment which is becoming transnational, global, virtual, and boundary-less. Syria is has been going through years of crisis and war that has torn the nation and reflected massive destruction and devastation. A considerable number of talented Syrian individuals left the country seeking better standards of living and secure environment. The prevalent organisational environment of Higher education in Syria could be strongly characterised by traditional and bureaucratic approaches which enforce uniformity, accountability and Machiavellian style of management. The predominant styles of management overlooks contemporary behavioural management approaches which would tend to emphasize teambuilding, people empowerment, collaboration and emphasis on outstanding performance.

The need for establishing a model of leadership approaches in higher education in Syria becomes evident. The need for contemporary management and leadership styles which could sustain time, place, geography, and the environment becomes evident. The purpose of this research is to develop a theoretical model of sustainable leadership behaviours which would build a positive relationship with organisational trust in Higher Education environment. The model builds relationships between a set of outstanding leadership styles and behaviours and its association with building trust, faith and confidence in organisational environment in Higher Education. The model builds on leadership styles which would emphasize teambuilding and dynamics, organisational vision, collaboration and service in higher education environment.

2 Leadership Behaviours in Higher Education

A study by Joo and associates investigated Bolman and Deal framework of leadership investigating a dean in a private university in Malaysia, applying LOS self-instrument which was administered to the dean, and LOS other-instrument which was administered to 35 staff who were responding directly to her. Results of the study shows a difference in leadership orientation between self-assessment and other assessment. Results of the study also show that it is necessary for future deans to be trained for leadership skills to meet demands of the industry [1].

Another study explored leadership styles among school principals applying the Leadership Orientation Questionnaire which has two dimensions: one is self-rated by principals, and the other is addressed to school teachers to rate their principals on two dimensions. These include leadership and behavior. The study is divided into two parts. The sample of the study in part one were 8 schools principals and 158 school teachers selected from four private schools and one public school in

Lebanon. In part two the sample was selected from two school principals and 40 school teachers from different schools. Results of the study showed that school principals crucially need creativity while school teacher need training [2].

There are internal and external factors to be considered when examining higher education institutions. One of these crucial factors is related to administrators' ability to exercise leadership qualities. The study examines the construct of instructional leadership in higher education institutions where a comparison between Turkish and Albanian universities' administrators is conducted. A questionnaire survey is administered among a sample of 613 lecturers in universities in Turkey and Albania. Results show no significant difference in the perception of administrator's instructional leadership roles, university mission, managing learning and teaching process. With regard to academic staff, there is a significant difference between Turkish and Albanian lecturers' perceptions of administrator instructional leadership, in the sense that Turkish lecturers have more positive perception than Albanians [3].

A study which examined the role of strategic leadership in building sustainable competitive advantage in academic environment found that there is a significant positive impact of strategic leadership capabilities on sustainable competitive advantage [4].

3 Higher Education in Syria

Higher Education is provided by state in Syria. However a legislation applied in 2001 allowed for the formation of private schools and colleges. Public higher education institutions in Syria are controlled and financed by state. The ministry of higher education and the Higher education Council administer and supervise the implementation higher education in Syria. The most influential legislative reforms for higher education in Syria was the presidential decree no. 36 for the year 2001, which governs the work of private universities in Syria. The other legal framework that governs higher education in Syria is Law No. 6 for the year 2006. This law governs the work of public universities in Syria which is called "The University regulation Law". The new law gives more autonomy to universities with regard to staff appointment and promotions. The ministry of the Higher Education is striving to apply reform, set priorities, set plans and implement them and continue the process of modernizing of HE industry in Syria [5].

The widespread aspects of organizational cultures and practices at Higher Education in Syria, particularly public universities, could be characterized by a traditional managerial approaches with strong bureaucratic environment, application of outdated methodologies, lack of individual recognition, lack of effective encouragement of outstanding performance; limited collaboration with international conferences and academic journals, and most important a turbulent political environment which goes back to the past 5 years, represented by a political and national crisis in Syria. Against this background, a theoretical framework of sustainable leadership and organizational trust in higher education is developed in this research.

4 Organisational Trust

Trust is conceptualised as individual willingness to have good intentions and have confidence in the words and actions of others; where trust is highly important factor in the long term stability of the organisation and the wellbeing of its members [6]. A study on organisational trust states that "trust is a psychological state comprising the intention to accept vulnerability based upon positive expectations of the intentions or behaviour of another" (p. 395) [7]. According to a study trust is defined as the willingness of one party to be vulnerable to the actions of another party based on the expectations that the other will comprise a specific action that is significant to the one who is trusting regardless of their ability to monitor or control this person [8].

4.1 Leadership and Organisational Trust

The prior literature indicates a significant relationship between leadership behaviours and organisational trust [9]. Leader's quality, transparency, resilience and optimism has a significant effect on followers' perceived trust in leader [10]. A study which examines the relationship between Leadership and organisational trust investigates the relationship between authentic leadership and organisational deviance and the moderating effects of trust and psychological contract violation on the relationship [11]. Findings indicate support for moderating effects of employee trust and psychological contract with regard to the relationship between authentic leadership and organisational deviance. Gillespie and Mann investigates relationship between leadership behaviours (transformational, transactional and consultative) and organisational members trust in their leader, in research and development teams. The results of the study indicates that trust is strongly correlated with leader's effectiveness [12]. A study by Joseph and Winston explored the relationship between employee perception of servant leadership and leader trust and organisational trust and found that organisations perceived as servant-led demonstrated higher levels of both leader and organisational trust [13]. A study examined the relationship between servant leadership, subordinates' trust in leader and job satisfaction. The study results indicates that trust in leader mediated the relationship between servant leadership and subordinates job satisfaction [14].

5 Sustainable Leadership in Higher Education

Sustainable leadership is a newly defined term in organisational leadership research [15, 16]. The term was coined by Hargreaves and Fink where sustainable leadership was stressed as a leadership paradigm which "matters, spreads and lasts. It is a shared responsibility that does not unduly deplete human of financial resources and that cares for and avoids exerting damage on the surrounding educational and community environment [17].

According to Hargreaves and Fink 2003 a model of Sustainable leadership in Higher education was developed which consists of seven components which includes depth, length, breadth, justice, diversity, resourcefulness and conversation. The term was introduced to develop a framework which could balance between short term organisational objectives and long term grand goal regardless the change of the individual leader represented by the institution rector or faculty dean or department head in the institution [17].

Lambert (2012) developed a model for sustainable leadership to be implemented as a tool for organisational capacity building in Higher Education institutions. The model consists of six components including capacity building in staff, strategic distribution, consolidation, building long term objectives from short term targets, diversity and conservation [16].

6 Model of Sustainable Leadership and Organizational Trust in Higher Education

The theoretical model examines a set of sustainable leadership behaviours and dimensions, which are building on prior research on leadership in Higher Education sector. The model builds on a set of behaviours of outstanding leadership which have positive association with organizational trust in Higher Education. The model of sustainable leadership at Higher Education builds on prior research of outstanding leadership in organizations emphasizing the importance of vision in organizations [18–23]. Organisational vision is defined as a set of idealized future goals developed by the leader which represents purpose and values shared by followers who embrace ideology of the leader [24–27]. To improve a business competitive advantage, managers and business leaders need greater strategic flexibility which is developed through several factors, two of which include firstly ability to manage change, and secondly developing organizational vision which could be translated into a strategic plan [28].

The model emphasises the significance of teambuilding in Higher Education and the importance of developing team leaders who can play crucial roles at individual, departmental and institutional levels. Team oriented leadership is defined as a leadership variable which emphasizes effective teambuilding and accomplishment of common goals among team members [29]. A team is composed of some number

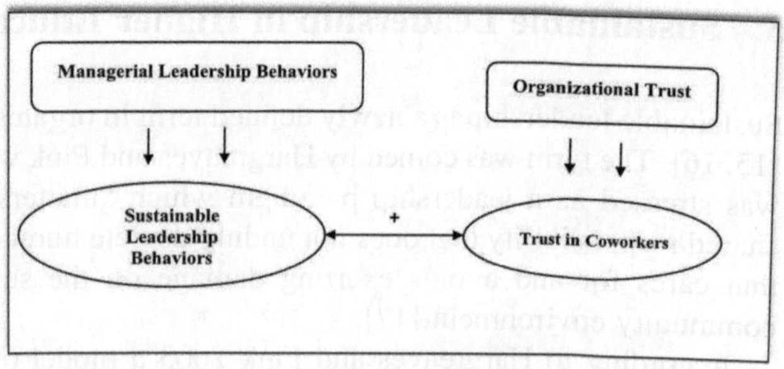

Fig. 1 Model of sustainable leadership and organizational trust in higher education. Source: Author

of relatively independent individuals who are connected together in a work activity and each have their own needs, goals and expected outcomes that motivate their behaviour [30–34]. The model emphasises the nature of service in the behaviour of the leader [13]. Sustainable leaders build trust and are reliable and dependable who earn subordinates' respect and demonstrates high levels of ethical standards and integrity [13, 14, 35]. Figure 1 illustrates a conceptual framework of sustainable leadership and organisational trust in private higher education institutions environment.

6.1 *Research Hypothesis*

The research hypothesis is developed based on prior literature which supports a positive relation between leadership and organizational trust.

H1 Perceived Sustainable Leadership is positively associated with organizational trust in co-workers in private higher education institutions in Syria.

7 Methodology Design

The planned research methodology for empirical testing of sustainable leadership and organisational trust model employs quantitative approaches, collecting primary data through self-administered questionnaire. The unit of analysis examined in this research is academic and administrative staff at the target institutions under investigation. The total number of observations in this research comprise 79 cases.

7.1 *Questionnaire Measurement Scale Development*

Leadership behaviours questionnaire is originated from prior leadership research [20, 35–38]. A study by Dalati examined, in a previous study the prior research and developed the final scale of managerial leadership. Sustainable Leadership scale comprises a set of 44 items measuring perception of sustainable leadership behaviours [39]. Sustainable leadership is developed as a composite construct. Organisational trust scale was developed by scholars Cook and Wall [6]. The measure consists of 12 items measuring faith in intentions and confidence in action in both peers and management. The scale was developed in Great Britain and its design is targeting blue-collar workers. It was reported that the scale has been shown to be "psychometrically adequate and stable" [6]. The organizational trust scale developed by Cook and Wall was originally developed as a multi-dimensional construct by two dimensions. In this research it is developed as a composite scale measuring members' organizational trust in their coworkers [6]. Constructing a measurement scale requires several factors which influence reliability, validity and practicality of the scale. These factors include response type, data properties, number of dimensions, balanced or unbalanced, forced or unforced, number of scale points and rater error [40]. The rating scale is employed through the application of a 5 points Likert scale, which was selected to measure respondents' attitude of the statements constructed in the questionnaire. The advantages of the Likert scale include simplicity and reliability [41]. The scale produces interval data. The leadership behaviour scale applied a 5 points Likert scale where 1 indicates strongly disagree, and 5 strongly agree. The organisational trust scale applied a 5 points Likert scale where 1 indicates strongly disagree and 5 strongly agree.

7.2 *Questionnaire back Translation*

Back Translation is constructed as the scale is originally developed in English. It is advisable to conduct back translation in cross cultural research, where the scale is designed and distributed in more than one language [42]. The original scale for organisational trust developed by Cook and Wall, 1980 follows a 7 points Likert scale. A pilot test was constructed to test the reliability and validity of the scale as it is applied in a different cultural environment representing different language. The results of the pilot test recommended that the 7 point scale is to be adjusted to 5 five points, as the translation of the responses were not clearly understood in Arabic. The scale for organisational trust was modified from 7 to 5 points Likert scale. The research on measurement and scaling indicates that 5 and 7 points scales make little difference. An analysis of variance could be applied comparing samples applying 5 and 7 points scale and comparing frequency distribution of responses between two sample groups of 5 and 7 points of Likert scale.

7.3 Sampling Design and Strategy

Sampling design employed a convenience sampling strategy. The questionnaire survey was distributed mainly to two target higher education institutions. Few respondents who are employed as part time academics at the first private sector institution are fulltime academic staff at a public university in Syria. They were included in the sample. The data was collected through paper and pencil questionnaire technique. The total sample size is 79 cases.

8 Data Analysis

This section comprises different stages in data analyses including conducting exploratory factor analysis to examine the validity of sustainable leadership and organizational trust scales, reliability analysis examining Cronbach alpha test, demographic analysis and correlation analysis to test the research hypothesis.

8.1 Exploratory Factor Analysis

To explore the sustainable leadership and organizational trust dimensionality in higher education environment in Syria, an exploratory factor analysis is conducted. The results of the EFA indicates that there are two factors with an Eigen value and factor loading which exceeded 1 and 0.30. The first factor indicates sustainable leadership behaviors as a composite construct which comprises 13 items. The second factor represent organizational trust as composite construct representing members' trust in coworkers, which comprises 5 items. Originally the organizational trust scale was developed by Cook and Wall, 1980 indicating two factors construct measuring faith of the intention and confidence of action of management and peers. The exploratory factor analysis combined both factors in composite factor producing a new factor which was defined as Trust in Co-workers (Table 1).

8.2 Reliability Analysis of the Scale

Cronbach alpha test is conducted to provide a measure of the internal consistency of the scales. Internal consistency describes the extent to which all the items measure the same construct and are connected to the interrelatedness of the items within the scale [43]. Cronbach alpha Reliability test shows optimal reliability ranging from 0.86 to 0.94 which to be is considered an excellent indication of internal consistency (Table 2).

Table 1 Exploratory factor analysis (n 79).

	Exploratory factor analysis		
Item description	Eigen value	% of variance	Factor loading
Factor 1: Sustainable leadership	8.544	47.466	
Act as role-model for team members			0.831
Has good comprehension and listens carefully to what people are saying			0.818
Has the ability to set future oriented tasks and goals			0.803
Deserves trust and is believed to keep their word			0.800
Has the ability to interpret and use the knowledge of the industry trends			0.798
Has a vision of future for the organization			0.793
Is aware of team members' abilities and what they can contribute to the team			0.791
acts according to what is right or fair			0.790
stimulates others to put forth efforts beyond the call of duty			0.769
Is capable of advocating and networking			0.752
Engages in activities involving great effort and energy			0.666
Uses simple, clear language in his/her conversation			0.655
Works towards one collective team identity			0.640
Factor 2: Trust in co-workers	**2.706**	**15.036**	
I can trust the people I work with to lend me a hand if I needed it			0.867
If I got into difficulty at work I know my workmates would try and help me out			0.843
I have full confidence in the skills of my workmates			0.784
Most of my workmates can be relied upon to do as they say they will do			0.781
Most of my fellow workers would get on with their work if Team and Group Leaders were not around			0.691

Extraction method: Principal component analysis. Rotation method: Varimax with kaiser normalization. Rotation converged in three iterations
Source: Author

Table 2 Cronbach alpha reliability test

Variable components	Number of items	Alpha (α) without deleting any item
Sustainable leadership	13	0.94
Organisational trust in co-workers	5	0.86

Source: Author

8.3 Demographic Profile of Respondents

Descriptive data analysis illustrates that the average mean for age for respondents is 42 years, work experience is in Higher Education industry is 11.64, and experience in the current institution is 5.32 years. Demographic analysis illustrates that 62% of respondents are male, 38% are female. 52.6% of the respondents have PhD, 16.7% have Masters Degrees, 19.2% have bachelor degrees and 11.5% have other degrees.

8.4 Correlation Analysis

To conduct a correlation analysis the variables were examined by normality test to determine if they were normally distributed. Shapiro–Wilk test are applied to examine normality distribution of data. Shapiro–Wilk test indicates that the study variables are not normally distributed. Shapiro–Wilk test of normality for Sustainable leadership indicates that data is not normally distributed where $p = 0.13$. Shapiro–Wilk test of normality for Trust in coworkers indicates that the data is not normally distributed where $p = 0.044$. Therefore, a non-parametrical correlation analysis is conducted to examine the relationship between the two variables. A spearman correlation analysis indicates a positive and significant relationship between sustainable leadership and organizational trust in co-workers where $rs = 0.388$, $p = 0.000$ (Table 3).

9 Discussion

The purpose of this research is to examine the relation between sustainable leadership and academic and administrative staff members' trust their in coworkers in the context of higher education environment in private institutions in Syria. The constructs of the study are developed for this research study. Sustainable leadership is developed as a composite construct which contains 13 items measuring perceived leadership behaviors which are examined and defined as sustainable leadership behaviors. Sustainable leadership comprises a set of behaviors, abilities and skills which are examined as outstanding and effective. Sustainable leadership emphasize behaviors and abilities including having vision of future for organization, being performance oriented, being communicative, collaborative, team oriented and above all ethical are behaviors and abilities associated with the term sustainable leadership. Organizational trust is examined in the context of perceived trust in co-workers including considering workmates as helpful, supportive, and reliable and having faith and confidence in the skills of coworkers.

The results of this research study indicates that as perceived sustainable leadership increases, trust in co-workers also increases. The research study emphasize on the importance of sustainable leadership and co-workers trust. Sustainable leader in higher education institutions is expected to apply a positive association with coworkers trust.

Table 3 Correlation analysis (n 79)

Research variables	1	2
Sustainable leadership	1	
Organizational trust in co-workers	0.388**	1

**Correlation is significant at the 0.01 level (2 tailed)
Source: Author

The research study provides contribution to the literature on sustainable leadership behaviors in higher education environment, by examining the effects of sustainable leadership of organizational trust.

10 Managerial Implication

The research study develops specific leadership behaviors which are defined as sustainable leadership behaviors. The research study emphasizes that behaviors and abilities including the state of being visionary, communicative, collaborative, team oriented, inspirational and ethical are strongly advised to be practiced, fostered and adapted among managers and educational leaders in higher education environment. The research study recommends emphasis of sustainable leadership behaviors among managers, heads of departments, faculty deans and institutional leaders and directors in higher education environment. The research study recommends that leadership development and training for functional level, mid-level and senior level managers and academics in leadership and management roles in higher education environment is crucial.

11 Research Limitation

The most important limitation in this research study is related to sample size. Obtaining an adequate sample size requires time and financial factor in the process of data collection to reach a convenient response rate levels. Data collection is usually hard process in any research and could require different research tools to obtain the data and response rate needed [44]. Limitation of the study could be related to the methodology used to gather data and select the sample. Although self-administered questionnaire are cost effective and less time consuming than other methods, there is a possibility for response bias [40]. A third limitation of the study is related to the scales of sustainable and organisational trust. There is a requirement to further improve the scales to produce a multi- dimensional scales of sustainable leadership and organisational trust.

12 Conclusion

This research investigated the relationship and effect of sustainable leadership behaviors on organizational trust in co-workers in higher education is Syria. The empirical testing of the model finds support for the hypothesis signifying an impact of sustainable leadership behaviors on staff members' trust in their co-workers in higher education environment.

References

1. Joo, M. T. H., Hee, T. F., & Piaw, C. Y. (2014). Leadership orientations of an educational leader in a private university in Malaysia. *Procedia—Social and Behavioral Sciences, 114* (1990), 681–686.
2. Al Chibani, W., & Al Chibani, P. H. (2013). Leadership styles of school principals in Lebanon: Multiple case study. *Procedia—Social and Behavioral Sciences, 93*, 174–176.
3. Sotirofski, K. (2011). Comparing the educational leadership roles of Albanian and Turkish higher education institutions administrators. *Procedia—Social and Behavioral Sciences, 15*, 3560–3565.
4. Mahdi, O. R., & Almsafir, M. K. (2014). The role of strategic leadership in building sustainable competitive advantage in the academic environment. *Procedia—Social and Behavioral Sciences, 129*, 289–296.
5. Ayoubi, R., Al-ahmar, A., & Ahmar-dakna, S. (2009, November). *The national project or the national programme: An evaluation of tempus programme contribution to the development of the higher education sector in Syria*. Stuttgart: University Stuttgart.
6. Cook, J., & Wall, T. (1980). New work attitude measures of trust, organizational commitment and personal need non-fulfilment. *Journal of Occupational and Organizational Psychology, 53* (1977), 39–52.
7. Rousseau, D. M., Sitkin, S. B., Burt, R. S., & Camerer, C. (1998). Not so different after all: A cross discipline view of trust. *Academy of Management Review, 23*(3), 393–404.
8. Tansley, C., & Newell, S. (2007). Project social capital, leadership and trust. *Journal of Managerial Psychology, 22*(4), 350–368.
9. Sendjaya, S., & Pekerti, A. (2010). Servant leadership as antecedent of trust in organizations. *Leadership and Organization Development Journal, 31*(7), 643–663.
10. Norman, S. M., Avolio, B. J., & Luthans, F. (2010). The impact of positivity and transparency on trust in leaders and their perceived effectiveness. *The Leadership Quarterly, 21*(3), 350–364.
11. Erkutlu, H., & Chafra, J. (2013). Effects of trust and psychological contract violation on authentic leadership and organizational deviance. *Management Research Review, 36*(9), 828–848.
12. Gillespie, N. A., & Mann, L. (2004). Transformational leadership and shared values: The building blocks of trust. *Journal of Managerial Psychology, 19*(6), 588–607.
13. Joseph, E. E., & Winston, B. E. (2005). A correlation of servant leadership, leader trust, and organizational trust. *Leadership and Organization Development Journal, 26*(1/2), 6–23.
14. Chan, S. C. H., & Mak, W. (2014). The impact of servant leadership and subordinates' organizational tenure on trust in leader and attitudes. *Personnel Review, 43*(2), 272–287.
15. Hargreaves, A. (2007). Sustainable leadership and development in education: Creating the future, conserving the past. *European Journal of Education, 42*(2), 223–233.
16. Lambert, S. (2012). The perception and implementation of sustainable leadership strategies in further education colleges. *The Journal of Leadership Education, 11*(2), 102–120.

17. Hargreaves, A., & Fink, D. (2003). The seven principles of sustainable leadership. *Educational Leadership, 61*(7), 8.
18. Tichy, N. M., & Devanna, M. A. (1986). The transformational leader. *Training and Development Journal, 40*(7), 27–32.
19. Bennis, W., & Biederman, W. (2009, November). The essential Bennis. *Harvard Business Review*, 465.
20. Conger, J. A., & Kanungo, R. N. (1998). *Charismatic leadership in organizations*. Thousand Oaks, CA: Sage.
21. Yammarino, F. J., Spangler, W. D., & Bass, B. M. (1993). Transformational leadership and performance: A longitudinal investigation. *The Leadership Quarterly, 4*(1), 81–102.
22. Kouzes, J. M., & Posner, B. Z. (1995a). *The leadership challenge: How to keep getting extraordinary things done in organizations* (Vol. 2). San Francisco, CA: Jossey-Bass.
23. Conger, J. A., & Hunt, J. G. (1999). Charismatic and transformational leadership. *The Leadership Quarterly, 10*(2), 121–127.
24. Strange, J. M., & Mumford, M. D. (2005). The origins of vision: Effects of reflection, models, and analysis. *The Leadership Quarterly, 16*(1), 121–148.
25. House, R. J. (1999). Weber and the neo-charismatic leadership paradigm. *The Leadership Quarterly, 10*(4), 563–574.
26. Collins, J. C., & Porras, J. I. (1994). SIOI ideology provides the glue together through time. *Harvard Business Review, 74*(5), 65–77.
27. Ergeneli, A., Gohar, R., & Temirbekova, Z. (2007). Transformational leadership: Its relationship to culture value dimensions. *International Journal of Intercultural Relations, 31*(6), 703–724.
28. Zaccaro, S. J., & Banks, D. (2001). Leadership, vision, and organizational effectiveness. In S. J. Zaccaro & R. J. Klimoski (Eds.), *The nature of organizational leadership: Understanding the performance imperatives confronting today's leaders* (pp. 181–218). San Francisco, CA: Jossey-Bass.
29. House, R. J., Hanges, P. J., Javidan, M., Dorfman, P. W., & Gupta, V. (2004). *Culture, leadership, and organizations: The globe study of 62 societies* (pp. 301–340). Thousand Oaks, CA: Sage.
30. Day, D. V., Gronn, P., & Salas, E. (2004). Leadership capacity in teams. *The Leadership Quarterly, 15*(6), 857–880.
31. Tolle, E. F. (1988). Management team building: Yes but! *Engineering Management International, 4*, 277–285.
32. Salas, E., Dickinson, T. L., Converse, S. A., & Tannenbaum, S. I. (1992). Toward an understanding of team performance and training. In R. W. Swezey & E. Salas (Eds.), *Teams: Their training and performance* (pp. 3–29). Norwood, NJ: Ablex.
33. Salas, E., Sims, D. E., & Burke, C. S. (2005). Is there a 'big five' in teamwork? *Small Group Research, 36*(5), 555–599. doi:10.1177/1046496405277134.
34. Cannon-Bowers, J. A., Salas, E., & Converse, S. A. (1993). Cognitive psychology and team training: Training shared mental models and complex systems. *Human Factors Bulletin, 33*, 1–4.
35. Mittal, R., & Dorfman, P. W. (2012). Servant leadership across cultures. *Journal of World Business, 47*(4), 555–570.
36. Kouzes, B., & Posner, J. (1995). The leadership challenge. *Nursing Standard, 24*(51), 24–25.
37. Strange, J. M., & Mumford, M. D. (2002). The origins of vision. Charismatic versus ideological leadership. *The Leadership Quarterly, 13*(4), 343–377.
38. Dickson, M. W., Den Hartog, D. N., & Mitchelson, J. K. (2003). Research on leadership in a cross-cultural context: Making progress, and raising new questions. *The Leadership Quarterly, 14*(6), 729–768.
39. Dalati, S. (2015). Leadership and sustainable entrepreneurship: Classical approaches and contemporary contexts. *Entrepreneurship and Sustainability Issues, 2*(4), 209–219.

40. Cooper, D., & Schindler, P. (2014). *Business research methods* (12th ed., p. 792). New York: McGraw-Hill.
41. Cooper, D. R., & Schindler, P. S. (2010). *Business research methods*. New York: McGraw-Hill.
42. Brislin, R. W. (1970). Back-translation for cross-cultural research. *Journal of Cross-Cultural Psychology, 1*(3).
43. Tavakol, M., & Dennick, R. (2011). Making sense of Cronbach's alpha. *International Journal of Medical Education, 2*, 53–55.
44. Zikmund, W., Babin, B., Carr, J., & Griffin, M. (2009). *Business research methods*. Boston, MA: Cengage Learning.

The Effect of Good Governance on Higher Education in Syria, Lebanon and Jordan for the Period (2000–2011)

Chadi Azmeh

Abstract Globally, the rules and regulations of higher education are for the betterment of economies and social uplift. The objective of this study is to develop a link between governance indicators and educational outcomes. The current study proposes a framework covering three broad categories of governance indicators: political governance, economic governance and institutional dimension of governance. These three categories are accompanied by five educational factors: higher education expenditures, higher education enrolment, higher education expenditures per student, literacy rate, scientific and technical journal articles and economic growth. The study covers three countries: Syria, Lebanon and Jordan for the period 2000–2011. The OLS model is employed for estimating the possible links between governance indicators and educational outcomes. The results show conflicting effects of governance on higher education indicators, but in most of the cases, it is not significant.

Keywords Higher education • Good governance • OLS

1 Introduction

Traditionally, the term 'governance' was understood as synonymous to government. However, recently, the term governance has acquired other meaning. It now refers to new processes, methods, or ways of governing society [1]. In fact, Governance refers to the processes in government actions and how things are done, not just what is done. It covers the quality of institutions and their effectiveness in translating policy into successful implementation. Institutions are in general understood to be the bodies setting formal rules (property rights, rule of law etc.) [2].

C. Azmeh (✉)
Faculty of Business Administration and Finance, International University for Science and Technology (IUST), Daraa, Ghabageb, Syria

Faculty of Business Administration, Jinan University, Tripoli, Lebanon
e-mail: Chadiazmeh@hotmail.com

J. Marx Gómez et al. (eds.), *Modernizing Academic Teaching and Research in Business and Economics*, Springer Proceedings in Business and Economics,
DOI 10.1007/978-3-319-54419-9_10

The World Bank was the first to adopt the concept of good governance as a condition for lending to developing countries" [3]. In fact, the World Bank considers the good governance as certain expectation of certain code of conduct. Good governance relates to democracy, the rule of law, human rights, decentralization, transparency, accountability, and reducing corruption to ensure maximum effectiveness of international development programs.

The World Bank has created and published a rich data to measure the level of governance for developed and developing countries. The Worldwide Governance Indicators [4] cover three groups of governance indicators, which include six different aspects of governance:

– Political Governance:

(a) Voice and Accountability and (b) Political Stability and Absence of Violence.

Voice and accountability include the assumptions that citizens are able to have a say in making their government, to have freedom of expression, to have freedom of association and to have a free open media. Stable political government and absence of violence/terrorism measures the perceptions that a government might be destabilized or dethroned illegally by violent means, including politically motivated violence and terrorism [4].

– Economic Governance:

(a) Government Effectiveness and (b) Regulatory Quality.

Government effectiveness includes the sense of the quality of public and civil services, as well as the extent to which they are insulated from political interference. It also consists of the government's ability for developing quality policies, their capacity to implement them and how much an individual government values such policies. Regulatory quality takes into account the government's capability to develop and execute good policies and rules that allow and promote private sector development [4].

– Institutional Dimensions of Governance:

(a) Rule of Law (ROL) and (b) Control of Corruption (CoC).

ROL measures the confidence of citizens that an agent will follow the norms and rules of society, particularly ones related to contract enforcement, property rights, the police, the courts and the possibility of crime and violence. By contrast, the CoC evaluates the interference of a country's bureaucracy—i.e., red-tapism, which has been defined as corrupt office bearers and other parties interfering with the implementation of policy [4].

Good governance has a positive and important effect on several aspect of social and economic life. It is considered as a universal condition for happiness [5]. It also contributes in the reduction of poverty [6] and in enhancing the level of economic growth [7, 8]. Furthermore, it plays a crucial role in increasing investment and promoting fiscal decentralization [9, 10].

The universities and other institutions are expected to create knowledge; to improve equity; and to respond to student needs—and to do so more efficiently. In a new and more complex environment, direct management by governments is no longer appropriate. How can the governance of higher education institutions assure their independence and dynamism while promoting key economic and social objectives? [11].

Good governance is critical to the effective operation of universities. It secures universities' success in achieving their missions, and in delivering benefits for economy, society and cultural wellbeing. Hence, the good governance of universities is about the effective definition and execution of universities missions and strategies [12]. The State is responsible for creating a regulatory environment which is aligned with the goals of higher education sector to meet the expectations of society. Regulations are embedded in virtually every tool available to government to influence the behavior of all actors within tertiary education systems [13].

There is a strong connection between governance and higher education. For example, Fried [14] points out that for the transformation processes in several European higher education systems,—the political and administrative ranks needs to be prepared to assume their new role to help achieving longer-term goals for national higher education institutions.

Mok [15] insists on the important role of government when it chooses its policy tools (such as the choice of market forces in higher education). In fact, governments should pay particular attention to the particular socio-economic and socio-political contexts of their countries when making such choices.

Magalhães et al. [16] concentrate on the EU's policies and their interaction on the national higher education sectors in several European countries. The study reveals that the efforts of the European governments and their practices are helping their educational systems to develop.

Middlehurst [17] studied the internal changes of educational institutions in the UK describing the similarity and differences in the policy and political conditions over time. He concludes that although institutional structures and roles had shifted in response to internal and external drivers, such changes needed to be aligned with strategy, skills, behaviors, performance and reward systems as well as the socio-emotional and symbolic aspects of institutional life if change was to become embedded and sustained.

This study inspects the relationship between governance and higher education in developing countries. It examines the connection between governance indicators and higher educational outcomes in Syria, Lebanon and Jordan for the period of 2000–2011. In the subsequent section, an empirical illustration has been made on the relationship between educational and governance indicators in Syria, Lebanon and Jordan by using the Ordinary least square (OLS) model. The study is divided into the following sections: Sect. 1, the introduction (see above); Sect. 2, the data source and methodological framework; Sect. 3, results; and finally, Sect. 4, our conclusion.

2 Data Source and Methodological Framework

The study employed OLS regression model to estimate the relationship between governance indicators and educational outcomes. The data were obtained from two sources: World Development Indicators which is published by World Bank [18] and World Governance Indicators [4] for the period of 2000–2011. It is no doubt that educational indicators improve economic gains. This study takes the initiative of using governance indicators to test its effects on indicators of higher education. The model takes the following form:

$$lnYt = \alpha + \beta Xi, t + \mu i,$$

The dependent variable Y reflects the five educational indicators (i.e., Expenditure on tertiary as % of government expenditure on education, Gross enrolment ratio, Government expenditure per tertiary student as % of GDP per capita, Literacy rate, Scientific and technical journal articles and GDP growth). The term 'i' indicates the number of governance indicators and 't' the time period. Independent variables X1–X6 reflect governance indicators, which cover three broad indicators, and each of the indicators comprises two sub-indicators: political governance comprises voice and accountability and political stability; economic governance comprises government effectiveness and regulatory quality; and finally, the institutional dimension of governance comprises rule of law and control of corruption (Table 1).

3 Results

As it is shown in Table 2, for the first variable (Voice), the estimated coefficients show a positive and significant impact on the enrollment and journal and scientific papers indicators. All the estimated coefficients for the second variable (political stability) are negative and not statistically significant. The impact of government effectiveness on the enrollment indicator is positive while it is negative on the level of expenditures per student. It is not statistically significant for other higher education indicators. For the fourth variable, regulatory quality has a negative and significant impact on the level of expenditures per student. Other results for this indicator are not statistically significant. The rule of law has a positive impact on the level of expenditures and the level of expenditures per student, but a negative impact on the enrollment rate. The last indicator, the control of corruption, has a positive and considerable impact on the level of economic growth. The results for other indicators are not statistically significant. Our results are not completely in conformity with the literature, which predicts a positive effect of all governance variables on higher education variables [19]. The negative effect of some variables

Table 1 Summery statistics

Variable	Mean	Median	Minimum	Maximum
Exp	24.8528	25.0544	19.8442	28.9752
Enroll	35.3880	39.7967	12.3787	49.7338
Exp_per	29.4684	17.7276	8.81529	102.114
Literacy	89.3779	90.5115	80.8445	95.9044
Journals	115.286	73.2500	21.0000	279.800
GDP%	5.33781	5.37398	0.600000	10.3009
Voice	−0.90589	−0.7172	−1.75000	−0.189702
Pol-stab	−0.68597	−0.4800	−2.13362	0.210000
Gov-eff	−0.32489	−0.2760	−1.16000	0.281031
Reg-Q	−0.338322	−0.175734	−1.38000	0.343240
R-law	−0.227385	−0.370000	−0.860000	0.458087
Con-corr	−0.452472	−0.603949	−1.08000	0.405914

Source: World Governance Indicators (WGI, 2012) and World Bank (2012)

and the statistically insignificance of the results are possibly due to lack of data for a longer period of time.

4 Conclusion

The objective of the study was to explore the possible links between governance indicators and educational reforms in Syria, Lebanon and Jordan. This study employed an OLS model over the period of 2000–2011. The analysis showed that governance indicators such as voice and accountability, political stability, government effectiveness, regulatory quality, rule of law and control of corruption have no clear effect on the development of higher education. The difference between the results of the precedent studies and the results of the present paper may be due to different measures of higher education (due to lack of data). Or it may be due to the period covered by this study. In fact, the period of 10 years, when testing the effect of governance on the higher education indicators, may not be enough. Furthermore, the difference in results may also be due the special case Syria, Lebanon and Jordan. Governments around the world are trying to develop strong relationships between the education sector and the society at large. Policymakers' objectives should be to ensure scientific achievement, and to place the teaching, research, economic and social sectors on one line. Universally, governments and authorities are trying to develop new rules and regulations to improve the performance of higher education institutions. Further research, which cover longer period of time and more higher education indicators, will help to clarify the real effect of governance on higher education in Syria, Lebanon and Jordan.

Table 2 Specification of OLS regression of governance indicators and educational outcomes in Syria, Lebanon and Jordan for the period (2000–2011)

	Exp	Enroll	Exp_per	Literacy	Journals	GDP%
Voice	0.014	**0.087***	−0.044	−0.026	**0.406********	−0.095
Pol-stab	−0.041	−0.010	−0.079	−0.015	−0.085	−0.286
Gov-eff	0.044	**0.309********	**−0.462********	−0.097	−0.193	−0.213
Reg-Q	−0.011	0.100	**−0.448********	0.128	0.045	0.0003
R-law	**0.148***	**−0.189***	**0.640********	−0.031	−0.249	−0.526
Con-corr	−0.028	−0.057	−0.006	0.050	−0.194	**0.915***
R^2	0.78	0.90	0.96	0.99	0.83	0.23
Obs	16	32	24	8	33	29

Source: Authors' calculations
Notes: the data were taken from the World Governance Indicators (WGI 2012) and World Bank (2012). All higher education variables are in a natural logarithmic form. Specifications of the model are Ordineray least square and are estimated using robust t-statistics. *Significant at the 1% level of significance and **significant at the 5% level of significance ***significant at the 0.01% of significance

References

1. Jolly, R. (2002). The history of development policy. In C. Kirkpatrick (Ed.), *Handbook on development policy and management*. MA: Edward Elgar Publishing Limited.
2. UN. (2008). *Guidebook on promoting good governance in public-private partnerships* [Online]. Available at: http://www.unece.org/fileadmin/DAM/ceci/publications/ppp.pdf
3. Simonis, U. E. (2004). *Defining good governance—The conceptional competition is on*. WZB Discussion Papers. Berlin: WZB.
4. WGI. (2012). *World governance indicator, 2011–12*. Washington, DC: World Bank.
5. Ott, J. C. (2009). Good governance and happiness in nations: Technical quality precedes democracy and quality beats size. *Journal of Happiness Studies, 11*(3), 353–368.
6. Chong, A., & Calderón, C. (1997). *Institutional change and poverty, or why is it worth it to reform the state?* Washington, DC: World Bank.
7. Levine, R. (1999). Law, finance and economic growth. *Journal of Finanicial Intermediation, 8* (1), 8–35.
8. Evans, P., & Rauch, J. (1999). Bureaucracy and growth: A cross-national analysis of the effects of "Weberian" state structures on economic growth. *American Sociological Review, 64* (5), 748.
9. Barro, R. (1991). Economic growth in a cross section of countries. *The Quarterly Journal of Economics, 106*(2), 407.
10. Huther, J., & Shah, A. (1998). *Applying a simple measure of good governance to the debate on fiscal decentralization*. Policy research working paper no. 1894. Washington, DC: World Bank.
11. OECD. (2003). *Chapter 3: Changing patterns of governance in higher education*. Education Policy Analysis, OECD [Online]. Available at: http://www.oecd.org/education/skills-beyond-school/35747684.pdf
12. *Review of higher education governance*. (2011). [Online]. Available at: http://www.universitiesscotland.ac.uk/uploads/US_GovResponse_FINALWEB031011.pdf
13. Henard, F., & Mitterle, A. (2009). *Governance and quality guidelines in higher education: A review of governance arrangements and quality assurance guidelines*. Paris: OECD/Directorate for Education.

14. Fried, J. (2006). Higher education governance in Europe: Autonomy, ownership and accountability—A review of literature. In J. Kohler & J. Huber (Eds.), *Higher education governance between democratic culture, academic aspirations and market forces* (pp. 79–133). Strasbourg: Council of Europe Strasbourg.
15. Mok, K. H. (2008). Singapore's global education hub ambitions. *International Journal of Educational Management, 22*(6), 527–546.
16. Magalhães, A., Veiga, A., Ribeiro, F. M., Sousa, S., & Santiago, R. (2012). Creating a common grammar for European higher education governance. *Higher Education, 65*(1), 95–112.
17. Middlehurst, R. (2013). Changing internal governance: Are leadership roles and management structures in United Kingdom universities fit for the future? *Higher Education Quarterly, 67* (3), 275–294.
18. World Bank. (2012). *World development indicators, 2011–12*. Washington, DC: World Bank.
19. Zaman, K. (2015). Quality guidelines for good governance in higher education across the globe. *Pacific Science Review B: Humanities and Social Sciences, 1*(1), 1–7.

University-Business Research Collaboration in Syria: An Empirical Assessment and Suggested Conceptual Model

Alaa Salhani and Victoria Khnouf

Abstract University-business research collaboration is an increasingly important innovation model (Johnson J. *Minister of state for universities and science in UK. The dowling review of business-university research collaborations in UK*, 2015). This study examines the research collaboration between universities and business sector in Syria, which is based on two different questionnaires, the first one is conceived for faculty members, and the second one is for the business sector. This study concludes that research which is conducted by faculty members and students in Syria does not significantly matching with the problems and the needs of business, also it shows that there is no significant difference between private and public universities in the above said domain, as well as between the social sciences and applied sciences faculties. Moreover, many faculty members are not so encouraged to achieve research for main reasons; poor income, no program to be invested within the research outcomes. In addition, Syrian business sector does not provide data easily and funding for most researchers. On the other hand, most of Syrian businesses do not benefit from research of Syrian universities, but they benefit more from foreign researches. This is due to the lack of trust with the ability of faculty members dealing and recommending adequate solution to businesses problems, they have no clue about the nature of research in the Syrian universities; in addition they consider the cooperation with universities as costly. However, most of the Syrian business sector is ready to participate into joint research programs with Syrian universities if it is financially supported. By considering the result, this research's aim is to suggest a new triple collaboration model that link Chambers, Universities and Business together through three interrelated elements ("Business collaboration case studies". University of Southampton, 2016). This will match the gap between universities research and the Syrian business sector needs, then advancing knowledge base, enhancing the relevance of

---

A. Salhani (✉)
Faculty of Business Administration, Department of Accounting and Finance, Arab International University, Damascus, Syria
e-mail: a-salhani@aiu.edu.sy

V. Khnouf
Faculty of Business Administration, Department of Management and Marketing, Arab International University, Damascus, Syria
e-mail: v-khnouf@aiu.edu.sy

J. Marx Gómez et al. (eds.), *Modernizing Academic Teaching and Research in Business and Economics*, Springer Proceedings in Business and Economics,
DOI 10.1007/978-3-319-54419-9_11

research programs, accelerating the application of innovation within the economy as well as contributing effectively and efficiently in the reconstruction phase of Syria.

Keywords University • Business • Collaboration • Model • Syria

1 Introduction

The concept of University-Business Research Collaboration (UBRC) is an increasingly important innovation mode that allows business and universities to tap into complementary skills of each other and thus potentially help with saving cost for business and universities, and enhancing research outcomes and innovations that can be applied into facts.

Improving knowledge transfer between universities, and business is essential for ensuring that investment in researches contribute to innovation and growth [1, 2].

The major benefits of research collaboration between business and universities are giving business better access to the cutting-edge research that is performed in academia and they speed up the development of applications for research [3, 4].

On the other hand, it makes universities better attuned to the needs of business and increases their innovation potential [5, 6].The research plan is based on:

Firstly, understanding the problem issues related to "University-Business Research Collaboration in Syria" (UBRC) by answering the following questions:

1. Does research that conducted by members of faculty deal with the problems and needs of the Syrian business sector.
2. Does research that conducted by universities students deal with the problems and needs of the Syrian business sector.
3. Are there any differences between research that conducted by social sciences and applied sciences faculties, dealing with the problems and needs of the Syrian business sector?
4. Are there any differences between research that conducted by Public universities and that conducted by private one dealing with the problems and needs of the Syrian business sector?
5. What are the barriers of any university-business research collaboration from the perspective of faculty members?
6. Do Syrian businesses benefit from research of Syrian universities?
7. Do Syrian businesses benefit from research of foreign universities?
8. Do Syrian businesses trust the ability of faculty members to deal and recommend solutions to businesses problems?
9. What factors represent barriers to any university-business research collaboration from the perspective of business?
10. Are Syrian businesses ready to collaborate in a joint research program with Syrian Universities if it is financially supported?

Secondly, building a new Syrian conceptual collaboration model in parallel with the needs of Syrian business sector and universities.

2 Literature Review

Gerry and Kharazmi [7] have discussed in their study, the problem issues related to University-Industry collaboration in Iran through an investigation of the factors from the literature, models and evidence from other countries. They have suggested three theoretical frameworks which has considered trust and culture as two important elements which contribute to the success or failure of an National Innovation System in general, and University-Industry Collaboration in particular. They have also suggested a conceptual model based on a combination of innovation systems theories with behavioral dimensions including empirically derived motivational factors, and culture and trust theories. According to this conceptual framework, trust is influenced by many factors including government activities, institutional structure, institutional culture, and also national culture of the country.

Huttner [8] in his case study has focused on a system launched an ambitious new approach to collaborating with industry under its Industry-University Cooperative Research Program (IUCRP).It used matching grants to catalyze hundreds of strategically focused partnerships, by increasing the number of faculties, students and companies participating in such joint collaborations. The approach promoted a new research and education paradigm and created an important new source of research funding across UC's nine campuses.

The grants bridged the gap between the university research community and California companies, advancing the scientific knowledge base, intensifying the relevance of research and education programmers, and accelerating the application of new discoveries in the economy.

Howell, Ramlogan, and Cheng [1] have discussed the main objective to develop a better understanding of the impacts of Higher Education Information Service (HEIs) on the innovativeness and competitiveness of regional economies in UK. They have identified the various avenues through which universities interact with local firms, businesses and other intermediaries in relation to research and innovative activity. They have analyzed how this, in turn, influences firm performance and the overall competitiveness of local and regional economies.

Lee [2] has explored the concept of university-industry collaboration as an important social experiment in the nation's innovation system, by examining the sustainability of this collaborative experience and focusing on the actual "give-and-take" outcomes between university faculty members and industrial firms. Based on two separate but similar surveys conducted in 1997, one for faculty members and another for industry technology managers, the study reports that participants in research collaboration appear to realize significant benefits, some expected and others unexpected.

Johnson [3] has discussed the Strategic business-university research collaborations that provide a myriad of benefits to their participants. For academics, these benefits can include the opportunity to address challenging research questions with real-world applications, see their research have tangible impacts and gain access to new skills, data or equipment. Companies can improve business performance through developing new techniques or technologies, de-risk investment in research, and extend the capabilities and expertise available to the firm. Investment in collaborative R&D also delivers real benefits to the UK, driving growth and productivity improvements for firms and high quality research outputs.

Borrell-Damian, Morais, and Smith [4] have concentrated on project collaborative research between European universities, and external partners from industry, enterprises and regional authorities. In particular, they have focused on the assessment tools which go beyond the traditional and widely used quantitative measurement indicators, towards better ways of measuring the more intangible aspects of research collaborations. The outcome of this approach sought to be a more comprehensive way of assessing university-business/enterprise cooperation, complementing quantitative outcomes with qualitative or semi-quantitative measurement tools. As a result the EUIMA project benefitted greatly from cooperation with the European Industrial Research Management.

Business collaboration case studies [5] provide a long history of successful business research collaborations examples of partnerships with a range of companies and organizations from UK, through an Access to Southampton's rich academic resource plus the availability of its extensive facilities in order to enable the project to push back the boundaries.

Forsythe and Cartwright [6] have discussed the objective of the way to document a set of practical recommendations and implementation steps that outline how industry-research collaboration in Western Australia, which can be improved within the context of available resources. These recommendations could provide the basis for the development of a number of pilot programs that may be rolled out in Sydney Chamber. While the outcomes of their discussion paper have application for businesses and research organizations across Australia Western Sydney, has been specifically identified by the Chambers as a region that can clearly benefit from a closer relationship between industry and the research sector.

Min and Bozeman [10] have examined the impact of researchers' previous industry experience on the research outputs and outcomes of Arizona State University faculty affiliated with NSF and DOE research centers. Using a data set combining curriculum vita and surveys. The results indicate significant differences between the researchers who have previous industry experience, and those who do not. Using a simple model of research productivity the findings were that academic researchers who had prior industry exposure produce fewer total career publications, but they support more students and research center personnel.

Bozeman, Fay, and Slade [11] have shown that research collaboration has become the norm in every field of scientific and technical research. They have provided a critical overview of the literature on research collaboration, focusing particularly on individual-level collaborations among university researchers, but also giving attention to university researchers' collaborations with researchers in other sectors, including industry. It considers collaborations aimed chiefly at expanding the base of knowledge (knowledge-focused collaborations) as well as ones focused on production of economic value and wealth (property-focused collaborations), the latter including most academic entrepreneurship research collaborations.

Moss-Kanter [12] has argued that a very different logic informs the practices of most high-performing and sustainable companies: An institutional logic. These companies believe that they are more than money-making machines; they are a vehicle for advancing societal goals. They deliver more than just financial returns; they also build enduring institutions. At great companies, institutional logic takes its place alongside economic logic in research, analysis, and managerial decision making. Six facets of institutional logic a common purpose, a long-term focus, emotional engagement, partnering with the public, innovation, and self-organization radically alter leadership, corporate behavior and form the building blocks of a more sustainable competitive advantage.

ICC International Chamber of Commerce, online Newsletter [13]. This document sets out why ICC is convinced that it is in a company's interest to make corporate responsibility a priority in today's competitive world of instant communication in which stakeholders have access to a wealth of information and enjoy an abundance of choice. Having stated the case for responsible business conduct, and its benefits to profitable business operations, this document aims to provide practical advice on how to make corporate responsibility to society an integral part of business conducts.

3 Empirical Study

The data was collected through two structured questionnaires the first one disseminated to 150 faculty members in Syrian universities and the second disseminated to 125 different private businesses.

We received 71 complete responses from the business sector, and 59 responses from faculty members.

3.1 *Measures and Characteristic of Two Samples*

Most of our survey items are measured on 5-points' likert scale. Characteristics of our two samples (business and faculty members) are reported in Tables 1 and 2.

Table 1 Characteristics of business respondents

	Frequency	Percent
Public Corporation	30	42.3
Private Corporation	11	15.5
LLC	14	19.7
Partnership	15	21.1
System Missing	1	1.4
Manufacturing	32	45.1
Services	29	40.8
Trading	10	14.1
Less than 10 employees	9	12.7
Between 10 and 50 employees	20	28.2
More than 50–100 employees	12	16.9
More than 100–150 employees	16	22.5
More than 150–200 employees	7	9.9
More than 250 employees	7	9.9
Less than 5 years	9	12.7
5–10 years	18	25.4
More than 10–20 years	28	39.4
More than 20 years	16	22.5
Total	71	100.0

Table 2 Characteristics of faculty members respondents

	Frequency	Percent
Private	32	54.2
Public	27	45.8
Social sciences	31	52.5
Applied sciences	28	47.5
Full time	37	62.7
Part Time	22	37.3
Total	59	100.0

4 Statistical Analysis and Results

4.1 The Reliability and Consistency Test of First Questionnaire (Faculty Members)

In order to test the reliability and consistency, the research used alpha Cronbach test, and found the following:

Table 3 shows a good reliability and consistency of data, because the value of alpha = (0.757), which is higher than the minimum acceptable level (0.6).

Table 3 Reliability statistics of first questionnaire

Cronbach's Alpha	No of Items
0.757	4

4.2 *Answering the Questions Related to Faculty Members in the First Questionnaire*

Questions (1, 2)

1. Does research that conducted by members of faculty deal with the problems and needs of the Syrian business sector?
2. Does research that conducted by university student's deal with the problems and needs of the Syrian business sector?

Table 4 shows that answers trend is neutral, with high significant level, and this indicates the necessity of reconsidering the method of research, which is conducted by both students and faculty members in order to be compatible with the needs of Syrian business sector.

Question (3)
Are there any differences between research that conducted by social science and applied science faculties, dealing with the problems and needs of the Syrian business sector?

In order to answer the above question, we defined a new variable that represents the mean of the above two question (1, 2), and tested the comparison of the new mean between two groups (social science, and applied science faculties).

By comparing the new means of the two groups of social science and applied science faculties, the results are:

The T-test shows (Table 5) that there is no significant confidence, so that the mean of social science faculties is different from the mean of applied science faculties. And this means that these faculties have the same problem.

Question (4)
Are there any differences between research that conducted by Public universities and that conducted by private one dealing with the problems and needs of the Syrian business sector?

In order to answer the above question, we defined a new variable that represents the mean of the above two question (1, 2), and tested the comparison of the new mean between two groups (Public, and private universities).

By comparing the new means of the two groups of private and public universities, the T-test shows that there is no significant confidence to say that the mean of private university is different from the mean of public university. And that means, both form of universities have the same problem (Table 6).

Question (5)
What are the barriers of any university-business research collaboration from the perspective of faculty members?

Table 4 The trend of answers for questions 1 and 2 with mean, standard deviation and significant level

Question	Mean	Standard deviation	Sig.	Trend
Research conducted by members of faculty and educational staff deals with the problems and needs of the Syrian business sector	2.75	0.975	0.009	Neutral
Research conducted by students deal with the problems and needs of the Syrian business sector	2.75	0.939	0.006	Neutral

Table 5 Descriptive statistics and T-test of equality of means for social science and applied science faculties

Faculty specialty	N	Mean	Std. deviation	Std. error mean
Social sciences	31	2.9355	0.78254	0.14055
Applied sciences	28	2.5357	0.97114	0.18353

T-test for Equality of Means

T	Df	Sig. (2-tailed)	Mean difference	Std. error difference	95% confidence interval of the difference	
					Lower	Upper
1.749	57	0.086	0.39977	0.22863	−0.05806	0.85760

Table 6 Descriptive statistics and T-test of equality of means for Public and private universities

Form of university	N	Mean	Std. Deviation	Std. Error Mean
Private	32	2.7813	0.85135	0.15050
Public	27	2.7037	0.95333	0.18347

T-test for Equality of Means

Sig.	T	Df	Sig. (2-tailed)	Mean Difference	Std. Error Difference	95% Confidence Interval of the Difference	
						Lower	Upper
0.352	0.330	57	0.743	0.07755	0.23500	−0.39304	0.54813
	0.327	52.736	0.745	0.07755	0.23730	−0.39847	0.55356

The first questionnaire is conceived for the faculty members (three different questions) in order to determine these barriers:

The first two questions are (Table 7).

The answers trend for the above two questions is disagree with high significant level. This means that the Syrian business sector does not provide data easily and the required funding for most researchers, this negatively affect the collaboration between universities and businesses.

The third question to the faculty members is to determine at most three main reasons why they are not so keen for research. The result shows in the Fig. 1.

Table 7 The trend of answers for question 5 with mean, standard deviation and significant level

Questions	Mean	Standard Deviation	Sig.	Trend
The Syrian business sector provides data easily for research held by university	1.93	0.666	0.000	Disagree

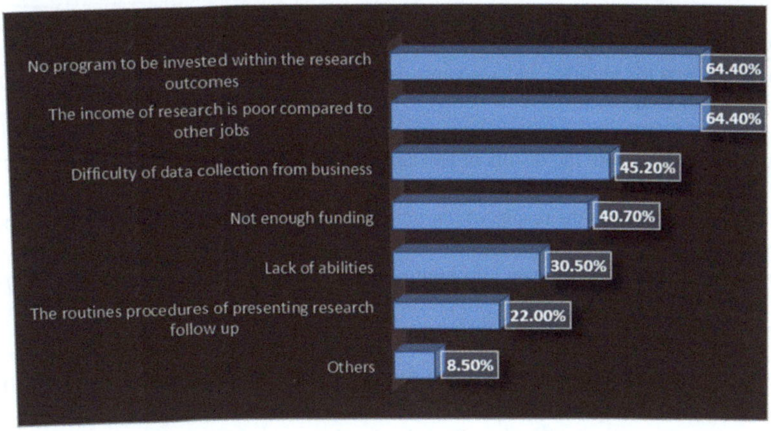

Fig. 1 The main reasons for not being so keen for research from the perspective of faculty members, Source: researchers

We can conclude from all of the above questions, that researches conducted by both students and faculty members do not significantly deal with the problems and needs of business, and many faculty members do not so keen for research due to the following:

The income of researchers is poor compared to other jobs (64.4%), there are no programs to be invested within the research outcome (64.4%), the difficulty of data collection from Businesses (52%), and not enough funding (40.7%). In addition, the Syrian business sector does not provide data easily and funding for most researchers which negatively affect the collaboration between universities and businesses.

The above results are considered as important to explore and build a new conceptual model that handles all of the following problems and difficulties.

4.3 *The Reliability and Consistency Test of Second Questionnaire (Business)*

In order to test the reliability and consistency, alpha Cronbach test is used:

Table 8 shows the value of alpha = 0.5, which is slightly less than the minimum acceptable level (0.6) because of the different trend and low average inter-items correlations. However, the standard deviation of each item (answer of each

Table 8 Reliability statistic

Cronbach's Alpha	No of Items
0.5	4

Table 9 Descriptive statistics answers of the second questionnaire

Question	N	Mean	Std. Deviation
The business trusts the abilities and academic experiences provided in Syrian universities and believes in its ability to present solutions to the Syrian business sector	71	2.03	1.042
The business benefits from the results of research conducted in Syrian universities	71	1.49	0.772
The business benefits from the results of research conducted in foreign universities	71	2.77	1.031
The business is ready to participate into joint research programs with Syrian universities if it is financially supported	71	3.90	1.030

question) is not high comparing to the mean (Table 9). This gives more confidence and reliability to the questionnaire.

Answering the questions related to the business in the second questionnaire

Question (6)
Do Syrian businesses benefit from researches of Syrian universities?

Table 10 shows the answer trend is: Disagree with high significant level, which indicates the very week collaborations between Syrian universities and business sector.

The above results show the need to establish many joint research programs between business sector and universities.

Question (7)
Do Syrian businesses benefit from researches of foreign universities?

Table 11 shows answer trend is neutral with high significant level. By comparing with Table 10, the research concludes that the Syrian business sector benefits more from researches of foreign universities than researches of Syrian universities.

In order to explain the above result, two relevant questions should be answered (8, 9).

Question (8)
Do Syrian businesses trust with the ability of faculty members to deal and recommend solutions to businesses problems?

Table 12 shows that the trend of answer is disagree with good significant level. This means most of Syrians business sector do not trust with the ability of faculty members to deal and recommend solution to businesses problems. The above answers explain one important cause of the weak collaboration between universities and Businesses.

Table 10 The trend of answers for question 6 with mean, standard deviation and significant level

Question	Mean	Standard Deviation	Sig.	Trend
The organization benefits from the results of research conducted in Syrian universities	1.49	0.772	0.001	Disagree

Table 11 Answer trend for question 7 with mean, standard deviation and significant level

Question	Mean	Standard Deviation	Sig.	Trend
The business benefits from the results of research conducted in foreign universities	2.77	1.033	0.003	Neutral

Table 12 The trend of answers for question 8 with mean, standard deviation and significant level

Question	Mean	Standard Deviation	Sig.	Trend
The organization trusts the abilities and academic experiences provided in Syrian universities and believes in its ability to present solutions to the Syrian business sector	2.03	1.042	0.04	Disagree

Question (9)
What factors represent barriers to any university-business research collaboration from the perspective of business?

The second questionnaire for the Syrian business sector: is to choose two important reasons explaining the weak bond between research conducted in Syrian universities and the Businesses. The result shows the following Fig. 2.

We can conclude that the main two barriers to any university-business research collaboration from the of business perspective are:

The Syrian business sector has no clue about the nature of research in Syrian universities (63.4%), and considers the cooperation with universities as costly (57.7%).

Question (10)
Do Syrian businesses ready to collaborate in a joint research program with Syrian universities if it is financially supported?

Table 13 shows that the trend of answer is agree with high significant level. Which means most of Syrian business sector is ready to be launched into joint research program with Syrian universities if it is financially supported.

All of the above results should be seriously considered to explore and build a new conceptual model that handles all difficulties faced by the business sector in Syria.

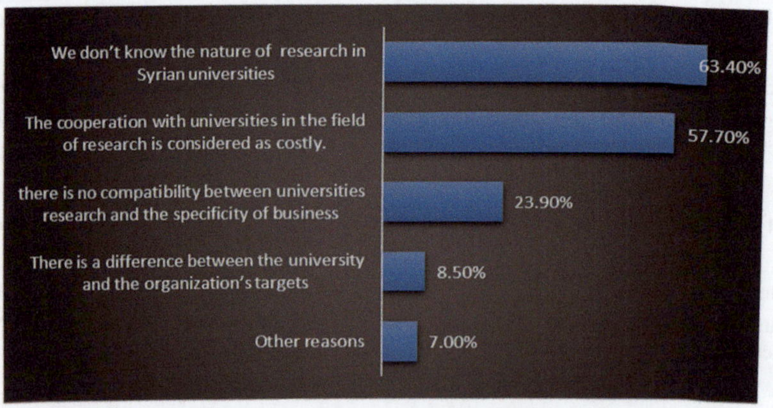

Fig. 2 Reasons explaining the weak bond between research conducted in Syrian universities and the businesses from the perspective of business, Source: researchers

Table 13 The trend of answers for question 8 with mean, standard deviation and significant level

Question	Mean	Standard Deviation	Sig. 3.2	Trend
The business is ready to participate into joint research programs with Syrian universities if it is financially supported	3.90	1.033	0.000	Agree

5 Triple Collaboration Model

University-Business-Chambers Research Collaboration (UBCRC).

This suggested model will overcome the gap between the universities researches and the Syrian business sector through advancing the basic knowledge, intensifying the relevance of research and education programs, and accelerating the innovation on in the economy and contributing effectively and efficiently in the reconstruction phase of Syria [6, 9].

The research suggests that chambers of industry and commerce, universities and business should work together and required to be linked through three interrelated elements to each other in order to enhance the level of innovation and economic growth of the country.

Programs link:

Establishing joint researches programs between universities and business that deal with needs of Syrian business sector, in order to find solutions, developing new products and technology [10].

Funding link:

Chambers of industry and commerce, industries and universities should collaborate in financing every joint research program, and that will decrease the investment risk for all parties and leverage the benefit of R&D expenses.

Resources link:

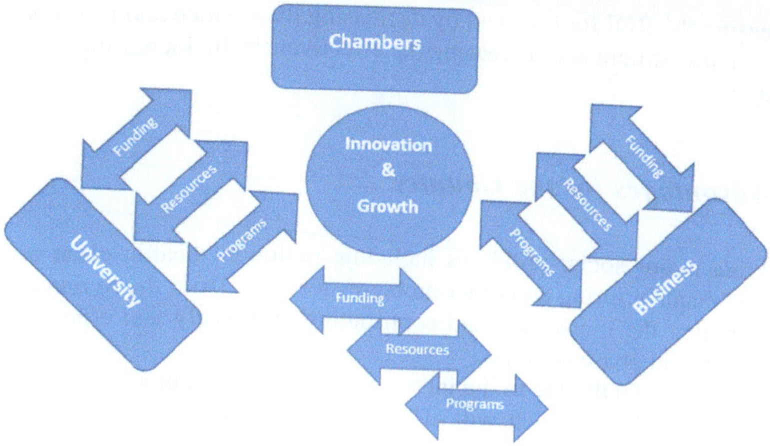

Fig. 3 Suggested triple collaboration model, University-Business-Chambers Research Collaboration (UBCRC), Source: researchers

The availability and accessibility of resources has a very important impact on the quality and relevancy of researches Fig. 3.

5.1 Advantages for Universities and Researchers

1. Leverage university R&D investment because of the triple co-funding and cooperation.
2. Improving universities ranking by improving their outputs, the quality and the number of researches.
3. Exposing universities to how R&D is planned and managed in the Syrian business sector.
4. A new and large funding stream for universities research.
5. Universities can recruit faculty members that can specialize only in research without incurring high expenses.
6. Increasing the compensations of researchers, and this might encourage them to exploit times and efforts towards joint researches programs.

5.2 Advantages for Businesses

1. Decreasing the investment risk for Business. The investment risk for business is mostly offset by chambers and universities matching funds and quality control.
2. Expanding Business sector access to the universities and increasing relevant research that could establish the foundation of entirely new technologies and products.

3. Increasing the ROI for business by decreasing the finance and time necessary to research investment and increasing the effectiveness by increasing the quality of research.

5.3 *Advantages for the Country*

1. Tackling major social problems including pollution, health, clean air, water, energy, manufacturing and other problems resulting from the Syrian crises.
2. Encouraging the innovation and contributing effectively and efficiently in the reconstruction phase of Syria.
3. Improving the GDP, due to the increase of the total output and the introduction of new technology, which will affect positively the productivity level of the Syrian business sector as a whole.
4. Creating new jobs, which will reduce the unemployment rate.

Business makes a huge contribution to economic and social development [11, 12]. This vital sector in Syria has to be in continuous and mutual collaboration with Syrian Universities and Chambers, in order to support the academic relevant researches progress, which will enhance the business investment opportunities that could establish the foundation of entirely new technologies, products and services [1, 8].

Business sector interest is to make corporate responsibility as priority in today's competitive world of instant communication in which stakeholders have access to a wealth of information and enjoy an abundance of choice [2, 13]. For academics, these benefits can include the opportunity to address challenging research questions with real-world applications, see their research have tangible impacts and gain access to new skills, data or equipment [3], improving Universities output, and the quality and the number of researches related to the needs of the industry [9]. Thus, Universities have to plan for a new approach of funding support with the business sector and chambers [6], which will help the effectiveness of research and development in Syria.

6 Conclusion and Recommendations

The paper's objective is to investigate the research collaboration between Syrian business sector and universities, and to suggest a new conceptual model based on investigation and findings. The majority of researches conducted by both faculty members and students in Syria, do not significantly deal with business needs; there is no significant difference between "Private and Public universities", as well as between "Social science and Applied science faculties" dealing with this issue. Moreover, many faculty members are not encouraged to achieve researches due to: poor income, the lack of structured and a mutual program to be invested within the research outcomes, the difficulties of acquiring data and funding from the Syrian business.

The Syrian business sector trust the international researches, more than the national one, this is due to the lack of trust with the ability of faculty members dealing and recommending adequate solution to businesses problems since there is no channel of communication and cooperation with the Syrian universities. In addition, it considers this cooperation with universities as costly, unless it is financially supported.

By considering the result, this paper suggested a new triple collaboration model that link Chambers, Universities and Business together through three interrelated elements, programs, resources and funding. This will match the gap between universities research and the Syrian business sector needs, then advancing knowledge base, enhancing the relevance of research programs, accelerating the application of innovation within the economy.

Two limitations of the study; Firstly the findings and the model are based only on Syrian universities and business sector; the samples were not big enough to represent the whole Syrian business sector and Universities. By expanding this study in the future and integrating more different faculties with their researchers staff, this study will enrich the findings which could be generalized. Secondly, the suggested model incorporate only the role of chambers to enhance the research collaboration, other organizations or institutions could also participate in this model like international chambers, banks, investments agencies and non-governmental organizations. Dealing with these limitations and the integration of one or more Organizations in this study, will be the scope of a future research.

References

1. Howells, J., Ramlogan, R., & Cheng, S.-L. (2015). *Benefits and challenges of university-industry interactions: A critical perspective*. Manchester: Manchester Institute of Innovation Research, University of Manchester.
2. Lee, Y. S. (2000). The sustainability of university-industry research collaboration: An empirical assessment. *The Journal of Technology Transfer, 25*(2), 111–133.
3. Johnson, J. (2015). *Minister of state for universities and science in UK. The dowling review of business-university research collaborations in UK.*
4. Borrell-Damian, L., Morais, R., & Smith, J. H. (2014). *University-Business collaborative research: Goals, outcomes and new assessment tools*. Brussels: European University Association. EUA Publication.
5. "Business collaboration case studies". University of Southampton. (2016). [Online]. Accessed June 9, 2016, from http://www.southampton.ac.uk/business/expertise/collaborate/business-case-studies.page
6. Forsythe, P., Cartwright, S., & Industry Research Collaboration. (2014). Sydney business chamber discussion paper, NSW Business Chamber.
7. Gerry, E., & Kharazmi, O. A. (2011). *A conceptual model of the role of university-industry collaboration in a national systems of innovation*. Stirling: Stirling Management School, University of Stirling.

8. Huttner, S. (2012). Partnerships that reinvent the role of the research university in the knowledge triangle. In G. Edmondson (Ed.), *Making industry-university partnerships work lessons from successful collaborations* (pp. 28–32). Brussels: Science|Business Innovation Board.
9. Joe, F., Hair, J.-R., Sarstedt, M., Hopkins, L., & Kuppelwieser, V.-G. (2014). Partial least squares structural equation modeling (PLS-SEM): An emerging tool in business research. *European Business Review, 26*(2), 106–121.
10. Min, W.-L., & Bozeman, B. (2006, March). Researchers' industry experience and productivity in university-industry research centers: A scientific and technical human capital explanation. *The Journal of Technology Transfer, 31*(2), 269–290.
11. Bozeman, B., Fay, D., & Slade, C.-P. (2013). Research collaboration in universities and academic entrepreneurship: The-state-of-the-art. *The Journal of Technology Transfer, 38*(1), 1–67.
12. Moss-Kanter, R. (2011). *How great company think differently Harvard Business review*. From the November 2011 Issue.
13. ICC International Chamber of Commerce online News letter. (2016). *Document, business in society: Making a positive and responsible contribution.*

Forging Research Links Between Academia, Business and Industry in Syria and Lebanon

Nabil Sukkar

Abstract Research links between academia, business and industry is extremely weak in both Syria and Lebanon. The reason is shortage of trust, mutual understanding, finance, competent human resources and competition in the market together with high presence of rent seeking activities, among other reasons. As a result, research that is produced in academia tends to be supply rather than demand oriented. The paper proposes a vision for needed research and development of research, and presents several suggestions to encourage research, to support cooperation between Arts and Science Faculties and to forge links between academia, business, industry and finance (including establishment of science and technology parks), and with research centers attached to the Matre Project EU partner institutions.

1 The State of Research Link Between Academia and Business

The research link between academia and business in Syria and Lebanon is extremely weak. The survey reports prepared by the academic teams of the Syrian and Lebanese business schools under the EU financed Matre project[1] identified the following main factors that hinder these links:

- Shortage of finance to support research
- Insufficient human resources to support collaboration, and
- Insufficient individual motivation on the part of academic staff (due to poor financial and promotion incentives).

---

[1]Serene Dalati and Louay Koulo (2014) MATRE Research Study on Academics at Higher Education in Syria and Anis Bou Diab (2014) Faculty Survey Reports of the Business Faculties at LU & MUBS, Lebanon.

N. Sukkar (✉)
Syrian Consulting Bureau for Development and Investment (SCB), Damascus, Syria

World Bank, Washington, DC, USA
e-mail: nsukkar@scbdi.com; nabil.scb@gmail.com

J. Marx Gómez et al. (eds.), *Modernizing Academic Teaching and Research in Business and Economics*, Springer Proceedings in Business and Economics,
DOI 10.1007/978-3-319-54419-9_12

To these factors we would like to add the following factors, based on our own observation:

– On the part of business, absence of sufficient competition in the market and a tendency on the part of business to go for easy rent seeking activities
– On the part of academia, shortage of the academic community's knowledge of the business sector and its problems and of the country's economic sector and their strategies and constraints. As a result most of academic research tends to be supply rather than demand oriented.

The above conclusion is supported by the empirical study presented in this Conference by A. Salhani and V. Khnouf[2] which points to a lack of confidence on both sides and concludes (a) that academic research in Syrian business schools do not respond to business needs and (b) that business does not benefit from research conducted in business schools (public and private). The reason for the gap according to the study's empirical research are the following:

On the business (demand) side, business says: (a) we do not trust the ability of Syrian faculty members to analyze problems and provide solutions to their problems, (b) we do not know enough about the nature of research in Syrian universities, and (c) we consider faculty research as costly. On the faculty (supply) side, faculty says: (a) business is not willing to release data, and (b) business is not willing to pay sufficiently for research.

2 The State of Research, Development and Link with Industry

The poor research link is even more serious in industry. Here the blame is more on industry which is not conducting and not requesting research and development, despite the low efficiency of industry in both Syria and Lebanon. This is reducing industry's ability to compete in world markets. This low efficiency is a result of high production and transaction costs, low technology in-use, and long history of protection in the case of Syria.

In the West, industry has always requested and financed scientific research and the recent globalization and digital revolution have increased R&D and Innovation efforts by industries because of intensified competitiveness in world markets.

[2]A. Salhani and V. Khnouf (2016), University–Business Research Collaboration in Syria: An Empirical Assessment and Suggested Conceptual Model, unpublished.

3 Factors Hindering R&D in Industry

For industry successful R&D should raise return on capital and for the country, successful R&D should improve a country's competitive advantage and allows it to integrate in the global economy. The shortage of R&D in Syria and Lebanon is hindered by the following factors: (a) absence of sufficient competition in the market which creates a sense of complacency, (b) small size of industries and hence shortage of resources to carry out research, (c) traditional mode of management, as the majority of industries are SME's and are traditionally and non-institutionally operated. In addition, there is a shortage of industrial knowledge on the part of academia, as academic curricula and faculty's knowledge are not oriented to the needs of industry.

4 What Should Be Done to Encourage Research and Forge Links

The following is proposed to respond to the shortage of research and of research links between academia, business and industry:

1. Developing a vision for research, one that should be developed through a joint effort of academia, business, industry, and government in both countries. This should also be done in collaboration with the main national research institutions in the two countries: The Higher Commission for Scientific Research in Syria and The National Council for Scientific Research in Lebanon.
2. This vision should focus, in our opinion, on the future of social, economic and business development in the two countries and their need for: (a) social equity, sustained growth and balanced urban and rural development, (b) competitive business and industry, (c) integration in the global economy, (d) ethical business practices and corporate social responsibility (e) domestic technological and skill upgrading, (f) minimizing technological dependency, (g) a focus on the knowledge economy, (h) enterprise development, (i) better investment environment, (j) avoiding rent seeking activities, and (k) combating poverty and corruption, among other targets. The vision should also focus, in our opinion, on coordinating the efforts in the two countries and seeking harmonization between the two economies. To all the above, we should include in the case of Syria, attending to the needs of economic recovery and reconstruction in post conflict.
3. There is a need for better understanding of business and industry on the part of academia and more trust between the two sides. This could be done through more visitations as well as through holding conferences and seminars on the subject in the two countries.

4. In the attempt to understand the business community, there is a need to differentiate between two types of business, the traditional business sector and the new knowledge economy sector (which is led by young entrepreneurs). These two sectors have different concerns, different needs and different priorities. The traditional business sector has concerns which have been discussed quite often in the past (issues of management, marketing, organizational behavior, consumer behavior, human resources, financial markets, and others), while the high tech knowledge economy sector has concerns which has not sufficiently been attended to, such as entrepreneurship, innovation, start up business, incubation, venture capital, propriety protection, information technology applications and integrating with the traditional business sector. In addition, industry's concerns which should be attended to include improving competiveness, innovation, developing new products and processes and enhancing use of IT applications.
5. Universities should take the initiative to reduce the increasing gap between their research and industry, including the creation of academic programs that are relevant to the needs of industry, involving both faculties and students.
6. There is a need to minimize monopolies and rent seeking activities in business and industry on one side and increasing competition in the market on the other.
7. There is a need to develop a Science, Technology and Innovation (S,T&I) Framework in both countries, linked to each country's national development objectives and plans.
8. For the sake of industrial research and development, there is a need for links between business, engineering and applied science Faculties on one side, and between these Faculties and the business and industrial communities on the other.
9. Government should offer tax incentives for research, improve protection of intellectual property rights and introduce competition policies. It should also reform the education system to enhance research and educational skills, to produce scientists, researchers, and to develop a curriculum responsive to industry needs
10. Government, Industry and Academia should all be willing to fund research and development.
11. In addition to research, we need to focus on commercializing research and development through collaboration with venture capital institutions and start up funds.
12. Finally, we need to establish Science and Technology Parks involving academia, business, industry and finance

5 Establishing Science and Technology Parks

We need to consider establishing S&T parks, bringing together academia, business, industry and financial institutions, along the lines of Berytech Technological Pole in Lebanon. The parks could include business and/or technology incubators for start up business which provide a work space, shared facilities and technical and business support services to tenants.

Berytech Technological Pole is a Lebanese business development center launched in 2008 by Saint Joseph University. It provides high tech hosting, incubation, training and counseling services to SME's. It has also set up several funds to provide seed capital for start up high tech knowledge economy business.

6 Linking MATRE Project Intended Research Centers in Syria and Lebanon with Centers in EU Partner Universities

The newly established research centers under the Matre Project should have close links with research centers in the EU partner universities in Oldenburg, Alicante and Vilnius or to centers linked to the three universities. It is noteworthy that all three universities have entrepreneurship, innovation and technology centers with close links with business and industry. They are the following:

1. Carlvon Ossietszky University of Oldenburg has links with the business sector through OFFIS and TGO
   (a) OFFIS (Oldenburg Research and Development Institute for Information and Technology Tools and Systems) is a leading institution for information technology, focusing on energy, health and transport. It works closely together with the Carlvon Ossietszky University of Oldenburg. It is an application oriented research and development institute and a center of excellence for selected areas of information technology and its fields of application.
   (b) TGO is a technology incubator for business starts up intended to support entrepreneurship.
2. Vilnius Gendiminas Technical University has a Sunrise Valley Science and Technology Park.
3. University of Alicante has a technology transfer park.

All these research and development centers as well as the three EU Partner universities could be a major source of support for the objectives of the intended research centers in Syria and Lebanon, as well as on the overall objective of forging research links between academia, business and industry.

References

1. European Commission. (2007). *Linking the world of work and education through tempus*. Brussels: European Commission.
2. Lebanese Industrial Association and The National Council for Scientific Research. (1999). *Academic research and industrial development conference*. Beirut: The National Council for Scientific Research.
3. National Tempus Office Syria. (2012). *Higher education in Syria*. Brussels: European Commission.
4. World Bank. (1998). *Education in the middle East and North Africa: A strategy towards learning for development*. Washington DC: World Bank.
5. World Bank. (2008). *The road not traveled : Education reform in the middle East and North Africa*. Washington DC: World Bank.
6. Dalati, S., & Koulo, L. (2014). *MATRE Research Study on Academics at Higher Education in Syria*. EU Tempus Matre Project (unpublished).
7. Diab, A. B. (2014). *Faculty Survey Reports of the Business Faculties at LU & MUBS*. Lebanon, EU Tempus Matre Project (unpublished).
8. Salhani, A., & Khnouf, V. (2016). *University-Business Research Collaboration in Syria: An Empirical Assessment and Suggested Conceptual Model*, EU Tempus Matre Project (unpublished).

MIX
Papier aus verantwortungsvollen Quellen
Paper from responsible sources
FSC® C105338

If you have any concerns about our products,
you can contact us on
ProductSafety@springernature.com

In case Publisher is established outside the EU,
the EU authorized representative is:
Springer Nature Customer Service Center GmbH
Europaplatz 3, 69115 Heidelberg, Germany

Printed by Libri Plureos GmbH
in Hamburg, Germany